STRESS EDUCATION FOR COLLEGE STUDENTS

STRESS EDUCATION FOR COLLEGE STUDENTS

JAMES H. HUMPHREY

Novinka Books
New York

Senior Editors: Susan Boriotti and Donna Dennis
Coordinating Editor: Tatiana Shohov
Office Manager: Annette Hellinger
Graphics: Wanda Serrano
Editorial Production: Marius Andronie, Maya Columbus, Vladimir Klestov,
　　　　　　　 Matthew Kozlowski and Tom Moceri
Circulation: Ave Maria Gonzalez, Vera Popovich, Luis Aviles, Melissa Diaz,
　　　　　　 Magdalena Nuñez, Marlene Nuñez and Jeannie Pappas
Communications and Acquisitions: Serge P. Shohov
Marketing: Cathy DeGregory

Library of Congress Cataloging-in-Publication Data
Available upon request

ISBN: 1-59033-616-X

Printed in the United States of America

CONTENTS

About the Author		**vii**
Introduction		**ix**
Chapter 1	The Meaning of Stress and Related Terms	**1**
Chapter 2	Understanding about Stress	**9**
Chapter 3	Dealing with Emotions	**21**
Chapter 4	Nutrition, Diet and Stress	**33**
Chapter 5	Physical Activity, Exercise and Stress	**47**
Chapter 6	Body Restoration and Stress	**59**
Chapter 7	Sexology and Stress	**65**
Chapter 8	Substance Use and Stress	**83**
Chapter 9	Stress in Childhood	**99**
Chapter 10	Stress Among Older Adults	**111**
Chapter 11	Job Stress	**125**
Chapter 12	Reducing Stress through Relaxation	**143**
Chapter 13	Reducing Stress through Meditation	**155**
Chapter 14	Reducing Stress through Biofeedback	**161**
Chapter 15	Reducing Stress through Self-Modification of Behavior	**167**
Chapter 16	Reducing Stress through Systematic Self-Desensitization	**175**
References		**183**
Index		**191**

ABOUT THE AUTHOR

James H. Humphrey is the author or co-author of 15 books about stress, and editor of more than 20 others. Considered a pioneers in stress education, he is the founder and editor of *Human Stress; Current Selected Research* and editor of the 16-book series on *Stress in Modern Society.* In the early 1980s he collaborated with the late Hans Selye, who is generally known as the father of stress, on certain aspects of stress research. Dr. Humphrey has received numerous educational honors and awards. He is a Fellow in the American Institute of Stress.

INTRODUCTION

STRESS! What is it? What causes it? How does it effect us? How do we react to it? Is it all bad? How do we deal with it? These, and countless other questions about this phenomenon of modern society confront all of us at one time or another.

Stress has no doubt been with us forever, and we can only speculate that the ancient caveman had to be concerned with it in the search for food and the prospect of fighting or fleeing from his enemies and wild animals.

It can engulf us from childhood through old age and it abounds in all environments - home, family, school and on the job.

Stress respects no population and it prevails among blue collar workers, employers and employees alike in business and industry, such professions as medicine, law, nursing, teaching, and the public services of law enforcement and fire fighting. And, of course, it is a concern of college students. No doubt about it, college life can be stressful. Stress levels may be particularly high for those entering their freshman year when they are suddenly separated from family and friends and thrust into strange surroundings. And as time goes on college students can encounter such stress inducing factors as academic pressure, financial problems, time constraints along with a host of others.

There are times when stress simultaneously effects the entire international community. A case in point is the terrorists attack on September 11, 2001. This event caused concern about an increase in the condition of Post Traumatic Stress Disorder. This could have occurred in those who survived or directly witnessed these destructive acts and others personally involved in subsequent rescue situations. Media and especially television coverage was so graphic and continuous in the aftermath, that tens of millions of Americans and hundreds of millions elsewhere may also have had these horrible scenes indelibly etched into their minds.

In various places throughout the book and especially in the final five chapters, a variety of techniques for coping with stress are presented. However, the reader should know that it is not absolutely necessary for everyone to be an expert in behavioral therapy in order to deal with stress. In this regard, there are certain *principles of living* that most persons can apply in helping to control stress. These principles are presented here to set the stage for a better understanding of the theme and content of the book.

Obviously, there are no resolute standard procedures that are guaranteed to relieve a person entirely from undesirable stress. There are, however, certain steps which may be applied as guidelines to help alleviate stressful conditions.

The term *principle* is interpreted to mean *guide to action*. Thus, the following principles should be considered as guidelines, but not necessarily in any particular order of importance. Moreover, it should be recognized that each principle is not a separate entity unto itself. This means that all of the principles are in some way interrelated and interdependent upon each other.

Principle: Personal Health Practices Should Be Carefully Observed

Comment:

This is an easy principle to accept, but sometimes it is difficult to implement. No one is against health, but not everyone abides by those practices that can help maintain a suitable level of health. Some jobs, with their imposing schedules, may cause workers to neglect the basic requirements that are essential for the human organism to reach an adequate functional level. Incidentally, many college students are guilty of not abiding by certain practices that are in the best interest of their health.

Current thinking, which suggests that the individual assume more responsibility for his or her own health, makes it incumbent upon all of us not to disregard such important needs as diet, adequate sleep and rest, sufficient physical activity, and balancing work with play, all of which can reduce one's ability to cope with the stressful conditions inherent in our daily lives.

Principle: There Should Be Continuous Self-Evaluation

Comment:

The practice of constantly taking stock of one's activities can help minimize problems encountered in various aspects of one's environment. This can be accomplished in part by taking a little time at the end of each day for an evaluation of the events that occurred during the day, and reactions to those events. Setting aside this time period to review performance is not only important to the achievement of goals, but it is also important to remaining objective. As a college student you might well consider this practice as a means of improving upon your school work. Those who take time to do this will be more likely to identify certain problems over which they have no control, and thus, will try to make an adjustment until such time that a positive change can be effected. The particular time that this task is performed is an individual matter; however, it is not recommended that it be done immediately at the end of the day. A little time should be taken to "unwind" before evaluating actions that took place during the day.

Principle: Learn to Recognize Your Own Accomplishments

Comment:

One must learn to recognize his or her own accomplishments and praise himself or herself for them, especially if such praise is not offered by others. This is generally known as "stroking" or "patting one's self on the back." In practicing this procedure one can develop positive attitudes and/or belief systems about his or her own accomplishments and thus reduce stress. All too often, many people "sell themselves short" and do not give themselves credit for the important things that they accomplish.

Principle: Learn to Take One Thing at a Time

Comment:

This is concerned with time budgeting and procrastination. Most persons, and particularly college students, are likely to put things off, and as a consequence, frustrations can build up as tasks pile up. There is a need to sort out those tasks in order of importance and attack them one at a time. Proper budgeting of time can help alleviate procrastination, which in itself can be a stress inducing factor. Think of the times you have delayed doing a term paper until the "last minute" or had to "cram" for an examination as a result of not keeping up with daily work. Budgeting of time can help eliminate worries of time urgency and the feeling of "too much to do in too short a time."

Principle: Learn to Take Things Less Seriously

Comment:

This should not be interpreted to mean that important things like school work should not be taken seriously. It does mean that there can be a fine line between what is actually serious and what is not. Sometimes when people look back at a particular event, they may wonder how they could have become so excited about it. Those persons who are able to see the humorous side in their various environments tend to look at a potentially stressful situation more objectively, and this can assist in keeping stress levels low.

Principle: Do Things for Others

Comment:

People can sometimes take their mind off their own stressful conditions by offering to do something for other persons. When individuals are helpful to others, in attempting to relieve them of stress, they in turn will tend to be relieved of stress themselves. Research tends to show that those persons who volunteer to help others often get as much, or more, benefit from this practice as those they volunteer to help. This even occurs in children because it has been clearly demonstrated that older children who have reading problems improve in their own reading ability when they assist younger children with these same problems.

Principle: Talk Things Over with Others

Comment:

People sometimes tend to keep things to themselves, and as a consequence, they may not be aware that others may be disturbed by the same things. Sometimes discussing something with a classmate or friend can help one to see things in a much different light. It is important to keep in mind that such discussion should be positive and objective lest it degenerate into idle gossip. This, of course, can tend to cause deterioration of a situation that is already at a low ebb.

Principle: Stress Should Not Be Confused with Challenge

Comment:

People often relate stress to producing tensions and therefore expect anxiety to result. Contrary to this, constructive stress in the right amounts can challenge a person and promote motivation, thinking, and task completion. Thus, recognizing stress as a natural phenomenon of life is no doubt one of the first and most important steps in dealing with it. This is a concept that parents should make every effort to develop with children at an early age.

The book is designed for use in the popular college course in stress management. Incidentally, it has been found that such courses have the potential to reduce symptoms of anxiety, depression, and hostility as well as to raise self-esteem among participants.[1] Moreover, instructional intervention of a stress management course seems to demonstrate that it can lead to improved scores for individuals in a Personal Life Style Survey, and Life Style Inventory.[2]

Each chapter of the book begins with an introductory overview, the purpose of which is to give the reader a compact idea of the content of the chapter. This is followed by a number of questions intended to serve a three-fold purpose: (1) it is expected that the questions will set forth a study guide at the outset of each chapter; (2) they should provide a convenient reference to problems considered in the chapter; and (3) they should provide a device by which the reader can evaluate his or her present knowledge of the content in the chapter.

At the end of each chapter are several *Suggested Activities,* which can be used in a variety of ways. The instructor may wish to have all or part of the activities completed depending upon the amount of class time available. In connection with these activities, it is perhaps appropriate to indicate the meaning of some of them. For example, an activity involving a *round table* discussion is similar to what many college students refer to a "rap session." On the other hand, in a *panel* discussion, each one of the four or five panel members prepares specific material for a presentation. At the end of either of these activities the subject is opened for discussion for all class members.

A book is seldom the sole product of the author. Granted, the author does most of the things concerned with actually putting a book together, from the germ of the idea to seeing it through to final publication. However, it is almost always true that many individuals participate, at least indirectly, in some way before a book is finally completed. This volume is no exception.

To acknowledge everyone personally is practically impossible. For example, thousands of individuals, including more than 2,500 college students participated in my extensive interviews and surveys in the acquisition of data that was pertinent to the content of the book. I express my sincere thanks to them collectively for taking their valuable time to provide this important information.

It is possible and practical, however, to cite certain individuals personally. To the late Dr. Hans Selye, one of the most distinguished scientists of the 20th century and world famous pioneer in the area of stress, I express my sincere thanks for his wise counsel in the writings I have undertaken in the stress field. Collaborating with him on certain aspects of stress research was an inspiring and rewarding experience.

A special debt of gratitude is due to Dr. Paul J. Rosch, President of the American Institute of Stress. A worldwide authority on the subject of stress, Dr. Rosch has shared important information with me on the subject and he has prepared the foreword for several of my books.

Chapter 1

THE MEANING OF STRESS AND RELATED TERMS

There is an unbelievable amount of confusion surrounding the meaning of stress and stress-related-terms. For this reason it appears important to attempt to arrive at some operational definitions and descriptions of some of these terms. If this can be accomplished, it will make for much easier communication in dealing with stress. It is the intent of this introductory chapter to provide information that will help to facilitate communication in the area of stress.

1. What is the difference between stress and anxiety?
2. Does stress cause anxiety or does anxiety cause stress?
3. What is meant by unlearned tensions?
4. What is meant by learned tensions?
5. What is the difference between physiologic and psychologic tension?
6. Does emotion stimulate stress or does stress stimulate emotion?
7. How are stress and depression related?
8. What is the difference between stress and burnout?

An intelligent discussion of any subject should perhaps begin with some sort of understanding about the terminology employed or, in other words, the language and vocabulary used to communicate about a given subject. There are several important reasons why a book on stress, in particular, should begin by establishing such a general frame of reference. For one thing, a review of several hundred pieces of literature concerned with stress revealed that the terminology connected with it is voluminous, sometimes contradictory and, to say the least, rather confusing. Many times, terms with different meanings are likely to be used interchangeably; conversely, the same term may be used under various circumstances to denote several different meanings. That this results in confusion for the reader is obvious, because such usage of terminology is likely to generate a situation of multiple meanings in the general area of stress. In this regard, my interviews and surveys of a large number of college students revealed a wide variety of understandings with reference to the meaning of stress.

It should be understood that we are not attempting to develop a set of standardized stress-related terms. This would be well-nigh impossible. The purpose is for communication only, and limited to the aims of this particular book. This is to say that if a term is used in the book you will know what is meant by it. The idea is to try to develop working descriptions of terms for the purpose of communicating with you, the reader. In no sense is it intended to impose a terminology upon you. If you prefer other terms you should feel free to use them in your communication with others.

For the discussion of terminology that follows, there will be an effort to resort in some instances to terms used by various authorities in the field, and in others, insofar as they may be available, to use pure technical definitions. It should be understood that many of the terms have some sort of general meaning. An attempt will be made in some cases to start with this general meaning and give it specificity for the subject at hand,

(NOTE: At this point would you please take a piece of scratch paper and complete the following sentence: Stress is_____. The reason for asking you to do this is so that you can compare your answer with the results of the previously-mentioned survey of college students about the meaning of stress. These results are reported in the following discussion).

WHAT STRESS MEANS TO COLLEGE STUDENTS

Since the term stress appears to mean so many different things to different people, it seemed appropriate to get some idea of college students' concepts of it. This was accomplished by having several hundred students fill in the above sentence completion item. It is to be expected that there would be a rather wide variety of responses among students as far as their concepts of stress are concerned. Consideration of students' concepts of stress focused on the number of times certain key words emerged in the responses. By identifying such key words it was felt that a fairly valid assessment could be made of how students conceived of what stress means to them.

The word *pressure* appeared in slightly more that 40 percent of the responses. This was by far the most popular key word and by almost a two to one margin over the second most popular key word. This is interesting because the word pressure rarely appears in the literature on stress except when it is used in connection with blood pressure. It is also interesting to note that the lead definition of the term in most standard dictionaries considers it in relation to the human organism by referring to pressure as "burden of physical and mental distress."

Some representative examples of how students used the word pressure in describing their concept of stress follow: Stress is

- important to release pressure you feel.
- constant pressure on the body.
- the pressure of problems we deal with every day.
- pressure that is put on you or your brain from a given situation.
- a feeling of having to deal with pressure.
- pressure that is harmful to you.

The key word appearing second most frequently at about 23 percent of the time was *tension*. Most often those students who used this term did so in the following manner: Stress is

- a lot of tension at one time, the combination of unfavorable events that cause tension.
- physical and mental tension.
- tension that gives one an annoying feeling in the stomach.

Following the key word tension were the key words *frustration* and *strain*, each used by slightly more than 13 percent of the respondents. Many of those students who conceived frustration as stress used the term as follows: Stress is

- frustration from doing poorly on an exam.
- the feeling of frustration you get when things are not going well.
- frustration caused by conflict within yourself.
- frustration that saps your energy.
- frustration caused when you did poorly on a test when you thought you did well.

Like the term pressure, the word *strain* is used very little in the literature on stress. However, as we shall see later the word strain derives from the same Latin word as stress. This being the case, it would be easy to rationalize that stress and strain might be considered the same thing. However, the term strain tends to be used in connection with unusual tension in a muscle caused by overuse or because of a sudden unaccustomed movement. (A strain is a milder injury than a sprain in which ligaments around a joint are pulled or torn, and swelling occurs.)

Examples of how students used the word strain in describing stress are listed below: Stress is

- mental strain from exams.
- strain caused by unknown sources.
- strain on physical health.
- excess strain on a person because of worry.

The key words *anxiety* and *emotion* were used slightly less than five percent of the students to describe their concept of stress. Typically, students used the term anxiety in connection with their concept of stress as follows: Stress is

- demands cause by anxiety a cause of anxiety.

As far as the key word emotion is concerned, various writers use the terms stress and emotion interchangeably, presumably to mean the same thing. In regard to their concepts of stress some students used the term emotion as follows: Stress is

- a bad emotional experience, when you have your emotions upset.

- a condition that causes emotional outbursts.
- emotion that has a negative influence.

In less that one percent of the cases, no particular key words were identifiable. For example, there were such responses as: Stress is

- an unnecessary thing that is blown out of proportion.
- something I don't think about.

In summarizing the responses of college students, two rather interesting bits of information emerged. First, there were relatively few who saw any aspect of stress as positive. That is, the responses were predominantly of a nature that conceived stress as always being undesirable with little or no positive effects. Second, in a large percentage of the cases, students' concepts tended to focus on the *stressor* rather than of the condition of stress itself. This would appear to be natural since it has been only in relatively recent years that literature on the subject of stress has become more plentiful in terms of describing what it is and how it affects the human organism. At any rate, the responses of students about their concepts of stress provided certain important guidelines for preparing content for the book. Because of this, the collection of such data was a worthwhile undertaking. (Before reading further please compare your concept of stress with the survey results; you will be asked to do more with your response in connection with the Suggested Activities at the end of the chapter).

STRESS

There is no solid agreement regarding the derivation of the term stress. For example, it is possible that the term is derived from the Latin word *stringere,* which means to bind tightly. Or is could have derived from the French word *destress,* anglicized to *distress.* The prefix *dis* could eventually have been eliminated because of slurring, as in the case of the word *because* sometimes becoming '*cause.*

A common generalized literal description of stress is "a constraining force or influence." When applied to the human organism, this could be interpreted to mean the extent to which the body can withstand a given force or influence. In this regard one of the most often quoted description of stress is that of the famous pioneer in the field, the late Hans Selye who described it as the "nonspecific response of the body to any demand made upon it."[1] This means that stress involves a mobilization of the body's resources in response to a stimulus (stressor). These responses can include various physical and chemical changes in the organism. This description of stress could be extended by saying that it involves demands that tax or exceed the resources of the human organism. (Selye's concept of stress will be explained in more detail in the following chapter.) This mean that stress not only involves these bodily responses but that it also involves wear and tear, brought about by these responses, on the organism.

In essence, stress can be considered as any factor, acting internally or externally, that makes it difficult to adapt and that indicates increased effort on the part of the individual to maintain a state of equilibrium between himself or herself and the external environment. It is emphasized that: stress is a *state* that one is in, and this should not be confused with any *agent* that produces such a state. Such agents are referred to as stressors.

Understanding the meaning of stress can be made more difficult because certain stress-related terms can cause confusion. Therefore, it seems appropriate at this point to review the meaning of such terms as tension, emotion, anxiety, depression, and burnout.

TENSION

The term tension is very frequently used in relation to stress and thus, attention should be given to the meaning of this term. It is interesting to examine the entries used for these terms in the *Education Index*. This bibliographical index of periodical educational literature records entries on the terms stress and tension as follows:

Stress (physiology)
  Stress (psychology) see *Tension* (psychology)
  Tension (physiology) see *Stress* (physiology)
Tension (psychology)

This indicates that there are physiological and psychological aspects of both stress and tension. However, articles in the periodical literature listed as "stress" articles seem to imply that stress is more physiologically oriented and that tension is more psychologically oriented. Thus, psychological stress and psychological tension could be interpreted to mean the same thing. The breakdown in this position is seen where there is another entry for tension concerned with *muscular* tension. The latter, of course must be considered to have a physiological orientation. In the final analysis, the validity of these entries will depend upon the point of view of each individual. As we shall see later, the validity of this particular cataloging of these terms may possibly be at odds with a more specific meaning of the term.

Tensions can be viewed in two frames of reference; first, as *physiologic* or *unlearned tensions,* and second, as *psychologic* or *learned tensions.* An example of the first, physiologic or unlearned- tensions would be "tensing" at bright lights or intense sounds. Psychologic or learned tensions are responses to stimuli that ordinarily do not involve muscular contractions, but that at sometime earlier in a person's experience were associated with a situation in which tension was a part of the normal response. In view of the fact that the brain connects any events that stimulate it simultaneously, it would appear that, depending upon the unlimited kinds of personal experiences one might have, he or she may show tension to any and all kinds of stimuli. An example of a psychologic or learned tension would be an inability to relax when riding in a car after experiencing or imagining too many automobile accidents.

In a sense, it may be inferred that physiologic or unlearned tensions are current and spontaneous, while psychologic or learned tensions may be latent as a result of a previous experience and may emerge at a later time. Although there may be a hairline distinction between stress and tension in the minds of some people, perhaps an essential difference between stress and tension is that the former is a physical and/or mental state concerned with wear and tear on the organism, while the latter is either a spontaneous or latent condition which can. bring about this wear and tear.

EMOTION

Since the terms stress and emotion are used interchangeably in some literature, consideration should be given to the meaning of the latter term. Emotion could be viewed as the response an individual makes when confronted with a situation for which he or she is unprepared or which is interpreted as a possible source of gain or loss. For example, if one is confronted with a situation for which he or she may not have a satisfactory response, the emotional pattern of fear could result. Or, if a person is in a position where desires are frustrated, the emotional pattern of anger may occur. Emotion, then, is not the state of stress itself but rather it is a stressor that can stimulate stress. (The subject of emotion will be discussed in detail in Chapter 3.)

ANXIETY

Another term often used to mean the same thing as stress is anxiety. In fact, some of the literature uses the expression "anxiety or stress" implying that they are one and the same thing. This can lead to the chicken and egg controversy. That is, is stress the cause of anxiety or is anxiety the cause of stress? Or, is it a reciprocal situation?

A basic literal meaning of anxiety is "uneasiness of the mind," but this simple generalization may be more complex than one might think. C. Eugene Walker, a notable clinical psychologist and a contributor to my *Human Stress Series,* points out the fact that psychologists who deal with this area in detail have difficulty in defining the term. He gives as his own description of it the "reaction to a situation where we believe our well-being is endangered or threatened in some way."[2] David Viscott, another authoritative source, considers anxiety as the "fear of hurt or loss." He contends that this leads to anger with anger leading to guilt, if unrelieved, leading to depression.[3]

DEPRESSION

The term depression, as used here, is thought of as a painful emotional reaction characterized by intense feelings of loss, sadness, worthlessness, failure, or rejection not warranted by an objective view of events. Depression is often a disproportionately intense reaction to difficult life situations. It may be accompanied by such physiological symptoms as tension, slowing of motor and mental activity, fatigue, lack of appetite and insomnia; that is, some of the same symptoms accompanying undesirable stress.

Depression can be a manifestation of many different psychomotor and physical disorders and a normal response to certain types of stress. Unless the cause of it can be clearly identified, depression usually represents a description rather than a diagnosis.

BURNOUT

Some persons become unable to cope with the physical and emotional trauma generated by the demands on their energy, emotions, and time. Current research conducted on people-oriented occupations indicates that some are characterized by several built-in sources of frustration, that eventually lead dedicated workers to become ineffective and apathetic; that is, burned out. Persons who experience burnout may begin to perceive their job as impossible. They may begin to question their ability. Feeling helpless and out of control, persons nearing burnout may tire easily and may experience headaches and/or digestive problems. In some cases they will view their tasks and their profession to be increasingly meaningless, trivial, or irrelevant.

With regard to burnout, a study of college athletes by William C. Thomas and colleagues is of interest.[4] They hypothesized that the personality trait known as *hardiness* could mediate the effects of stress that lead to burnout. And further, that hardiness is one characteristic that could differentiate between individuals who are able to effectively manage environmental and internal demands and those who burn out.

The purpose of the study was to examine a theoretical model in which hardiness was posited to act as a stress buffer in the stress-burnout relationship. Participants were 181 National Collegiate Athletic Association Division I athletes who completed questionnaires containing stress, hardiness, and burnout instruments.

The study revealed that hardiness did appear to act as a buffer against the effect of stress. Given the positive consequences of having a hardier personality, it was concluded that athletes could benefit from purposefully structured experiences to enhance hardiness and improve their ability to cope with the many situational demands placed on them.

So much for terminology. Although the above brief discussion of certain terms does not exhaust the vocabulary used in relation to stress, it is hoped that it will serve to help the reader distinguish the use of terms basic to an understanding of the general area of stress. Other terminology will be described as needed when dealing with certain specific topics in subsequent discussions in the book.

SUGGESTED ACTIVITIES

1. Pool your response of the sentence completion item Stress is _____ with other class members. Compile the data and find out how it compared with the survey reported in the chapter.
2. Have a round table discussion on one or more of the following topics:
   a. Stress and anxiety.
   b. Emotion and anxiety.
   c. The relationship of frustration to stress.
   d. The relationship between stress and tension.
   e. The difference between physiologic and psychologic tensions.

Chapter 2

UNDERSTANDING ABOUT STRESS

In recent years the study of stress (stressology) has become widespread. Physicians, psychiatrists, psychologists, sociologists, nurses, teachers, in fact, individuals in almost all professional fields are becoming more and more concerned with the subject. In addition, leaders in business and industry have seen such an important need for stress management that many of these organizations are beginning to provide services to help employees cope with stress.

The area of stress is complicated and complex; however, there is a need for a better understanding of it by all segments of the population. It is the purpose of this chapter to provide basic information to assist in improving the knowledge of the reader about this phenomenon.

1. What are some physiological reactions to stress?
2. What are some behavioral reactions to stress?
3. What are some of the ways in which stress can be classified?
4. What is the meaning of eustress and distress?
5. How are physical stress and psychological stress related?
6. What is meant by social stress?
7. What are some of the effects of stress?
8. What are some of the general causes of stress?

THEORIES OF STRESS

It should perhaps be mentioned at this point that it is not the intent to get into a highly technical discourse on the complex aspects of stress. However, there are certain basic understandings that need to be taken into account, and this requires the use of certain technical terms. For this reason, it appears appropriate to provide an "on-the-spot" glossary of terms used in the discussion to follow.

ACTH - (AdrenoCorticoTropic Hormone) secreted by the pituitary gland. It influences the function of the adrenals and other glands in the body.

ADRENALIN - A hormone secreted by the medulla of the adrenal glands.

ADRENALS - Two glands in the upper posterior part of the abdomen that produce and
                secrete hormones. They have two parts, the outer layer, called the *cortex* and
                the inner core called the *medulla.*

CORTICOIDS - Hormones produced by the adrenal cortex, and example of which is
                cortisone.

ENDOCRINE - Glands that secrete their hormones into the blood stream.

HORMONE - A chemical produced by a gland, secreted into the blood stream, and
                influencing the function of cells or organs.

HYPOTHALAMUS - The primary activator of the autonomic nervous system, it plays a
                central role in translating neurological stimuli into endocrine processes
                during stress reactions.

PITUITARY - An endocrine gland located at the base of the brain about the size of a pea. It
                secretes important hormones, one of which is the ACTH hormone.

THYMUS - A ductless gland that is considered a part of the endocrine gland system, located
                behind the upper part of the breast bone.

Although there are various theories of stress, one of the better known and widely accepted ones is that of the previously-mentioned Hans Selye.[1] Selye's description. of "stress has already been given as the "nonspecific response of the body to any demand made upon it." The physiological processes and the reactions involved in Selye's stress model is known as the *General Adaptation Syndrome* and consists of three stages of *alarm reaction, resistance stage,* and the *exhaustion stage.*

In the first stage (alarm reaction), the body reacts to the stressor and causes the hypothalamus to produce a biochemical "messenger," which in turn causes the pituitary gland to secrete ACTH into the blood. This hormone then causes the adrenal gland to discharge adrenaline and other corticoids. This causes shrinkage of the thymus with an influence on heart rate, blood pressure, and the like. It is during the alarm stage that the resistance of the body is reduced.

In the second stage, *resistance* develops if the stressor is not too pronounced. Body adaptation develops to fight back the stress or possibly avoid it, and the body begins to repair damage, if any.

The third stage of *exhaustion* occurs if there is long-continued exposure to the same stressor. The ability of adaptation is eventually exhausted and the signs of the first stage (alarm reaction) reappear. Selye contended that our adaptation resources are limited, and, when they become irreversible, the result is death (our objective, of course, should be to keep our resistance and capacity for adaptation, and this is part of what this book is about).

Selye's stress model, which places emphasis upon "nonspecific" responses, has been widely accepted. However, the nonspecific nature of stress has been questioned by some. This means that psychological stressors activate other endocrine systems in addition to those activated by physiological stressors such as cold, electric shock, and the like.

As in the case of all research, the search for truth will continue, and more and more precise and sophisticated procedures will emerge in the scientific study of stress. Current theories will be more critically appraised and evaluated, and other theories will continue to be advanced. In the meantime, there is abundant evidence to support the notion that stress in modern society is a most serious threat to the well being of man if not controlled, and of course the most important factor in such control is man himself.

REACTIONS TO STRESS

There are various ways in which reactions to stress may be classified, and, in any kind of classification, there will be some degree of unavoidable overlapping. In the discussion here, I arbitrarily suggest two broad classifications as *physiological* and *behavioral.*

Physiological Reactions

Although all individuals do not always react in the same way physiologically as far as stress is concerned, the following generalized list suggests some of the more or less standard body reactions.

1. Rapid beating of the heart, which has sometimes been described as "pounding of the heart." We have all experienced this reaction at one time or another as a result of great excitement, or as a result of being afraid.
2. Perspiration, which is mostly of the palms of the hands, although there may be profuse sweating in some individuals at various other parts of the body.
3. The blood pressure rises, which may be referred to as a hidden reaction because the individual is not likely to be aware of it.
4. The pupils of the eyes may dilate, and, again, the individual will not necessarily be aware of it.
5. The stomach seems to "knot up," and we tend to refer to this as "feeling a lump in the pit of the stomach." This of course can have a negative influence of digestion.
6. Sometimes individuals experience difficulty in swallowing, which is often characterized as a "lump in the throat."
7. There may be a "tight" feeling in the chest and when the stressful condition is relieved one may refer to it as "getting a load of my chest."

What these various bodily reactions means is that the organism is gearing up for a response to a stressor. This phenomenon is called the *fight or flight* response and was first described as an *emergency* reaction by Walter B. Cannon[2], the famous Harvard University Professor of Physiology several years ago. The fight or flight response prepares us for action in the same way that it did for prehistoric man when he was confronted with an enemy. His responses were decided on the basis of the particular situation, such as fighting an opponent for food or fleeing from an animal that provided him with an overmatched situation. In modern times, with all of the potentially stressful conditions that provoke a fight or flight response, modern man uses these same physiological responses to face up to these kinds of situations. However, today, we generally do not need to fight physically (although we might feel like it sometimes), or run from wild animals, but our bodies still react with the same fight or flight response. Physiologists point out that we still need this means of self-preservation occasionally, but not in response to the emotional traumas and anxieties of modern living.

Behavioral Reactions

In discussing behavioral reactions, it should be mentioned again that various degrees of unavoidable overlapping may occur between these reactions and physiological reactions. Although behavioral reactions are, for the most part physically oriented, they are likely to involve more overt manifestations than are provoked by the physiological reactions. For purposes of this discussion, I will consider *behavior* to mean anything that the organism does as a result of some sort of stimulation.

An individual under stress will function with a behavior that is different from ordinary behavior. These are subclassified as: (1) *counter* behavior (sometimes referred to as defensive behavior, (2) *dysfunctional* behavior, and *(3) overt* behavior (sometimes referred to as expressive behavior).

In counter behavior, a person will sometimes take action that is intended to counteract the stressful condition. An example is when an individual takes a defensive position; that is, a person practicing an "on-the-spot" relaxation technique, but at the same time, being unaware of it. He or she may take a deep breath and silently "count to ten" before taking action, if any.

Dysfunctional behavior means that a person will react in a manner that demonstrates impaired or abnormal functioning, which results in a lower level of skill performance than he or she is ordinarily capable of accomplishing. There may be changes in the normal speech patterns, and there may be a temporary impairment of the systems of perception, as well as temporary loss of memory. Many of us have experienced this at one time or another due to a stress inducing situation, with a "mental block" causing some degree of frustration while we attempt to get back on the original train of thought.

Overt behavior involves such reactions as distorted facial expressions; that is, tics and twitches and biting the lip. There appears to be a need for the person to move about, and thus, pacing around the room is characteristic of this condition. Incidentally, there is a point of view that suggests that overt behavior in the form of activity is preferable for most individuals in most stressful situations, and can be highly effective in reducing threat and distress.

CLASSIFICATIONS OF STRESS

The difficulty encountered in attempting to devise a foolproof classification system for the various kinds of stress should be obvious. The reason for this, of course, lies in the fact that it is practically impossible to fit a given type of stress into one exclusive category because of the possibilities of overlapping. As in the case of attempting to classify reactions to stress in the immediately preceding discussion we are confronted with the same problem in trying to classify various kinds of stress. However, an attempt will be made to do so, and, as been mentioned before, any such classification on the part of the author is arbitrary. Others may wish to use different classifications than those used here, and, in the absence of anything resembling standardization, it is their prerogative to do so. With this idea in mind, some general classifications of stress that will be dealt with in the following discussion are (1) desirable and undesirable stress, (2) physical stress, (3) psychological stress, and (4) social stress. It should be understood that this does not exhaust the possibilities of various kinds of stress classifications. That is, this particular listing is not necessarily theoretically complete, but for purposes here it should suffice.

Desirable and Undesirable Stress

The classic comment once made by Selye that "stress is the spice of life" sums up the idea that stress can be desirable as well as devastating. He went on to say that the only way one could avoid stress would be to never to do anything and that certain kinds of activities have a beneficial influence in keeping the stress mechanism in good shape. Certainly the human organism needs to be taxed in order to function well, and it is a well-known physiological fact that muscles will soon atrophy if not subjected to sufficient use.

At one time or another most of us have experienced "butterflies in the stomach" when faced with a particularly challenging situation. Thus, it is important that we understand that stress is a perfectly normal human state and that the organism is under various degrees of stress in those conditions that are related to happiness as well as those concerned with sadness.

In the literature, undesirable stress may be referred to as *distress*. It is interesting to note that Selye referred to the pleasant or healthy kind of stress as *eustress* and to the unpleasant or unhealthy kind as *distress*.

Some of the desirable features of stress have been mentioned, but like any factor involving the human organism, most anything in excess is not good for it. Of course, this holds true for an abnormal amount of stress. When stress becomes prolonged and unrelenting and, thus, chronic, it can result in serious trouble. In the final analysis, the recommendation is not necessarily to avoid stress, but to keep it from becoming a chronic condition.

Although both *good* stress and *bad* stress reactions place specific demands for resources on the body, does this mean that good stress is *safe* and bad stress *dangerous?* Two prominent psychologists, Israel Posner and Lewis Leitner[3] have made some interesting suggestions in this regard. They feel that two psychological variables, *predictability* and *controllability* play an important role. Let us examine this premise.

It can be reasoned that *predictable* pain and discomfort is less stressful because under this condition a person could be capable of learning when it is safe to "lower his or her guard" and relax. Since periods of impending pain are clearly signaled, the person can safely relax at times when the warning is absent. These periods of psychological safety seem to insulate individuals from harmful effects of stress. Obviously, persons receiving unsignaled pain have no way of knowing when it is safe to relax and, thus, are more likely to develop serious health problems as a result of chronic psychological stress.

The second psychological variable, *controllability* of environmental stressors, which is closely related to coping behavior, also plays a major role in determining stress effects. The ability to control painful events may insulate individuals from experiencing damaging stress effects. However, such coping behavior is beneficial only if a person is given a feedback signal that informs him or her that the coping response was successful in avoiding an impending stressor. Without the feedback of success, active coping behavior, as such, may increase stress effects since it calls upon the energy reserves of the body and leaves it in a state of chronic stress.

The research on predictability and controllability of stressful events may help to answer *why* people who seek out stressful and challenging types of jobs do not appear to develop stress illnesses from this form of stress. In contrast, when essentially similar body reactivity is produced by *bad* stress, then stress-related illnesses can be the result. Perhaps *good* stress does not produce illness because typically the events associated with it are planned in advance (they are predictable) or otherwise scheduled to integrate (they are controlled) into the individual's life. However, even activities that are generally considered to be pleasant and exciting (good stress) can produce illness if the individual is not forewarned or has little control over the events. And unpleasant events (bad stress) may result in stress-related illness because they generally come without warning and cannot be controlled.

In closing this section of the chapter, it should be mentioned that some persons have taken the middle ground on this subject by saying that stress is neither good not bad, indicating that the effect of stress is not determined by the stress itself but how it is viewed and handled. That is, we either handle stress properly or we allow it to influence us negatively and, thus, become victims of undesirable stress.

Physical Stress

In discussing physical stress it is important to differentiate between the two terms *physical* and *physiological*. The former should be considered a broad term and can be described as "pertaining or relating to the body." On the other hand, physiological is concerned with what the organs do in relation to each other. Thus, physical stress could be concerned with unusual and excessive physical exertion, as well as certain physiological conditions brought about by some kind of stress.

Although there are many kinds of physical stress, they can perhaps be separated into two general types, to which the organism may react in different ways. One type may be referred to as *emergency* stress and the other to *continuing* stress. In emergency stress, the previously described physiological phenomenon takes place. That is, when an emergency arises such as bodily injury, hormones are discharged into the blood stream. This involves an increase in heart rate, rise in blood pressure, and dilation of the blood vessels in the muscles to prepare themselves for immediate use of the energy that is generated.

In continuing stress, the body's reaction is somewhat more complex. The physiological involvement is the same, but more and more hormones continue to be produced, the purpose of which is to increase body resistance. In cases where the stress is excessive, such as an extensive third degree burn, a third phase in the form of exhaustion of the adrenal glands can develop, sometimes culminating in fatality.

It was mentioned that physical stress can also be concerned with unusual and excessive physical exertion. This can be depicted in a general way by performing an experiment involving some mild physical exertion. First, try to find your resting pulse. This can be done by placing your right wrist, palm facing you, in your left hand. Now, bring the index and middle fingers of your left hand around the wrist and press lightly until you feel the beat of your pulse. Next, time this beat for ten seconds and then multiply this by six. This will give your resting pulse rate per minute. For example, if you counted 12 beats in ten seconds, your resting pulse will be 72 beats per minute. The next step is to engage in some physical activity. Stand and balance yourself on one foot. Hop up and down on this foot for a period of about 20 seconds, or less if it is too strenuous. Then, take your pulse rate again in the same manner as suggested above. You will find that, as a result of this activity, your pulse will be elevated above your resting pulse. Even with this small amount of physical exertion, the body was adjusting to cope with it, as evidenced by the rise in pulse rate. This was discernible to you;

however, other things, such as a slight rise in blood pressure were likely involved and you were not aware of them.

Psychological Stress

The essential difference between physical stress and psychological stress is that the former involves a real situation, while psychological stress is more concerned with foreseeing or imagining an emergency situation. As an example, a vicarious experience of danger may be of sufficient intensity to cause muscle tension and elevate the heart rate. A specific example of psychological stress is seen in what is commonly called "stage fright." Incidentally, it is interesting to note that this type of psychological stress may start when one is a child. For example, my studies of stress inducing factors among children have indicated that "getting up in front of the class" is an incident that causes much concern and worry to a large number of children. It has been my experience that this condition also prevails with large numbers of adults.

It has been clearly demonstrated that prolonged and unrelenting nervous tension developing from psychological stress can result in psychosomatic disorders, which in turn can cause various serious diseases.

It should be mentioned that physiological and psychological conceptions of stress have evolved independently within their respective fields. One writer on the subject, Anis Mikhail, once proposed the following holistic definition of stress for the purpose of emphasizing the continuity between psychological and physiological theorizing, "Stress is a state which arises from an actual or perceived demand-capability imbalance in the organism's vital adjustment actions, and which is partially manifested by a nonspecific response."[4]

Social Stress

Human beings are social beings. They do things together. They play together. They work together for the benefit of society. They have fought together in time of national emergencies in order to preserve the kind of society in which they believe. This means that life involves a constant series of social interactions. These interactions involve a two-way street, in that the individual has some sort of impact upon society, and, in turn, society has an influence upon the individual. There are obviously many levels of social stress in life situations. For example, economic conditions and other social problems have been found to be very stressful for many people.

Negative attitudes about social interactions will almost always generate hard feelings and hostility among groups, making for more stressful conditions for all concerned. Also a neutral or *laissez faire* attitude often degenerates into one of tolerance, and, as such, can become almost as devastating as a negative attitude. In fact, the development of an "I don't care" attitude can often make life intolerable and bring about stress. People themselves hold the key to avoidance of undesirable social stress in any kind of environment, and good social relationships are more likely to be obtained if one assumes a positive attitude in such relationships.

CAUSES OF STRESS

A fair question to raise might be, What doesn't cause stress? This is mentioned because most human environments, including the worksite and society as a whole, are now seen as stress inducing to some degree. In recent years so many causes of cancer have been advanced that many persons have almost come to the conclusion that *everything* causes cancer. Perhaps the same could be said of stress. Because it has reached near epidemic proportions, it is easy to believe that *everything* causes stress.

Factors that induce stress are likely to be both general and specific. This means that certain major life events can be stress inducing. Also, in our day-to-day environments, many specific causes of stress can elevate undesirable stress levels.

A number of researchers have studied certain *life events* as causes of stress. They have attempted to find out what kinds of health problems are associated with various events, normal and abnormal, that afflict people either in the normal course of events or as a result of some sort of misfortune.

One of the best known studies is the early original work of T. H. Holmes and R. H. Rahe[5] - a social readjustment scale. Following is a list of their ten most serious events causing stress.

1. Death of a spouse
2. Divorce
3. Marital separation
4. Jail term
5. Death of a close family member
6. Personal injury or illness
7. Marriage
8. Fired at work
9. Marital reconciliation
10. Retirement

As important as life event scales are as a means of determining causes of stress, some specialists feel that rather than life events, a better measure is that which is concerned with day-to-day problems. Prominent in this regard is Richard Lazraus[6] the distinguished stress researcher at the University of California at Berkeley. He and his associates once collected data from a number of populations on what he identified as "daily hassles." Following is the list of hassles for one of these populations - 100 white, middle-class middle-aged men and women.

1. Concern about weight
2. Health of a family member
3. Rising prices of common goods
4. Home maintenance
5. Too many things to do
6. Yard work, or outdoor maintenance
7. Property, investment, or taxes

8. Crime
9. Physical appearance

Some Causes of Stress Among College Students

In my studies of college students three major stress inducing factors that emerged were (1) academic problems, (2) time constraints, and (3) finances. In the area of academic problems more than 90 percent of college students were stressed by such factors as tests and examinations, and preparing papers for classes. Various factors related to time were a series cause of stress with more than 60 percent saying there was insufficient time for planning. Like most everyone else college students are stressed by financial problems and this was a cause of stress for more than half of them.

EFFECTS OF STRESS

The viewpoint that prompts the comment "almost everything causes stress," could be applied with the assertion that "stress causes everything." A tragic consequence is that stress-related psychological and physiological disorders are viewed as primary social and health problems. Compelling evidence from studies and clinical trials, as well as many standard medical textbooks, attribute anywhere from 50 to 80 percent of all diseases at least in part to stress-related origins.

The literature by various medical authorities shows that among other conditions, the following in some way could be stress related: diabetes, cirrhosis of the liver, high blood pressure, peptic ulcer, migraine headaches, multiple sclerosis, lung disease, injury due to accidents, mental health problems, cancer, and coronary heart disease.

Some Effects of Stress-on College Students

It has already been mentioned that stress can result in many serious health problems. This is especially true of prolonged and unrelenting stress that becomes chronic. Although not all college students are immediately at risk for serious stress-related conditions, there is some evidence that they could be affected in some way later in life. Also, we are well aware of some older adults who have vivid memories of a poor school performance that they have recalled and which has troubled them for years - and therefore has created stress for them over time.

My studies showed effects of stress among college students impacting on mental/emotional health and on physical health. They cited such factors as outbursts of anger, excessive anxiety, frustration, conflict, irritation, and fear. As far as impact on physical health was concerned, many mentioned such factors as not enough sleep, continuous tension, fatigue, headaches, and digestive problems.

PERSONALITY AND STRESS

Before commenting on personality as it pertains to stress, it seems appropriate to discuss briefly my own conception of personality. Ordinarily, personality is often dealt with only as a psychological entity. I think of it in terms of a broad frame of reference, which is the *total* personality. I view this total personality as consisting of physical, social, emotional, and intellectual aspects. This conforms more or less with what has become a rather common description of personality - *existence as a person* and this should be interpreted to mean the whole person or unified individual.

There appears to be general agreement that personality can influence how individuals handle stress. On the other hand, there is much less agreement regarding personality as a causal factor in disease. One specific example of this is the difference of opinion regarding the extent to which certain types of personality are associated with heart disease. A case in point is that which concerns the early work of Meyer Friedman and Ray H. Rosenman, who designated Type A behavior and Type behavior. A person with Type A behavior tends to be aggressive, ambitious, competitive, and puts pressure on himself or herself in getting things done. An individual with Type B behavior is more easy going, relaxed, and tends not to have self-imposed pressure. With regard to these two type of behavior, the authors have commented, "In the absence of Type A Behavior Pattern, coronary heart disease almost never occurs before 70 years of age, regardless of the fatty foods eaten, the cigarettes smoked or the lack of exercise. But when the behavior pattern is present, coronary heart disease can easily erupt in one's thirties and forties." [7]

This point of view has been challenged by some, the main point of contention being that there is little in the way of solid objective evidence to support the hypothesis. In this connection it is interesting that many heart specialists have noted that death from heart disease is on a downward trend and may be expected to continue. They credit this, among other things, to diet, control of high blood pressure and particularly to exercise.

It is interesting to note that in a special symposium on the interaction between the heart and brain at an American Psychiatric Association meeting a few years ago, Rosenman reported that a 22-year research project found that Type As were twice as likely as Type Bs to develop coronary heart disease.[8] In addition, however, the highly competitive nature found in Type A people increases the likelihood that important warning signs of heart disease, such as chest pain, will be denied. It is estimated that Type As also survive better than Type Bs, and it is speculated that this may have something to do with Type As' adeptness at denial. This is to say that once a heart attack has occurred, Type A people tend to deny their symptoms, and therefore may be better at suppressing the health anxieties that often accompany recovery from heart attack. According to Rosenman, with less anxiety there is less adrenaline release and a greater feeling of control over life.

In another frame of reference, Benjamin Newberry and his associates[9] writing in my series, *Stress in Modern Society,* reported that Type As are highly susceptible to many stress responses, including hostility and aggression. It is suggested that the consequences of the Type A behavior pattern depends upon other aspects of personality and temperament. It is hypothesized that the Type A behavior pattern will be associated with dysphoric emotion and disease susceptibility in individuals who are high in reactivity (roughly, high in biological predisposition to introversion). The social environments of these people will have imposed the Type A behavior pattern on them despite its compatibility with their underlying temperament.

There is general agreement that one manifests his or her personality through certain behavior traits and characteristics. This being the case, if these traits and characteristics can be positively identified as being detrimental to one's health, it may be possible to modify behaviors that cause the problems.

SUGGESTED ACTIVITIES

1. Hold a panel discussion on the likenesses and differences between physiological and psychological stress.
2. Make a list of those factors which are stress inducing for you. Pool your list with other class members and compile the results of the entire class.
3. Make a list of your own physiological and behavioral reactions to stress. Pool your list with other class members and compile the results of the entire class.
4. Hold a round table discussion on one or more of the following topics:
   a. Selye's General Adaptation Syndrome
   b. Social interaction and social stress
   c. Personality and stress
   d. The causes of eustress and distress.

Chapter 3

DEALING WITH EMOTIONS

In introducing the subject of emotion, we are confronted with the fact that, for many years, it has been a difficult concept to define and, in addition, there have been many changing ideas and theories as far as the study of emotion is concerned. Obviously, it is not the purpose of a book of this nature to attempt to go into any great depth on a subject that has been one of the most intricate undertakings of psychology for many years. However, a general overview of the subject appears to be in order to help the reader have a clearer understanding of the emotional aspect of personality, particularly with regard to its involvement in stress.

1. Why is more literature devoted to unpleasant emotions than to pleasant emotions?
2. What causes people to manifest emotional behavior?
3. What are some of the ways researchers have attempted to assess emotional reactivity?
4. What is the difference between frustration and conflict?
5. What are some characteristics of emotionality?
6. What is the difference between the emotional patterns of fear and anger?
7. What are some factors that influence emotionality?
8. What are some of the ways to develop emotional stability in various kinds of environment?
9. What are some of the characteristics of the emotionally healthy person?

Emotional stress can be brought about by the stimulus of emotional patterns. For example, the emotional pattern of anger can be stimulated by such factors as the thwarting of one's wishes, or a number of cumulative irritations. Response to such stimuli can be either *impulsive* or *inhibited*. An impulsive expression of anger is one that is directed against a person or an object, while the inhibited expressions are kept under control, and may be manifested by such overt behaviors as skin flushing.

Generally speaking, emotional patterns can be placed into the two broad categories of *pleasant* emotions and un*pleasant* emotions. Pleasant emotional patterns include such things as joy, affection, happiness, and love - in the broad sense, while included among the unpleasant emotional patterns are anger, sorrow, jealousy, fear, and worry - an imaginary form of fear.

It is interesting to note that a good proportion of the literature is devoted to emotions that are unpleasant. It has been found that, in most basic psychology books, much more space is given to such emotional patterns as fear, hate, and guilt, than to such pleasant emotions as love, sympathy, and contentment.

At one time or another all of us have manifested emotional behavior as well as ordinary behavior. Differences in the structure of the organism and in the environment will largely govern the degree to which each individual expresses emotional behavior. Moreover, it has been suggested that the pleasantness or unpleasantness of an emotion seems to be determined by its strength or intensity, by the nature of the situation arousing it, and by the way the individual perceives or interprets the situation.

The ancient Greeks identified emotions with certain organs of the body. In general, sorrow was expressed from the heart (a broken heart); jealousy was associated with the liver; hate with the gall bladder; and anger with the spleen. In regard to the latter, we sometimes hear the expression "venting the spleen" on someone. This historical reference is made because in modern times we take into account certain conduits between the emotions and the body. These are by way of the *nervous* system and the *endocrine* system. That part of the nervous system principally concerned with the emotions is the *autonomic* nervous system, which controls functions such as the heart beat, blood pressure, and digestion. When there is a stimulus of any of the emotional patterns, these two systems activate in the manner explained in Chapter 2. By way of illustration, if the emotional pattern of fear is stimulated, the heartbeat accelerates, breathing is more rapid, and the blood pressure is likely to rise. Energy fuel is discharged into the blood from storage in the liver, which causes the blood sugar level to rise. These, along with other bodily functions serve to prepare the person to cope with the condition caused by the fear. He or she then reacts with the fight or flight response, also discussed in Chapter 2.

When we attempt to evaluate the emotional aspect of personality, we encounter various degrees of difficulty, because of certain uncontrollable factors. Included among some of the methods used for attempting to measure emotional responses are the following:

1. Blood pressure: It rises when one is under some sort of emotional stress.
2. Blood sugar analysis: Under stressful conditions, more sugar enters the blood stream.
3. Pulse rate: Emotional stress causes it to elevate.
4. Galvanic skin response: Similar to the lie detector technique, and measurements are recorded in terms of perspiration on the palms of the hands.

These, as well as others that have been used by investigators of human emotion, have various and perhaps limited degrees of validity. In attempting to assess emotional reactivity, we often encounter the problem of the extent to which we are dealing with a purely physiological response or a purely emotional response. For example, one's pulse rate would be elevated by taking some sort of physical exercise. It could be likewise be elevated if a person were the object of an embarrassing remark by another. Thus, in this illustration, the elevation of pulse rate could be caused for different reasons, the first being physiological and the second emotional. Then, too the type of emotional pattern is not identified by the measuring device. A joy response and an anger response will likely show the same or nearly the same rise in pulse rate. These are some of the reasons why it is a most difficult thing to arrive at a high degree of objectivity in studying the emotional aspect of personality.

FACTORS CONCERNED WITH EMOTIONAL STABILITY

Modern society involves a sequence of experiences that are characterized by the necessity for us to adjust. Consequently, it could be said that normal behavior is the result of successful adjustment, and abnormal behavior results from unsuccessful adjustment. The degree of adjustment that one achieves depends upon how adequately he or she is able to satisfy basic needs and to fulfill desires within the framework of his or her environment and the pattern or ways dictated by the society.

As mentioned in the first chapter, stress may be considered as any factor acting internally or externally that renders adaptation difficult, and which induces increased effort on the part of the person to maintain a state of equilibrium within himself or herself and with the environment. When stress is induced as a result of the individual's not being able to meet needs (basic demands) and satisfy desires (wants or wishes), *frustration* or *conflict* results Frustration occurs when a need is not met, and conflict results when choices must be made between nearly equally attractive alternatives or when basic emotional forces oppose one another. In the emotionally healthy person, the degree of frustration is ordinarily in proportion to the intensity of the need or desire. That is, he or she will objectively observe and evaluate the situation to ascertain whether a solution is possible, and if so, what solution best enables him or her to achieve the fulfillment of needs and desires. However, every person has a *zone of tolerance* or limits for emotional stress within which he or she normally operates. If the stress becomes considerably greater than the tolerance level, or if the individual has not learned to cope with his or her problems and objectively and intelligently solve them, some degree of maladjustment possibly can result.

It could be said that the major difference between you, as a normal college student, and some young criminal confined to prison is that you have the ability to control your emotional impulses to a greater extent than he. Perhaps many of us at one time or another have experienced the same kinds of emotions that have led the abnormal individual to commit violence, but we have been able to hold our powerful and violent emotions in check. This may be an extreme example, but it should suggest something of the importance of emotional control in modern society.

An important aspect of controlling the emotions is becoming able to function effectively and intelligently in an emotionally charged situation. Success in most life situations hinges on this ability. Extremes of emotional upset must be avoided if the individual is to be able to think and act effectively.

It is sometimes helpful to visualize your emotions as being forces within you that are in a struggle for power with your mind as to which is to control you, your reason, or your emotions. Oftentimes, our basic emotions are blind and unconcerned with the welfare of other people, or sometimes, even with our own welfare. Emotional stability has to do with gaining increased mastery over our emotions - not, of course, eliminating them - so that we may behave as intelligent and civilized human beings rather than as savages or children in temper tantrums.

In order to pursue a sensible course in our efforts to acquire desired emotional stability, there are certain factors that need to be considered as follows: (1) characteristics of emotionality, (2) emotional arousals and reactions, and (3) factors that influence emotionality.

Characteristics of Emotionality

1. *There are variations in how long emotions last.* A child's emotions may last for a few minutes or less and then terminate rather abruptly. The child gets it "out of his system" so to speak by expressing it outwardly. In contrast, some adult emotions may be long and drawn out. As children get older, expressing the emotions by overt action is encumbered by certain social restraints. This is to say that what might be socially acceptable at one age level is not necessarily so at another. This may be a reason for some children developing moods, which in a sense are states of emotion drawn out over a period of time and expressed slowly. Typical moods may be that of "sulking" due to restraint or anger, and being "jumpy" from repressed fear. Of course, it is common for these moods to prevail well into adulthood.

2. *There are differences in the intensity of emotions.* You will probably recall in your own experience that some persons may react rather violently to a situation that, to you might appear insignificant. This kind of behavior is likely to reflect one's background and past experience with specific kinds of situations.

3. *Emotions are subject to rapid change.* A young child is capable of shifting quickly from laughing to crying, or from anger to joy. Although the reason for this is not definitely known, it might be that there is not as much depth of feeling among children as there is among adults. In addition, it could be due to lack of experience that children have had, as well as their state of intellectual development. We do know that young children have a short attention span, which could cause them to change rapidly from one kind of emotion to another. As we mature into adults rapid change in emotions is likely to wane.

4. *Depending on the individual, emotions can appear with various degrees of frequency.* As individuals grow and mature, they manage to develop the ability to adjust to situations that previously would have caused an emotional reaction. This is, no doubt, due to the acquisition of more experience with various kinds of emotional situations. As far as children are concerned, they learn through experience what is socially acceptable and what is socially unacceptable. This is particularly true if a child is reprimanded in some way following a violent emotional reaction. For this reason, a child may try to confront situations in ways that do not involve an emotional response. You probably know some adults who tend to react in much the same way.

5. *People differ in their emotional responses.* One person confronted with a situation that instills fear may run away from the immediate environment (hit and run driver), while another may try to hide. Different reactions of people to emotional situations are probably due to a host of factors. Included among these may be past experiences with a certain kind of emotional situation, willingness of parents and other adults during childhood to help them become more independent, and family relationships in general.

6. *Strength of people's emotions are subject to change.* At some age levels certain kinds of emotions may be weak and later become stronger. Conversely, with some young children, emotions that were strong may tend to decline. For example, small children may be timid among strangers, but later when they see there is nothing to fear, the timidity is likely to diminish. This may be true of some adults who experienced insecurity in childhood.

Emotional Arousals and Reactions

If we are to understand the nature of human emotions, we need to take into account some of those factors of emotional arousal and how people might react to them. Many different kinds of emotional patterns have been identified. For purposes here the patterns arbitrarily selected for discussion are fear, worry, anger, jealousy, and joy.

1. *Fear.* The term fear from the Old English *fir* may have been derived originally from the German word *fahr*, meaning danger or peril. In modern times fear is often thought of in terms of anxiety caused by present or impending danger or peril. For example, fear can generally be defined as a more generalized reaction to a vague sense of threat in absence of a specific or realistic dangerous object. However, the terms fear and anxiety are often used loosely and often interchangeably. When fearful or anxious, individuals experience unpleasant changes in overt behavior, subjective feelings (including thoughts), and physiological activity.

Fears differ from anxiety in that the former are negative emotional responses to any specific environment factor. But fears and anxiety are similar in the feelings they arouse; rapid heartbeat, sweating, quivering, heavy breathing, feeling weak or numb in the limbs, dizziness or faintness, muscular tension, the need to eliminate, and a sense of dread -the "fight or flight" response mechanism. Not all people experience all these signs of fear, but most experience some of them.

There are various ways of classifying fears. For purposes of discussion here the two broad classifications of *objective* fears and *irrational* fears will be cited.

Many objective fears are useful and necessary and it is logical that we be afraid of such things as: (1) touching a hot stove, (2) falling from a high place, (3) running into the street without looking for oncoming cars, and (4) having a tooth drilled without anesthesia. These kinds of fears are referred to as *rational* and *adaptive.*

Some fears are said to be *irrational* and *maladaptive.* It is an irrational fear when the objective danger is. in disproportion to the amount of distress experienced. These kinds of fears are called *phobias* or *phobic disorders,* among which are (1) fear of high places, (2) fear of closed-in places, (3) fear of receiving injections, (4) fear of working with sharp instruments, (5) fear of the dark, and (6) fear of being alone.

Irrational fears or phobias do not necessarily have to interfere with our lives. It matters little if you are afraid of heights if your life style permits you to avoid high places. However, some irrational fears can be debilitating experiences and interfere greatly with your attempt to lead your daily life. For instance, if one has no tolerance for the sight of blood or being in an environment of medical procedures, one may find his or her health or life endangered if he or she refrains from seeking treatment for an injury or disease. In such cases it would clearly be of benefit to do something about such fears. In another frame of reference it should be mentioned that behavioral explanations of the development and maintenance of fears are based on learning principles. That is, basically it is assumed that all behavior, and thus the individual's fear responses, are learned from the environment.

Reporting in Volume 1 of my series on *Stress in Modern Society,* D'Ann Whitehead and her associates[1] suggested three paradigms by which learning takes place: respondent conditioning, operant conditioning, and the two-factor theory of learning.

In *respondent conditioning* if a neutral stimulus is presented simultaneously with presentation of a fear provoking stimulus, the neutral stimulus will become a conditioned stimulus for fear. Thus, on subsequent occasions, the previously neutral stimulus will evoke a fear response. The classic experiment by J. B. Watson and R. Raynor[2] more than eight decades ago illustrates this process. In the experiment, a child learned to fear a white rat. Initially, the child, Little Albert, was shown the white rat for which he showed no fear. While the child was paying attention to the rat, he was frightened by a loud sound (striking a steel bar with a hammer held a safe distance behind the child's head). Following several repetitions of this, the child was noticed to be afraid of the rat. The original neutral stimulus (rat), therefore, became a conditioned stimulus to elicit fear. It was later noticed that the child generalized this fear to other "furry" objects, (e. g. his mother's fur neckpiece). Watson and Raynor whimsically noted that a dynamically oriented child psychologist examining this child might produce many speculations as to the origin of the fear, but almost certainly would not state in his report that the child was obviously frightened by striking a steel bar behind his head as a white rat was placed in front of him - yet that is how the fear was produced.

Operant conditioning can account for the development of fear or the basis of reinforcement through the environmental contingencies that follow a fear response. For example, the child's fear of the dark may lead to such social reinforcement in terms of parental attention (including bedtime stories, snacks, and the like) at bed time. Similarly, a fear of bugs or dirt may make in "impossible" for the child to help pull weeds in the garden.

The *two-factor theory* was advanced by O. H. Mowrer[2] in the late 1930s and both respondent and operant conditioning are embodied in this concept. According to this theory, fears first develop by respondent conditioning are maintained by operant conditioning. A neutral stimulus is paired with a fear-provoking stimulus and the neutral stimulus becomes a conditioned fear stimulus. The individual then engages in behavior which enables him or her to escape or avoid the conditioned fear stimulus. If such maneuvers are successful, they decrease the level of experienced anxiety or fear. This fear reduction serves to reinforce the behaviors that were instrumental in reducing the fear. For example, if a child is taking a bath and gets water in the nose, the child may develop fear of baths. In order to reduce the fear and anxiety, he or she may hide until just before bed time, fall asleep in the living room, or throw a tantrum when told to take a bath. The anxiety reduction experienced by avoiding the bath reinforces continued avoidance of baths.

In my interviews and surveys of college students the following fears were the most prominent: Fear

- of failing in school
- of letting my parents down
- of not getting a good job after college
- of not keeping my health
- of not having enough money to finish college

2. *Worry.* This might be an imaginary form of fear, and it can be a fear not aroused directly from one's environment. Worry can be aroused by imagining a situation that could possibly arise; that is, one could worry about other family members. Since worries are likely to be caused by *imaginary* rather than *real* conditions, they are not likely to be found in abundance among very young children. Perhaps the reason for this is that they have not reached a stage of intellectual development where they might imagine certain things that

could cause worry. Among some college students worry is a constant problem, and many will find things to worry about. Controlling worry is a difficult problem for those college students who have problems in adjusting. In my surveys of college students the following were the most prominent worries: Worry

- about passing my courses
- about failing examinations
- about my financial position
- about not being a success
- about where the country is headed

3. *Anger.* This emotional response tends to occur more frequently than fear. This is probably due to the fact that there are more conditions that incite anger. In the case of children, they quickly learn that anger may get attention that otherwise would not be forthcoming (can you think of any "spoiled" adults who react in this manner?) It is likely that as children get older they may show more anger responses than fear responses because they soon see that there is not as much to fear as they originally thought.

Because of individual differences in people, there is a wide variation in anger responses, and as mentioned previously, these responses are either impulsive or inhibited. It should be recalled that in impulsive responses, one manifests an overt action against another person or an object, such as kicking a door. This form of child behavior is also sometimes manifested by some "adults." In discussing anger, the condition of *aggression* should also be taken into account. Aggression literally means "to attack." This ordinarily is provoked by anger and can result in hostile action. Thus, anger is the emotional pattern and it is outwardly demonstrated by aggression. It is important to point out the difference between aggressive behavior and *assertive* behavior. The latter form of behavior has received a great deal of attention in recent years, and rightly so. Self-assertiveness should be considered a basic role in one's life. All of us have a need for self-reliance and confidence in our abilities. This need can be met by asserting ourselves in a manner that we pursue our personal goals without too much dependence on others. Certainly one can be assertive without being aggressive.

My studies reveal that the following things seem to cause the most anger among college students:

1. People who cheat on examinations.
2. People who think they are better than I am.
3. People who try to tell me what to do.
4. People who are always complaining.
5. Having to wait too long in line for almost everything.

4. *Jealousy.* This response usually occurs when one feels a threat of loss of affection. Many psychologists believe that jealousy is closely related to anger. Because of this, a person may build up resentment against another person. Jealousy can be very devastating and every effort should be made to avoid it.

Jealousy is concerned with social interactions that involve persons one likes. There are various ways in which the individual may respond. These include: (1) being aggressive toward the one of whom he or she is jealous, (2) withdrawing from the person whose affections he or she thinks have been lost, and (3) possible development of an "I don't care" attitude,

In some cases, individuals will not respond in any of the above ways. They might try to excel over the person of whom they are jealous. In other words, they might tend to do things to impress the person whose affections they thought had been lost.

5. *Joy.* This pleasant emotion is one that we strive for because it is so important in maintaining emotional stability. Causes of joy differ from one age level to another, and from one person to another at the same age level. This is to say that what might be a joyful situation for one person might not necessarily be so for another.

Joy is expressed in various ways, but the most common are laughing and smiling, the latter being a restrained form of laughter. Some people respond to joy with a state of body relaxation. This is difficult to detect because it has little or no overt manifestation. However, it may be noticed when one compares it with body tension caused by unpleasant emotions.

GUIDELINES FOR THE DEVELOPMENT OF EMOTIONAL STABILITY

It is important to set forth some guidelines if we are to meet with any degree of success in our attempts to provide for emotional stability. The reason for this is to assure, at least to some extent, that our efforts at attaining optimum emotional stability will be based somewhat on a scientific approach. These guidelines might well take the form of *valid concepts of emotional stability.* The following list of concepts is submitted with this general idea in mind.

1. *An emotional response may be brought about by a goal's being furthered or thwarted.* Serious attempts should be made by those responsible to assure successful experience in a given environment such as home, school, or job. In the school setting, this can be accomplished in part by attempting to provide for individual differences within given school experiences. The school, home, or job setting should be such that each person derives a feeling of personal worth through making some sort of positive contribution.

2. *Self-realization experiences should be constructive.* The opportunity for creative experiences that afford the individual a chance for self-realization should be inherent in the home, school, or on the job. Individuals should plan with others to see that specific environmental activities are meeting their needs, and as a result, involve constructive experience,

3. *In the case of children, as they develop the emotional reactions tend to become less violent and more discriminating.* A well planned program of school experiences and wholesome home activities should be such that they provide for release of aggression in a socially acceptable manner.

4. *Emotional reactions tend to increase beyond normal expectancy towards the constructive or destructive on the balance of furthering or hindering experiences of the individual.* For some persons the confidence they need to be able to face the problems of life may come through physical expression. Therefore, such experiences as recreation in the form of pleasurable physical activity in the away-from-work situation have tremendous potential to help contribute toward a solid base of emotional stability.

5. *Depending on certain factors, one's own feelings may be accepted or rejected by the individual.* All environmental experiences should make people feel good and have confidence

in themselves. Satisfactory self-concept is closely related to body control; physical activity oriented experiences might be considered as one of the best ways of contributing to it.

OPPORTUNITIES FOR THE DEVELOPMENT OF EMOTIONAL STABILITY IN VARIOUS KINDS OF ENVIRONMENTS

Environments, such as the school, home, and work situations, have the potential to provide for emotional stability. The extent to which this actually occurs is dependent primarily upon the kind of emotional climate provided by individuals responsible for it, such as teachers, parents, and others. For this reason, it appears pertinent to examine some of the potential opportunities that exist for the development of emotional stability in these environments. The following descriptive list is submitted for this purpose.

1. *Release of aggression in a socially acceptable manner.* This appears to be an outstanding way in which school activities such as physical education can help provide college students with opportunities to improve upon emotional stability. For example, batting a softball or engaging in a combative stunt can afford a socially acceptable way of releasing aggression. The same can be said for a home or campus environment where students are provided with wholesome recreational opportunities.

2. *Inhibition of direct response to unpleasant emotions.* This does not necessarily mean that feelings concerned with such unpleasant emotions as fear and anger should be completely restrained. On the contrary, the interpretation should be that such feelings can take place less frequently in a wholesome school, home, or work environment. This means that opportunities should be provided to relieve tension rather than to aggravate it.

3. *Promotion of pleasant emotions.* Perhaps there is too much concern with suppressing unpleasant emotions and not enough attention given to promotion of pleasant ones. This means that the college experience should provide a range of activities where all students can succeed. Thus, all students should be afforded the opportunity for success at least most of the time.

4. *Recognition of one's abilities and limitations.* It has already been mentioned that a wide range of activities should provide an opportunity for success for all. This should make it easier in the college setting to provide for individual differences among students so that all of them can progress within the limits of their own skill and ability. This calls for provision of counseling that will help guide students into appropriate major areas of study and career pursuits.

5. *Understanding about the ability and achievement of others.* In the educational experience emphasis can be placed upon achievement of the group. Team play and group effort is important in most situations, whether it be in school or on the job.

6. *Being able to make a mistake without being ostracized.* In the school setting, this requires that the teacher serve as a catalyst who helps students understand the idea of trial and error. Emphasis can be placed on *trying* and that one can learn not only from his or her own mistakes but from the mistakes of others as well. The classroom is *not* the "real world" but preparation for it.

EVALUATING INFLUENCES OF THE ENVIRONMENT ON THE DEVELOPMENT OF EMOTIONAL STABILITY

What we are essentially concerned with here is how an individual can make some sort of valid evaluation of the extent to which a particular environment contributes to emotional stability. This means that some attempt should be made to assess an environment with reference to whether or not these experiences are providing for emotional stability.

One such approach would be to refer back to the list of "opportunities for the development of emotional stability in various kinds of environments" suggested in the immediately preceding discussion. These opportunities have been converted into a rating scale as follows:

1. The environmental experience provides for release of aggression in a socially acceptable manner.
    4 most of the time
    3 some of the time
    2 occasionally
    1 infrequently
2. The environmental experience provides for inhibition of direct response of unpleasant emotions.
    4 most of the time
    3 some of the time
    2 occasionally
    1 infrequently
3. The environmental experience provides for promotion of pleasant emotions.
    4 most of the time
    3 some of the time
    2 occasionally
    1 infrequently
4. The environmental experience provides for recognition of one's abilities and limitations.
    4 most of the time
    3 some of the time
    2 occasionally
    1 infrequently
5. The environmental experience provides for an understanding about the ability and achievement of others.
    4 most of the time
    3 some of the time
    2 occasionally
    1 infrequently
6. The environmental experience provides for being able to make a mistake without being ostracized.
    4 most of the time
    3 some of the time

2 occasionally

1 infrequently

If one makes these ratings objectively and conscientiously, a reasonably good procedure for evaluation is provided. Ratings can be made periodically to see if positive changes appear to be taking place. Ratings can be made for a single experience, a group of experiences, or for the total environmental experience. This procedure can help one identify the extent to which environmental experiences and/or conditions under which the experiences take place are contributing to emotional stability.

THE EMOTIONALLY HEALTHY PERSON

It seems appropriate to close this chapter by mentioning some of the characteristics of emotionally healthy persons. As we look at some of these characteristics we must recognize that they are not absolute nor static. We are not always happy, and we sometimes find ourselves in situations where we are not overly confident. In fact, sometimes we may feel downright inadequate to solve commonplace problems that occur in our daily lives.

1. Emotionally healthy persons have achieved basic harmony within themselves and a workable relationship with others. They are able to function effectively, and usually happily, even though they are well aware of the limitations and rigors involved in human existence.

2. Emotionally healthy persons manage to adapt to the demands of environmental conditions with emotional responses that are appropriate in degree and kind to the stimuli and situations and that fall, generally, within the range of what is considered "normal" within various environments.

3. Emotionally healthy persons face problems directly and seek realistic and plausible solutions to them. They try to free themselves from excessive and unreal anxieties, worries, and fears, even though they are aware that there is much to be concerned with and much to be anxious about in our complex modern society.

4. Emotionally healthy persons have developed a guiding philosophy of life and have a set of values that are acceptable to themselves and that are generally in harmony with those values of society that are reasonable and conducive to human happiness.

5. Emotionally healthy persons accept themselves and are willing to deal with the world as it exists in reality. They accept what cannot be changed at a particular time and place and they build and derive satisfaction within the framework of their own potentialities and those of their environment.

6. Emotionally healthy persons tend to be happy, and they tend to have an enthusiasm for living. They do not focus their attention exclusively upon what they consider to be their inadequacies, weaknesses, and "bad" qualities. They view those around them in this way too.

7. Emotionally healthy persons have a variety of satisfying interests and they maintain a balance between their work, routine responsibilities, and recreation. They find constructive and satisfying outlets for creative expression in the interests that they undertake.

This list of characteristics of emotionally healthy persons presents a near-ideal situation and obviously none of us operate at these high levels at all times. However, they might well be considered as suitable guidelines for which we might strive to help us deal with and possibly prevent unpleasant emotional stress.

SUGGESTED ACTIVITIES

1. List as many things as you can think of that arouse *fear* in you. Pool your list with other class members to determine the percent of times these fears occur.
2. List as many things as you can think of that arouse *anger* in you. Pool your list with other class members to determine the percent of times these forms of anger occur.
3. Complete the following: Happiness is _____
   Compare your statement with other class members.
4. Complete the following: Sadness is_____
   Compare your statement with other class members.
5. Using the rating scale in the chapter, select an environment such as the classroom, dormitory, or dining hall and make ratings of "opportunities provided for the improvement of emotional stability." Compare your ratings with class members who selected the same environment. Compile the data for the entire class.

Chapter 4

NUTRITION, DIET AND STRESS

The 18th century gastronomist Anthelme Brillat-Savarin, famous for his book, *The Physiology of Taste,* once said, "Tell me what you eat and I will tell you what you are." The more modern adage "You are what you eat" could well have been derived from this old quotation. And, of course, it is true.

At one time eating was fun and enjoyable - until recent years when many of us have become victims of the "don't eat this, don't eat that" syndrome. The fact is that because certain aspects of nutrition and diet have become so controversial, many people in the general public have become more or less confused about the entire matter. Therefore, it is the purpose of this chapter to attempt to clear up at least some of this confusion, as well as to consider nutrition and diet as they are concerned with stress.

At the outset it is stated forcefully and unequivocally that any consideration of one's nutritional problems, eating habits, dietary concerns and the like should be undertaken in consultation with, or under the supervision of a physician and/or a qualified nutritionist.

1. What are the processes of nutrition?
2. What are the essential nutrients?
3. How does stress affect digestion?
4. What is the function of proteins in the body?
5. What are some of the food elements one should consider consuming after a stressful situation?
6. How is diet concerned with stress?
7. What is the theory underlying blood sugar deficiency as it concerns stress?

NUTRITION

Nutrition can be described as the sum of the processes by which a person takes in and utilizes food substances; that is, the nourishment of the body by food. These processes consist of (1) ingestion, (2) digestion, (3) absorption, and (4) assimilation.

Ingestion is derived from the Latin word *ingestus,* meaning "to take in," and in this context it means taking in food, or the act of eating. The process of digestion involves the breaking down or conversion of food into substances that can be *absorbed* through the lining of the intestinal tract and into the blood and used by the body. *Assimilation* is concerned with the incorporation or conversion of nutrients into *protoplasm,* which is the essential material making up living cells.

Essential Nutrients and Their Function in the Body

The body needs many nutrients or foods to keep it functioning properly. These nutrients fall into the broad groups of proteins, carbohydrates, fats, vitamins, and minerals. (Although water is not a nutrient in the strictness sense of the word it must be included, because nutrition cannot take place without it.)

Three major functions of nutrients are (1) building and repair of all body tissues, (2) regulation of all body functions, and (3) providing fuel for the body's energy needs. Although all of the nutrients can do their best work when they are in combination with other nutrients, each still has its own vital role to play.

Protein

Protein is the protoplasmic matter from which all living animal cells and tissues are formed. It is the source of nitrogen, and it is from nitrogen that the building blocks of protein are formed. These basic substances are called *amino acids,* and they are to be found in plant and animal food sources.

The amino acids are acted upon and released during the digestive process, absorbed, and then rebuilt into new protein forms. For example, when you eat a protein food such as meat, the digestive process promptly breaks down into various amino acids. The body chemistry then goes to work to reassemble these amino acids into a new protein form. Some of the combinations are used to make cells for different tissues, such as muscle, blood, bone, and the soft tissues of the vital organs. Other amino acid combinations form the various hormones for the endocrine system, and still others are utilized to form enzymes. Enzymes are internal secretions necessary for the proper functioning of the blood, stomach, and other: organs of the body. They are highly specialized and are responsible for such varied functions as aiding in the clotting of the blood and turning starches into sugar.

Protein is the basic raw material necessary for growth from the very beginning of life. It is necessary for the building of new tissues and the repairing of worn-out tissue. It can also serve as a fuel for muscular work when needed, and we never outgrow our need for it. Since the metabolic process of the body is continuous, it is imperative that we have a continual supply of protein, so that the functions of the body can be successfully accomplished.

Although most Americans obtain their protein from both plant and animal sources, certain religious groups, vegetarians, and people in countries where producing meat is not economically feasible have demonstrated that various plants provide many of the amino acids that are needed by humans. Plants have the ability to synthesize all of the amino acids they need for growth, but humans are not self-sufficient. There are at least eight out of the more than 25 amino acids necessary to human health and growth that he or she is capable of synthesizing satisfactorily from other foodstuffs. The amino acids that the body tissues cannot manufacture and must be obtained from outside sources are called "essential."

"Complete" protein foods are those which contain all of the essential amino acids. Animal meats are complete in this sense, as are also milk and milk products and eggs. Fish, too is a good source of complete proteins. On the other hand, the fact is that large segments of the world population never eat meat and in some cases not even dairy products -but still grow into active adulthood. Thus, it is clear that some vegetable foods likely provide all necessary proteins. Grain foods, nuts, peanuts, soy beans, peas, beans, and yeast are among the more important sources of non-animal proteins. Combinations of proteins seem to be especially valuable for meeting the body's needs.

Although proteins are essential for life, and are needed regularly, their importance should not lead to their being exaggerated in the diet. They are especially important during such times as when bodily tissues are being rebuilt following debilitating illnesses. Still, it is known that people can do without food of any kind for well over a week and have no ill effects. In other words, we would not wish the comments concerning a continuous supply of protein or any other food to lead one to think that they could not stand to miss an occasional meal, or several meals for that matter. After all, "three meals a day" is more a conditioned response than a nutritional necessity. And it seems likely that the quality of one's food intake over a period of time - say several days - is more important than a meal-by-meal evaluation. However, efforts have been made by nutritionists to provide guidance as to what, roughly, the body needs daily.

Carbohydrates

The carbohydrates that occur in our foods chiefly as sugars and starches are combinations of the chemical elements of carbon, hydrogen, and oxygen. These foods are broken down during the digestive process into simple sugars absorbed into the blood. It is from the blood that the tissue cells can withdraw sugar according to their energy needs.

Our main source of carbohydrates is foods composed of grain. These include breads and cereals some of which are also rich in protein, minerals, and vitamins), spaghetti, macaroni, pastries, and the like. Potatoes are also a source of starch, but they contain other important food values as well.

Another important aspect of carbohydrates is that they provide fiber (once generally referred to as roughage), which adds bulk and helps to move the bowels. In recent years the lack of fiber in the diet has been of some concern because on the average we consume only about 40 percent of the fiber that is necessary.

Generally speaking, usable carbohydrates have at least two fates in the body. The first is the formulation of glucose. Glucose is the major energy source for the body and the only form of energy used by the brain, nerves, and lung tissue.

One gram of carbohydrate yields four calories of energy. The second fate of carbohydrates is the formation of glycogen from glucose. Glycogen is a form of stored energy with the principal stores being in the liver. Smaller reserves are found in the muscles. Blood glucose comes from dietary complex carbohydrates and simple carbohydrates.

Carbohydrates are the fuel foods that provide us with most of the energy to carry on bodily activities, including those associated with the basic metabolic processes. All foods provide energy to some extent, but the starches and sugars are the most economical and most easily digested foods that can be obtained for this purpose.

Fats

Fats are derived from the same chemical elements as carbohydrates, but the combination of the carbon, hydrogen, and oxygen is different. Fats contain more carbon but less oxygen than carbohydrates, and they are a more concentrated energy source than either carbohydrates and proteins. They also contribute to the bodily functioning in other important ways and should not, therefore, be considered as substances to be eliminated entirely from the diet.

Fat deposits in the body serve as insulation and shock-absorption material and as reserve energy in storage. Individuals whose energy expenditure is likely to exceed that provided by their carbohydrate intake are especially in need of the "slower burning" fats in their diet. Individuals who wish or need to reduce their weight or who have certain circulatory disorders and risks usually are advised to restrict their fat intake more or less sharply. For several decades the consumption of fat has been about 40 percent of the diet. Because of the relationship to fat intake and heart disease, it is generally recommended that on the average the diet not exceed more than 30 percent fat. And 20 percent is considered to be a low-fat diet.

Minerals

The mineral elements of the body are often referred to as ash constituents, for they are the residue left from the oxidation process of the organic compounds we eat in the form of food. In simpler terms, we may liken them to the ashes remaining after the burning of wood or coal. The mineral elements compose about four percent of the total body weight, with calcium accounting for approximately half of that.

Included among the minerals are calcium, phosphorous, potassium, sulfur, chlorine, sodium, iron, iodine, manganese, copper, cobalt, nickel fluorine, and magnesium. The last mentioned one, magnesium, has important implications for stress. It protects against the cardiac damage caused by stress-related hormones like adrenaline and noradrenaline. During acute stress, there is an increase in fatty acids in the blood, which slows down blood flow and promotes clot formation. Magnesium tends to bind these fatty acids, making less of the active, or ionizable form available. A high fat intake increases blood lipids that similarly bind magnesium, and dairy products, which are also rich in calcium, can seriously aggravate the problem. When calcium is high and magnesium is low, blood clotting is accelerated, further impeding blood flow. Magnesium also appears to be particularly important in preventing heart attacks. In fact, the incidence of coronary disease is lowest in those areas with the highest drinking water concentrations of magnesium.

The majority of the minerals are needed in minute quantities that are plentiful in a good diet. However, calcium, iron, and iodine are needed in appreciable quantities and therefore may require special consideration in the diet.

The major function of minerals in the body are to serve as building and regulatory substances. As structural constituents they operate in three general ways: (1) they give rigidity to the hard tissues of the bones and teeth, (2) they serve as components of soft tissues in muscle and nerve, and (3) they often serve as the crucial element necessary for the production of hormones such as iodine and thyroxin. As a regulatory of body processes, minerals serve many ways, examples of which are (1) they (calcium) are essential for the coagulation of blood, (2) they protect against the accumulation of too much acid or alkali in the blood and body tissues, (3) they are involved in the maintenance of the normal rhythm of the heartbeat, (4) they aid in the exchange of water in the tissues, and (5) they are involved in the transmission of nerve impulses.

Minerals have an important and diverse use in human metabolism. Since many of them are required in carbohydrate, fat and protein metabolism, they would be important in the energy reaction required during the stress response. However, it is important to take minerals in balanced proportions and not in excessive amounts since they can be toxic in high doses.

Since calcium accounts for approximately one-half of the body weight in minerals, it should receive special consideration in this discussion. Although it is one of the very important minerals in the diet, many persons, particularly women, tend to have about one-half of the calcium intake needed.

Calcium is the basis for strong bones and teeth, with the bones containing 99 percent of the body calcium and the blood the other one percent. The latter is very important because calcium assists with proper heartbeat, contractions of muscles, and as previously mentioned, blood clotting.

In aging, the bones will tend to become more brittle. This is primarily due to loss of calcium from the bones because if there is insufficient amount of calcium intake the calcium is taken from the bones for other uses in the body. Therefore, as one grows older it is very important to consume sufficient amounts of calcium so that bone strength will not be decreased. At one time it was thought that 800 milligrams of calcium was sufficient for older persons. However, more recent recommendations suggest that this is increased to 1,500 milligrams daily to compensate for possible calcium bone loss to other body parts.

Some people like their food well-seasoned with salt and they sometimes wonder why they are cautioned to use less of it. Salt is made up of the two elements of sodium (40 percent) and chloride (60 percent). The former is important to the body because it helps one to have a balance between body fluids and cells. It is also important for transmission of nerve impulses and muscular relaxation.

The U. S. Daily Recommended Allowance is not more than 2,000 milligrams of sodium per day. Unfortunately, on the average we consume a great deal more than this - sometimes in amounts as high as 7,000 milligrams per day. Because high sodium intake is associated with high blood pressure and abnormal fluid retention, persons with high blood pressure and other types of heart disease are ordinarily cautioned by their physician to reduce their salt intake. Other forms of food seasoning are certain herbs and spices such as garlic powder, dill, basil, and thyme.

Vitamins

From an historical point of view, the realization that vitamins are basic nutrients stands as a milestone in the emergence of the field of nutrition as a scientifically based discipline. Unlike such nutrients as carbohydrates, fats, and proteins, vitamins do not become a part of the structure of the body, but rather they serve as catalysts that make possible various chemical reactions within the body. These reactions have to do with converting food substances into the elements needed for utilization by the various cells of the body. For example, vitamin D needs to be present if calcium is to be metabolized and made available for use in the blood and bones.

The vitamins with which we are familiar today are commonly classified as fat soluble or water soluble. This designation means that the one group requires fatty substances and the other water if they are to be dissolved and used in the body. Although a large number of vitamins have been identified as being important in human nutrition, the exact function of many of them has not yet been determined.

In countries such as the United States it should not be difficult for people to select a diet sufficiently varied to include all necessary vitamins. However, poor dietary practices can lead to vitamin inadequacy, and as a precaution many people supplement their diets with vitamin pills. Even though such a supplement may not be needed, when taken in small amounts the vitamins may do no harm. This is particularly true of the water-soluble vitamins in that if one gets more than needed they will pass right through the body. (Recently, some scientists have been disputing this claim, especially if water-soluble vitamins are taken in extra large doses). On the other hand, some of the fat-soluble vitamins may be toxic and overdoses could render possible harm. Of course, extra vitamins may be prescribed by a physician for a variety of reasons.

Water

By far the greatest proportion of the body weight of human beings is water. This water, evaporating and flowing from the surface of the body, and breathed out as vapor on the breath, must be continuously replenished if one is to remain alive. The chemical changes that make life possible can take place only in solution, and it is water that provides the necessary solvent.

The body secures the water it needs from fluids as drink, from foods that are eaten, and from the water formed by the combustion of foods in the body. The body loses water in the form of urine from the kidneys, fecal discharge from the intestinal tract, perspiration from the skin, and exhaled breath from the lungs.

Physical activity, environmental heat, and the normal bodily processes lead more or less rapidly to water loss. If this loss is not balanced by water intake, dehydration can occur. For short periods this loss is harmless and leads to thirst and restoration of normal water level and body weight with copious drinking. However, if the dehydrated state continues over an extended period of time, bodily functions become seriously jeopardized since water is involved in all of them.

The inevitable question is: How much water should one drink daily? Perhaps we should consider this in terms of liquids rather than water as such, because fruits and vegetables contain water. Recommendations by physicians are likely to vary on the amount of water intake one should have daily. Some will recommend that one start and end the day with an eight-ounce glass of water with the same amount at each meal. Others suggest that six to eight glasses of water per day be consumed.

In fact, many such arbitrary recommendations have been made concerning the desirable water intake per day. However, there are many factors that affect the need for it, such as the fluid content of other foods, how active a person is, and the environmental temperature. For younger persons, possibly, thirst could be the guide. However, this is not necessarily true for all older persons. Therefore, some physicians are now recommending that periodic water-drinking periods be scheduled daily to make sure one receives sufficient water. Some physicians have told me that they recommend two and one-half quarts of water daily, mainly for the dissolution of calcium to help prevent the formation of kidney stones.

Calories

Many people labor under the misconception that a calorie is a nutrient just as carbohydrates, fats, and proteins. Actually, a calorie is a unit of measurement just like an ounce or an inch. The body requires energy to function, and heat is the by-product of this energy. A calorie is the amount of heat necessary to raise the temperature of one kilogram (2.2 pounds) of water one degree centigrade. Since food is our source of fuel, scientists have been interested in computing the number of calories different foods provide, as well as the number of calories the body must utilize in the performance of various activities. The results of these studies have furnished information telling how many calories or heat units of the food we eat must produce in order to provide us with enough energy to meet our needs. These energy needs may be classified into two categories, those which are voluntary and those which are involuntary. Voluntary activities are those over which we have control, but the involuntary energy demands are those which take place continuously, whether we are awake or asleep. Among the latter are digestion, heart function, elimination, breathing, and such special demands automatically brought on by emotional excitation, stress, and environmental heat.

One way to assess your caloric needs is: If you are completely sedentary, multiply your weight by 10; that is, if you weigh 150 pounds you would probably need 1,500 calories per day. If you are fairly active, multiply your weight by 12 or 13, and if you are extremely active multiply your weight by 15.

Digestion

The digestive system of the body is more than 30 feet long from beginning to end, and the chemical processes that occur within the walls of the mucus-lined hollow tube are extremely complex in nature. From the moment that food is taken into the mouth until waste products are excreted, the body's chemical laboratory is at work. The principal parts of this system are the alimentary canal, consisting of the oral cavity, pharynx, esophagus, stomach, small intestine, and large intestine. Two additional organs are necessary to complete the digestive system. These are the liver and the pancreas, both of which connect to the small intestine. It is from these two organs that many of the essentially digestive juices are secreted.

As mentioned previously, the function of the digestive system is to change the composition of foods we ingest. Reduced to simpler chemical substances, the foods can be readily absorbed through the lining of the intestines for distribution by the circulatory system to the millions of body cells. These end products of digestion are in the form of simple sugars, fatty acids, amino acids, minerals, and vitamins.

Digestion is also accomplished by mechanical action. First, the food is broken down by the grinding action of the teeth. This increases tremendously the food surface area upon which the various digestive juices can act. It is then swallowed and eventually is moved through the alimentary canal by a process called peristalsis. This is a series of muscular contractions, which mix the contents of the digestive tract and keep it on the move.

Some people have trouble digesting milk because of what is called lactose intolerance. This means that the enzyme lactate may be decreasing, and this enzyme is needed to break down lactose, a form of sugar found in milk. One may wish to use a substitute for regular milk such as buttermilk, yogurt, or cheese. Also there is a product called Lactaid, which is a reduced lactose milk.

Digestion and Stress

You may recall that some college students reported digestive disturbance when they are under stress. This is commonly known as *nervous indigestion*. In this regard, the digestive tract is exceedingly responsive to one's emotional state. Food eaten under happy conditions tends to be readily digested. On the contrary, digestion may be impeded and even stopped for a considerable period of time (as much as a day or more) if severe emotional stress occurs. Extensive nervous connections in the digestive tract tend to make its organs especially susceptible to disorders caused by stress. Examples of some of these disorders are nausea, diarrhea, and colitis (inflammation of the large bowel). In such disorders the organs involved may not necessarily be diseased and there may only be an impaired functioning of the organ. However, many authorities agree that prolonged emotional stress can lead to serious diseases of the digestive tract. Two of my collaborators on a stress project, Donald Morse and Robert Pollack[1] contend that stress is the principal reason for digestive disturbance. For example, in their work on stress and saliva it was found that stress causes dry mouth. This is particularly important since digestion starts in the mouth and saliva is needed to start the digestion of starch.

DIET

The term *diet* is an all inclusive one used to refer to foods and liquids regularly consumed. The question often raised is: What constitutes a balanced diet? A balanced diet means, essentially, that along with sufficient fluids, one should include foods from the four basic food groups. These are the dairy group, the meat group, the vegetable and fruit group, and the bread and cereal group.

A guide to a balanced diet was prepared by the staff of the United States Senate Select Committee on Nutrition and Human Needs. This committee spend a great deal of time on hearings and research, and some of its recommendations are listed as follows:

1. Eat less meat and more fish and poultry.
2. Replace whole milk with skim milk.
3. Reduce intake of eggs, butter and other high-cholesterol sources.
4. Cut back on sugars to 15 percent of daily caloric intake.
5. Reduce intake of salt to a total of three grams per day.
6. Eat more fruit, vegetables, and whole grain.

The above recommendations are directed to the general population. However, one important fact must be remembered, and this is that eating is an individual matter. The problem may not be so much one of following an arbitrary diet, but one of learning to know on what foods and proportions of foods one functions best.

It was mentioned previously that you are what you eat. This old adage has been brought more clearly into focus because researchers now know that our bodies synthesize food substances known as *neurotransmitters*. Prominent nutritionists tend to be of the opinion that these neurotransmitters relay messages to the brain that, in turn, affect our moods, sex drive, appetite, and even personality. This is to say that adding a certain food or omitting another could be just what a person might need. It is believed that when a person is stressed the body becomes less able to make use of protein. Therefore, the general recommendation is that after any kind of stress one should eat more lean meat, fish or milk products. Also since stress depletes the supply of vitamin C and potassium, these should be replaced by eating extra portions of citrus products.

The diets of some families include too much of certain foods that can be potentially harmful. A case in point is the intake of *cholesterol*. Excessive amounts of this chemical component of animal oils and fats are deposited in the blood vessels and may be a factor in the causation of hardening of the arteries leading to a heart attack.

Cholesterol has become one of the health buzzwords in recent years. The importance of cholesterol as a risk factor prompted the first National Cholesterol Conference, held November 9 to 11, 1988. This meeting was sponsored by the National Cholesterol Education Program Coordinating Committee, which includes some 25 member organizations. This conference was a somewhat unique forum in that researchers, physicians, and policy and program experts shared new knowledge and program successes in the rapidly changing field of cholesterol.

The universal interest in this risk factor is certainly justified by such estimates as:

1. Over 50 percent of Americans have a cholesterol level that is too high.
2. Only about eight percent of Americans know their cholesterol level.
3. As many as 250,000 lives could be saved each year if citizens were tested and took action to reduce their cholesterol.
4. For every one percent you lower your cholesterol, you reduce your risk of a heart attack by two percent.
5. If your cholesterol level is 265 or over, you have four times the risk of heart attack as someone with 190 or less.
6. Nine out of 10 people can substantially reduce their cholesterol level by diet.

Physicians vary widely in their beliefs about safe levels of cholesterol and a few years ago a very broad range of 150 to 300 was considered normal. However, thoughts on this matter have changed radically. For example, the National Heart, Lung and Blood Institute has announced more stringent guidelines. That is, it is now believed that total blood cholesterol should not go over 200 (this means 200 milligrams of total cholesterol per deciliter of blood).

It should be mentioned that not all cholesterol is bad. Actually, there are two kinds of lipoproteins, low-density lipoproteins (LDL) and high-density (HDL). The former is considered "bad" because the cholesterol it carries in the blood is associated with an increased risk of atherosclerosis (hardening of the inner lining of the arteries). HDL (good) appears to clear excess cholesterol from the arteries while LDL (bad) can lead to cholesterol buildup in the artery walls. (There are certain approved drugs that a physician can recommend to lower abnormally high cholesterol levels.)

It should be mentioned that it is not absolutely necessary to have a balanced diet every day. The body is capable of compensating for an imbalance in the nutrients one fails to get if the shortage is made up within a reasonable period of time. In other words, it is not necessary to have an exactly balanced diet at every meal. Indeed, it is possible to miss meals -even go for several days without food - and show little or no signs of malnutrition. The important consideration seems to be the quality of total intake over periods of time.

Diet and Stress

Most writers on the subject of stress emphasize the importance of diet as a general health measure. However, the following question arises: Are there any specific forms of diet that can contribute to the prevention of stress and/or help us cope with it? In this regard, J. Daniel Palm[2] once developed the theory that many stress-initiated disorders are related to problems that originate in the regulation of the blood sugar level. This theory, developed as an extension of the data derived from controlled research, states that an insufficiency of sugar in the blood supplied to the brain is enough of a detrimental condition, and therefore a stress, to initiate physiological responses and behavioral changes that develop into a variety of disorders. A deficiency of blood sugar, which is known to be associated with a variety of disorders, is seen not as a consequence of the disease but a primary and original physiological stress. Behavioral changes may be inadequate or inappropriate attempts of the stress-affected persons to compensate. It is believed that if the stress of an insufficiency of blood sugar can be prevented, various kinds of abnormal behavior can be controlled. To eliminate this stress of a deficiency of blood sugar a dietary program was proposed. This diet was based on the metabolic characteristics of *fructose* (fruit sugar) and its advantageous use when exchanged for glucose or other carbohydrates, which are digested to glucose and then absorbed (fructose itself is a normal constituent of sucrose, which is ordinary table sugar; it also occurs naturally in many fruits and constitutes half the content of honey).

Writing in my series on *Stress in Modern Society,* Donald Morse and Robert Pollack[3] cautioned that an excess of fructose can also be a problem. This occurs more from the ingestion of soft drinks and processed foods where the concentration of fructose is often higher than it is in fruits and juices. It has also been found that when fructose intake is raised about 20 percent of a person's daily diet (up from the average of 10-12 percent), total cholesterol may increase over 11 percent and triglycerides are elevated slightly above 56 percent.

For some time a great deal of controversy has emerged as a result of what has been called *megavitamin therapy* which concerns the use of certain vitamins in massive doses - sometimes as much as 1,000 times the U. S. Recommended Daily Allowances. The proponents for megavitamin therapy believe that massive doses of such vitamins, particularly vitamin C, and in some cases the B complex vitamins, will prevent certain diseases and very significantly extend life. On the contrary, opponents of the practice maintain that it is not only useless, but in some instances, harmful as well.

There is support in some quarters for massive dosages of certain vitamins as an important factor in surviving stress. In fact, there is a classification of vitamins sold over the counter that are called *stress formula vitamins,* and they go by a variety of brand names. The formula for these is one that includes large amounts of vitamin C and vitamin B complex (anyone contemplating utilizing a vitamin supplement over and above the U. S. Recommended Daily Allowance should do so in consultation with a physician and/or a qualified nutritionist).

It is certainly interesting that one of the most popular claims for nutritional supplements is that they can effectively eliminate or reduce stress. Several years ago governmental regulatory agencies cautioned vitamin manufacturers that implied this on their labels. However, as mentioned, the word stress still appears on some products, and the Food and Drug Administration has been petitioned to ban vitamins and "stress formulas," because there was no proof that their ingredients were beneficial in this regard. Most claim protection against the effects of daily stress, or overwork, and usually contain large amounts of vitamins, as well as minerals, or herbal products. While generally not harmful, some formulations have enough vitamin C to cause diarrhea, and dosages of vitamin B6 that can produce nerve damage if taken over long periods of time.[4]

Practically all theories have enthusiastic proponents as well as equally enthusiastic opponents, and this sometimes results in a great deal of confusion among all of us. The fact that the human organism is so complicated and complex makes any kind of research connected with it extremely difficult. Nevertheless, scholars in the scientific community continue to make important inquiries into the study of human needs. It is emphasized again, and forcefully, that individuals concerned in any way with their own specific dietary problems should consult a physician and/or a qualified nutritionist for guidance.

EATING HABITS OF COLLEGE STUDENTS

At best, college students' eating habits can be described as *irregular*. In fact, a recent study[5] found that only 25 percent of college students ate the recommended five servings per day of fruits and vegetables.

My own studies of college students have revealed that they are aware of foods that are *best* for health and those that are *worst* for health. Those foods identified as "best" were: vegetables, 80 percent; fruits 26 percent; meat, 24 percent; bread, eight percent, and somewhat surprisingly, milk only two percent. As for the "worst" foods for health: 71 percent said candy and other sweets. 10 percent said junk food; eight percent said salt; six percent said coffee; and four percent said fats. (This might well be a question of health knowledge and not necessarily health practice.)

It was also found that the favorite foods of college students in order of preference were: pizza, hamburgers, ice cream, and hot dogs. Of course, these results should not be interpreted to mean that these foods consist primarily of college students' diet, but rather that they are foods that are best liked. Nonetheless, a disturbing estimate is that Americans take as many as one-half of their meals out - and these out-of home meals are likely to be taken at "fast food" establishments. Singling out hot dogs in the above list, according to the National Hot Dog and Sausage Council - a trade association in Westchester, Illinois - American eat 50 million hot dogs a day, an average of 80 hot dogs per person per year. One of the problems with hot dogs is that there does not seem to be much good about them except taste. For example, the Center for Science in the Public Interest - a Washington, DC based health advocacy group- claims that a typical one and one-half ounce hot dog contains 13 grams of fat, 500 milligrams of sodium, and 145 calories. Moreover, about 80 percent of the calories are derived from fat and more than one-third of this is saturated fat. In this general regard, it is interesting to note that some scientists are exploring the effect of hot dog consumption on certain diseases of children, such as leukemia. For example, some estimates suggest that children who eat a dozen or more hot dogs monthly develop childhood leukemia at nine times the usual rate. However, these studies are preliminary in nature and are without definitive conclusions.

Nutritional and Dietary Disorders in College Students

It has already been reported that some college students suffer digestive disorders because of stress. However, a much more serious nutritional and dietary disorder is *anorexia nervosa,* The condition of anorexia nervosa is characterized by an obsession with losing weight. The following criteria for this disorder have been determined by the American Psychiatric Association.[6]

1. Intense fear of becoming obese, which does not diminish as weight loss progresses.
2. Disturbance in the way in which one's body weight, size, or shape is experienced (claiming to "feel fat" when the individual is thin or even emaciated; belief that one area of the body is "too fat" even when obviously underweight)
3. Refusal to maintain body weight over a minimal normal weight for age and height (e.g., weight loss leading to maintenance of body weight 15 percent below expected; failure to make expected weight gain during period of growth, leading to body weight 15 percent below expected)
4. In females, absence of at least three consecutive menstrual cycles when otherwise expected to occur (primary or secondary amenorrhea)

This condition is about ten times more prevalent among females than males, because a higher percent of females are preoccupied with thinness.

Anorexics use all sorts of ways to lose weight, such as drastically reducing food intake and self-induced vomiting. This is a very serious condition and when it is identified it should be treated immediately.

The condition among some female college athletes, particularly in such sports as swimming, gymnastics, and track and field, is said to be due in part to the type of apparel used in participation; that is, the "skintight" uniform tends to display one's figure in detail. The perception of the athletes is that they want to be seen as lean and fit, especially when an athletic competition is viewed by a significant number of spectators.

Another condition known as *bulimia nervosa,* while not as prevalent, at the same time is extremely serious. Bulimia can best be described as binge eating, or rapid ingestion of large quantities of food over a short period of time. The American Psychiatric Association has established the following criteria for this disorder.[7]

1. Recurrent episodes of binge eating (rapid consumption of a large amount of food in a discrete period of time, usually less than two hours)
2. Fear of not being able to stop eating during eating binges.
3. Regular occurrences of either self-induced vomiting, use of laxatives, or rigorous dieting or fasting to counteract the effects of the binge eating.
4. A minimum average of two binge-eating episodes per week for at least three months

Again, this is an extremely serious condition and requires immediate medical attention. And, of course it is not too difficult to discern the relationship of stress to these disorders.

FOOD FADS

Regardless of the extent to which they may or may not be concerned with stress, any discussion about nutrition and diet would not be complete without some mention of food fads. A fad is a passing fancy or fashion or a hobby. It will be thought of here as it is commonly used to designate dietary practices that deviate more or less from popular practices.

Intelligent people properly take an interest in what they eat. Such individuals are, of course, on the alert for the especially beneficial foods that they enjoy and that can be added to their regular diet. Some, who may seem rather extreme to their more conventional friends, have merely succeeded in discovering foods that, they are convinced, help them feel good, vigorous, and alive. Or they may have identified certain foods, food preservatives, or insecticide-bearing foods that they have reason to believe are undesirable or possibly lethal. Although such individuals are sometimes called such things as "food-faddists" because they may not eat just like everyone else, at least some of them could be called thoughtful eaters.

George Bernard Shaw, the famous Irish playwright and critic who lived until the age of 96 refused to eat meat and he said that he had no special philosophy on this subject but merely expected that a large number of animals, would, one day, follow his funeral procession to his grave in tribute to a man who had not eaten them.

Serious vegetarians are likely to argue their case on nutritional *and* moral grounds. As yet there does not seem to be experimental data that unequivocally supports the contention of some of them that meats are poisonous to the body and should be replaced by vegetable products. On the other hand, we might profess to a paradox that some vegetarians have pointed out. How, they ask, is it possibly to justify teaching children to be kind to animals as well as to people, when animals are being slaughtered to supply us with meat? It is obviously possible for some people to decide that they want no part of such goings on and become vegetarians.

Not all so-called "food faddists" are scientifically informed, thoughtful eaters. In fact, most are probably not. That is, the dietary practices of many make little sense except from the perspective of compensatory psychology. For example, there are people who for various reasons have rejected their childhood religion and have, in effect, made a substitute religion of "health foods." On grounds having little or nothing to do with nutrition, certain foods and ways of preparing them have become a kind of fountain of youth, an elixir.

From time to time someone proposes a dietary plan based on local traditions, personal experience, or a kind of divine inspiration that is designed to add vigor to and extend life. As a matter of fact, some such plans make more or less sense in terms of what is known about nutrition, and perhaps actually anticipate future scientifically based knowledge, just as some useful medical practices have anticipated scientific validation. Other plans make no sense at all by available criteria. Good or bad, the extent of their acceptance by the public tends to be based more upon their merits. But, then, this is true in politics and in all product advertising; the only answer is an educated discerning, and critical public.

Various traditions are very much alive today and affect the eating practices of many people. You probably remember having been told that eating or mixing certain foods is likely to be bad of even lethal. How about cucumbers with the skins on? Hot with cold foods? Fish with milk? Many of us seemed to have lived through violating most of these taboos.

Another tradition is quite forceful in terms of the time of day when various foods should be eaten. Thus, in many places it is futile to order pancakes at dinner time; and dinner foods are often not accessible in the early morning because they are not supposed to belong there. Incidentally, some nutritionists recommend the practice of eating untraditionally for some individuals whose appetites have waned for one reason or another.

Some inconclusive scientific research has also been responsible for starting or encouraging some fads and traditions. Some foods have been glorified and made to appear indispensable even though it is possible to get along very well without them. Of course, in most such cases, certain business interests have had a lively interest in keeping such traditions alive.

SUGGESTED ACTIVITIES

1. Compile a list of the foods you like and dislike and compare it with other class members. Try to determine why certain foods are liked or disliked.
2. Hold a round table discussion on the advantages and disadvantages of megavitamin therapy.
3. Make a survey of some of the eating habits of students on campus. Present your findings to the class.
4. Keep a record for a week of the foods you consume. Make particular reference to those foods in the four basic food groups. Compare your findings with other class members.
5. Hold a panel discussion on the pros and cons of "stress foods."

Chapter 5

PHYSICAL ACTIVITY, EXERCISE AND STRESS

When used in connection with the human organism, the term *physical* means a concern for the body and its needs. The term *activity* derives from the word "active," one meaning of which is the requirement of action. Thus, when the two words physical and activity are used together, it implies body action, This is a broad term and could include any voluntary and/or involuntary body movement. When such body movement is practiced for the purpose of developing and maintaining *physical fitness,* it is ordinarily referred to as *physical exercise.* This chapter is concerned with both the broad area of physical activity and the more specific area of physical exercise, and will take into account how these factors are concerned with all around health as well as how they relate to stress.

1. How would you define physical fitness?
2. What are the basic components of physical fitness?
3. What are the three major body types?
4. In what ways do size of bodily segments bear upon physical performance?
5. What is the main difference between isotonic and isometric exercises?
6. What is involved in proprioceptive-facilitative exercises?
7. What are some factors to take into account in developing your own physical activity program?
8. Why is physical exercise important in reducing stress?

THE PHYSICAL ASPECT OF PERSONALITY

One point of departure in discussing the physical aspect of personality could be to state that "everybody has a body." Some are short, some are tall, some are lean, and some are fat. People come in different sizes, but all of them have a certain innate capacity that is influenced by the environment.

As far as human beings are concerned - from early childhood through adulthood - it might be said that the body is our base of operation, what could well be called our "physical base." The other components of the total personality -social, emotional, and intellectual - are somewhat vague. Although these are manifested in various ways, we do not actually see them as we do the physical aspect. Consequently it becomes all important that starting as children, that a serious attempt be made to gain control over the physical aspect, or what is known as basic body control. The ability to do this of course will vary from one person to another. It will depend to a large extent upon our status of physical fitness.

The broad area of physical fitness can be broken down into certain components, and it is important that individuals achieve to the best of their natural ability as far as these components are concerned. There is not complete agreement as far as identification of the components of physical fitness are concerned. However, the following information provided by the President's Council on Physical Fitness and Sports considers certain components as basic:

1. *Muscular strength.* This refers to the contraction power of muscles. The strength of muscles is usually measured with dynamometers or tensiometers, which record the amount of force particular muscle groups can apply in a single maximum effort. Man's existence and effectiveness depend upon his muscles. All movements of the body or any of its parts are impossible without action by muscles attached to the skeleton. Muscles perform vital functions of the body as well. The heart is a muscle; death occurs when it ceases to contract. Breathing, digestion, and elimination are dependent upon muscular contractions. These vital muscular functions are influenced by exercising the skeletal muscles; the heart beats faster, the blood circulates through the body at a greater rate, breathing comes deep and rapid, and perspiration breaks out on the surface of the skin.

2. *Muscular endurance.* Muscular endurance is the ability of muscles to perform work. Two variations of muscular endurance are recognized: *isometric,* whereby a maximum static muscular contraction is held and *isotonic,* whereby the muscles continue to raise and lower a submaximal load as in weight training or performing push-ups. In the isometric form, the muscles maintain a fixed length; in the isotonic form, they alternatively shorten and lengthen. Muscular endurance must assume some muscular strength. However, there are distinctions between the two; muscle groups of the same strength may possess different degrees of endurance.

3. *Circulatory-respiratory endurance.* Circulatory-respiratory endurance is characterized by moderate contractions of large muscles groups for relatively long periods of time, during which maximal adjustments of the circulatory-respiratory system to the activity are necessary, as in distance running and swimming. Obviously, strong and enduring muscles are needed. However, by themselves they are not enough; they do not guarantee well-developed circulatory-respiratory functions.

As far as the physical aspect of personality is concerned a major objective of modern man should be directed to maintaining a suitable level of physical fitness, the topic of the ensuing discussion.

MAINTAINING A SUITABLE LEVEL OF PHYSICAL FITNESS

Physical fitness presupposes an adequate intake of good food and an adequate amount of rest and sleep, but beyond these things, activity involving all the big muscles of the body is essential. Just how high a level of physical fitness should be maintained from one stage of life to another is difficult to answer because we must raise the following question: Fitness for what? Obviously, the young varsity athlete needs to think of a level of fitness far above that which will concern the average middle-aged individual.

Physical fitness has been described in different ways by different people; however, when all of these descriptions are put together it is likely that they will be characterized more by their similarities than their differences. For purposes here, physical fitness will be thought of as the level of ability of the human organism to perform certain physical tasks or, put another way, the fitness to perform various specified tasks requiring muscular effort.

A reasonable question to raise at this point is: Why is a reasonably high level of physical fitness desirable in modern times when there are so many effort-saving devices available that, for many people, strenuous activity is really not necessary anymore? One possible answer to this is that all of us stand at the end of a long line of ancestors, all of whom lived at least long enough to have children because they were fit and vigorous, strong enough to survive in the face of savage beasts and savage men, and able to work hard. Only the fit survived. As a matter of fact, not very far back in your family tree, you would find people who had to be rugged and extremely active in order to live. Vigorous action and physical ruggedness are our biological heritage. Possibly because of the kind of background that we have, our bodies simply function better when we are active.

Most child development specialists agree that vigorous play in childhood is essential for the satisfactory growth of the various organs and systems of the body. It has been said that "play is the business of childhood." To conduct this "business" successfully and happily, the child should be physically fit. Good nutrition, rest, and properly conducted physical activities in school can do much to develop and maintain the physical fitness of children and youth. Continuing this practice throughout life should be an essential goal of all mankind.

The word *exercise* may tend to have strong moralistic overtones. Like so many things that are said to be "good for you," it also tends to give rise to certain feelings of boredom and resentment. Thus, many people draw more than facetious pleasure in repeating the old sayings: "When I feel like exercising, I lie down quickly until the feeling goes away," and "I get my exercise serving as pall-bearer for my friends who exercised."

As an "old gym teacher," I can summarize my feelings about exercising and maintaining some level of physical fitness by saying that doing so makes possible types of meaningful experiences in life that are not otherwise available to you. These experiences include all manner of physical activity and exercise, including indoor and outdoor sports; and they also include the rich and satisfying interpersonal relationships that are usually associated with these activities. But maintaining some level of physical fitness has still another value that is usually not fully appreciated. This value has to do with the idea that the entire personality of every individual rests upon, and is dependent up, its physical base. The entire personality -which is to say, all of social, emotional, and intellectual components - is threatened when the physical component, the base of operation is weak or unreliable. It has been claimed by fitness enthusiasts that academic performance, emotional control, and social adjustments are improved when an adequate level of physical fitness is improved; and many case histories and clinical data would tend to support this contention. However, at the moment, it could be argued that a reasonably solid physical base is more likely than a shaky one to serve you as a successful launching pad for other personality resources. In other words, you will be likely to do better in everything you undertake if you feel good, your vitality is high, and you are capable of prolonged effort.

BODY TYPES AND SEGMENTS AND PHYSICAL FITNESS

Body Types

One of the fundamental things about understanding yourself is understanding something about the structure and proportions of your own body. Body builds have been classified in several ways, but they reduce to three major types: (1) the heavy, broad-hipped, relatively, narrow-shouldered type (endomorph); (2) the broad-shouldered, narrow-hipped muscular type (mesomorph); and (3) the lean, straight up-and-down type (ectomorph). Of course, the "average" woman is not the same as the "average" man, but the same general classifications apply to women too.

It is interesting to note that these body types are associated with different emotions and behaviors. For example, the endomorph is said to be jovial, enjoys eating and sensual pleasures and tends to be extraverted (Viscerotonic). The mesomorph is competitive, aggressive enjoys athletics and tends to be ambiverted (Musculoskeletonic). The ectomorph is serious, intellectual, enjoys reading and tends to be introverted (Cerebrotonic). Not to worry, because any body can deviate from the standard.

Most people are a mixture of the first and second type (endomorph-mesomorph) or of the second and third type (mesomorph-ectomorph). However, occasional individuals approach being "pure types" in the sense of being very much one type or another, for example, an upper body of one type and a lower body of another. By way of illustration take the case of an individual who was somewhat self-conscious and uncomfortable about having what seemed to him to be mesomorphic arms and trunk on relatively ectomorphic legs. However, it occurred to him one day that the present arrangement managed somehow to serve him quite well, or at least did not prevent his doing most of the things he wanted to do, so he stopped worrying about it. By then, too, he had given up the idea that he might someday pass as a Greek god.

Heredity, chance blending of genes, and undoubtedly other factors, not completely known to us, present you, finally with your basic body type. This being the case, individuals had better decide that it is acceptable because there is little they can do to change the basic structure.

What can be done, however, is to learn to make the most of what you have. In the first place, no matter what type you may have, you can elevate it to, or maintain it at a satisfactory level of physical fitness. Even though you should happen to be very endomorphic (inverted V) or ectomorphic (straight up and down), you can be strong, have good endurance, and learn to be skillful in the activities that you like. Most heavily built people can control their weight by minimizing the starches and fats in their diets and being physically active regularly. Most lean people can elevate their weight, putting in on "in the right places," by following the basic recommendations for increasing and keeping their protein and carbohydrate food intake reasonably high. Even if the weight does not jump up, the main point is that one feels well enough and enjoys the things he or she likes to do.

No matter what your own particular body type, you can participate successfully in most activity programs where the emphasis is on having an active, pleasurable experience. However, if you wish to excel in a sport, you should pick one in which your body type is not against you. Of course, the "athletic type" (mesomorph) stands to have a chance in most sports; but his weight and leanings toward endomorphy or ectomorphy are important factors that determine where he is likely to perform the best. However, the well-developed lean individual (ectomorph) tends to excel in non-contact sports such as middle- and long-distance running and tennis. The well-muscled heavy person (endomorph) has a chance in such sports as football (lineman), and often excels in distance swimming where his buoyancy and insulation against cold may be a major advantage. Some individuals of high endomorphic components have been outstanding weight lifters and heavyweight wrestlers.

In brief, there is no reason why one's body type should exclude him or her from any but a few recreational sports. At the highly competitive level, the athletic types have the greatest range of possibilities open to them; but the interested endomorph or ectomorph has opportunities too.

Body Segments

The sizes of the various bodily segments have an important bearing upon physical performance. For example, even though two men have equal leg strength, other things being equal, the one with the longer legs will win in a race because the longer stride provides a mechanical advantage. In effect, he is able to go into high gear while the shorter man must roar along in low. However, of probably greater interest to the general student is the role of the size of the various segments of the body in determining one's bigness or smallness. If you have several people of about the same overall size sit on the edge of a desk and compare the length of their necks, trunks, upper legs and lower legs, you will probably find that these measurements vary widely from person to person. It is soon likely to become apparent that one person may have the height in one segment of the body while another may have it in a different segment. Thus, some "tall" men and women are really not big anywhere except in their long bones. Some "shorties" are just as big as their friends except that their necks are short.

By tradition, we seem prone to equate bigness with "best-ness." Because we might have the biggest buildings and biggest cities, drive the biggest cars, and so on, we feel somehow superior. Similarly, this is true with "bigness" in people, especially men - although tall long-legged women are fashion able too. The point is that this "bigness is best" idea is a completely arbitrary standard that does not necessarily have any bearing upon either the quality of the car of the humanness of the person. Moreover, when we consider that one's bigness or smallness may be entirely a matter of long lower leg bones, the whole business begins to seem relatively unimportant. Incidentally, these arbitrary standards of what is "best" for people to be sometimes get pretty complicated. Some individuals not only tend to prize bigness but not being very "different" as well. Thus, one is about as likely to be considered an "odd ball" if he is very bright or quite dull. And we like to fit comfortably within the "norms" our various statisticians calculate for us. But, in connection with our body size, we can remember before basketball made it permissible for men (and women) to be very tall, tall young men and women sometimes had poor posture because they were forever slouching down so as to appear "normal."

It is of course possible, within limits, to cultivate one's body, to make it serviceable and reasonably attractive by keeping it fit and learning to use it with skill. People should be inclined to consider doing so on a par with "cultivating the mind." To repeat the opening comments in this general discussion -understanding and accepting our bodies as they are, including those aspects that we can do nothing about, are fundamental factors in accepting ourselves as human beings whose personalities are our own and not really the business of arbitrary standardization.

TYPES OF EXERCISES

Generally speaking, there are three types of exercises: (1) *proprioceptive-facilitative,* (2) *isotonic,* and (3)*isometric* (In reading this section of the chapter the reader is asked to reflect back to the discussion of the components of physical fitness - muscular strength, muscular endurance, and circulatory-respiratory endurance.)

Proprioceptive-Facilitative Exercises

These exercises are those that consist of various refined patterns of movement. Important in the performance of these exercises are those factors involved in movement: (1) time, (2), force, (3) space, and (4) flow.

Time is concerned with how long it takes to complete a movement. For example, a movement can be slow and deliberate, such as a child attempting to create a body movement to depict a falling snowflake. On the other hand, a movement might be made with sudden quickness, such as starting to run for a goal on a signal.

Force needs to be applied to set the body or one of its segments in motion and to change its speed and/or direction. Thus, force is concerned with how much strength is required for movement. Swinging the arms requires less strength than attempting to propel the body over the surface area with a standing long jump.

In general, there are two factors concerned with *space*. These are the amount of space required to perform a particular movement and the utilization of available space.

All movements involve some degree of rhythm in their performance. Thus, *flow* is the sequence of movement involving rhythmic motion.

The above factors are included in all body movements in various degrees. The degree to which each is used effectively in combination will determine the extent to which the movement is performed with skill. This is a basic essential in the performance of proprioceptive-facilitative exercises. In addition, various combinations of the following are involved in the performance of this type of exercise.

1. *Muscular power.* Ability to release maximum muscular force in the shortest time. Example: Standing long jump.
2. *Agility.* Speed in changing body position or in changing direction. Example: Dodging run.
3. *Speed.* Rapidity with which successive movements of the same kind can be performed. Example: 50-yard dash.
4. *Flexibility.* Range of movement in a joint or sequence of joints. Example: Touch floor with fingers without bending knees.

5. *Balance.* Ability to maintain position and equilibrium both in movement (dynamic balance) and while stationary (static balance). Examples: Walking on a line or balance beam (dynamic); standing on one foot (static).

6. *Coordination.* Working together of the muscles and organs of the human body in the performance of a specific task. Example: Throwing or catching an object.

Isotonic Exercises

These are the types of exercises with which most people are familiar. An isotonic exercise involves the amount of resistance one can overcome during one application of force through the full range of motion in a given joint or joints. An example of this would be picking up a weight and flexing the elbows while lifting the weight to shoulder height.

Isotonics can improve strength to some extent. They are also very useful for increasing and maintaining full range of motion. Such range of motion should be maintained throughout life if possible, although it can decrease with age with such musculoskeletal disorders as arthritis. This disease can cause shortening of fibrous tissue structures and this is likely to limit the normal range of motion.

Another important feature of isotonic exercise is that it can increase circulatory-respiratory endurance in such activities as running (jogging) and swimming.

Isometric Exercises

Although isometrics do not provide much in the way of improvement or normal range of motion and endurance, they are most useful in increasing strength and volume of muscles. In isometrics the muscle is contracted, but the length of the muscle is generally the same during contraction as during relaxation. The contraction is accomplished by keeping two joints rigid while at the same time contracting the muscle(s) between the joints. A maximal amount of force is applied against a fixed resistance during one all-out effort. An example of this is pushing or pulling against an immovable object. Let us say if you place your hands against a wall and push with as much force as you can, you have effected the contraction of certain muscles while their length has remained essentially the same.

DEVELOPING YOUR OWN ACTIVITY PROGRAM

In recommending physical activity - vigorous pleasurable physical activity - to college students, one should do so not only in the sense that it will be likely to reduce, eliminate, or avoid chronic fatigue and lessen the impact of acute fatigue. It is recommended too, on the basis that that the ability to move the body skillfully in a wide variety of ways and for appreciable periods of time is a dimension of human experience that is fundamental, pleasurable, and meaningful. It is a part of being human and alive. To deprive ourselves of this category of living is as silly as closing the door to music, art, and good books.

As a college student you probably have available to you instructional services and facilities designed for your participation in regularly scheduled physical activities. If this is the case you have a distinct advantage over those for whom such services are not provided.

However, you may also be interested in some of those factors that are concerned with embarking on a program as a supplement for your own individual use. It should be mentioned here that my studies show that upwards of 90 percent of college students believe that physical activity and exercise are very good techniques to use for the purpose of reducing stress. However, only about 60 percent of them follow this practice on a regular basis. In those institutions where physical education activity courses are required it is obvious that almost all students participate. After fulfilling this requirement, there is a rather large decrease in participation because students are not as likely to exercise on their own.

The traditional recommendation has been to consult a physician before undertaking a physical activity program. It is likely that a physician will recommend the program without restriction, or if a problem is found, he or she will take steps to correct it - and there may be suggestions for modifying the program to make it more suitable to you as an individual.

The next consideration is that a program be an individual matter and one that fits your own needs and wishes. In other words, if a person is not happy with the program, it will be unlikely that it will meet with success as far as personal goals are concerned. Each individual will have to determine which particular approach is best for him or her - specified physical exercises, recreational sports, or a combination of both. Having supervised numerous personal exercise programs, I believe that there are three very important factors to consider when formulating an exercise program for yourself: (1) *frequency,* (2) *persistence and adherence,* and (3) *positive reinforcement.*

Once you have decided what you are going to do for your exercise program, whether prescribed exercises or recreational sports, (or both), you will need to determine how many times a week to engage in these activities. It is best to avoid the extremes of the "once in a while" or "always without fail" spurts and try to maintain a regular schedule of three to four times a week. It is a good idea to work out on alternate days - Monday, Wednesday, and Friday, or Tuesday, Thursday, and Saturday. Sunday can then be used as a makeup day. The hour of the day does not necessarily matter. However, it should be remembered if you have already decided that your fitness program is going to be number one of your priority list of things to do, it should not be difficult to get into the habit of putting regular workouts into your weekly schedule.

Persistence and adherence are as important to any exercise program as the activities or exercises themselves. You will obtain much better and much more lasting results from a program of three or four steady and regular workouts each week than a program where you go all out every day for one week and then do nothing at all the following two or three weeks. Once you commit yourself to your program, stay with it and do not let anything interfere with it. Your maintenance program, once you have reached your desired level of fitness, might be less strenuous and/or slightly less frequent, but you will lose whatever results you have built up or gained if your activity program ceases completely or becomes too sporadic.

Psychological research has discovered that a response that is reinforced by some means is more apt to be repeated than one that is not. When this kind of research was first studied, it was thought that the reward of desired behavior and the punishment of undesired behavior created equal and opposite effects. It was soon discovered that this was not the case. Punishment seems to have a less permanent effect than reward, and punishment may even bring about the opposite results from the intended one. Therefore, it is positive reinforcement that we are seeking. Although there seems to be plenty of positive reinforcement built right into your fitness program (looking feeling better), you will also need to be reassured that you will be receiving praise and encouragement from people around you as you get started and continue in your fitness program. This also works both ways. If some members of your family or someone you know is attempting to change in his or her fitness condition, by all means offer encouragement and praise. Make them feel good about what they are doing or trying to do. Obviously, it should go without saying that criticizing or belittling are the easiest ways to put a damper on or even wipe out completely, a person's confidence in himself or herself and enthusiasm for the program.

IMPORTANCE OF PHYSICAL EXERCISE IN REDUCING STRESS

Exercise can provide a variety of stress reduction benefits for many individuals. Many people under stress experience a "fight or flight" response characterized by increased muscle tension, blood pressure, and heart rate due to the release of stress-related hormones and increased sympathetic nervous system activities. These are designed to increase alertness and improve strength for fight, or greater speed for flight. However, if this state persists, or is not followed by a period of relaxation, a variety of physical and emotional problems can ensue. Exercise may relieve stress by providing an outlet for increased energy stores which have not been utilized. In some instances, exercise may provide emotional benefits, as stressful thoughts are replaced by focusing on the activity being pursued. There may also be increased endorphin secretion, which promotes a sense of well-being or euphoria, and greater resistance to pain. We often hear of the "runner's high" and people feeling good about themselves after exercising. When we stop exercising, heart rate and blood pressure fall, breathing becomes slower and more regular, and muscle tension is dissipated. In addition, during the post-exercise period, we are apt to fall into a relaxed and contemplative state that provides other emotional benefits.

For years the value of exercise as a means of reducing stress has been documented by various sources. Walter McQuade and Ann Aikman[1] suggested that one of the many stresses people suffer from is stress resulting from their own pent-up aggressive drives. When people express these drives in physical action, they are better off because exercise not only dispels this form of stress, but it also enables the body to hold up better against stress in general.

Similarly, Beata Jencks[2] once reported that physical and emotional trauma upset balance of body and mind, and that much energy is wasted in muscular tension, bringing on unnecessary tiredness and exhaustion. This could mean that if stress reactions become habit patterns, then the muscles and tendons shorten and thicken and excessive connective tissue is deposited, causing a general consolidation of tissues. As mentioned before, excess energy released by action of the sympathetic nervous system, if not immediately dissipated by muscular action, produces muscular tension and this tension should be dissipated by muscular action in the form of exercise.

In a different frame of reference, C. Eugene Walker[3] suggested that exercise is very effective in reducing anxiety. He theorized that it may be that it satisfies the evolutionary need of man to engage in large muscle, physically aggressive activity that was very adaptive for primitive man, but with our highly civilized, sedentary, and confined lifestyle, has fewer acceptable outlets.

As far as objective scientific inquiry is concerned, a number of controlled studies, some as far back a three decades ago provide evidence that physical activity contributes to one's capacity to reduce stress. One representative example is the work of Richard Driscoll.[4] He used 40 minutes of stress treatment and a combination of physical exertion and positive imagery to determine their effect upon anxiety reduction. High-anxiety students were tested in six conditions, including one group that, received standard systematic desensitization (discussed in the final chapter of the book), one that received the exercise and imagery treatment, and a control group that received no treatment. After witnessing a sequence of stressful scenes, the group that was most successful in effectively reducing anxiety was the one that used the physical exertion of running, plus positive imagery of themselves being calm and tranquil. It was found that the combination of positive imagery and physical exertion reduced the anxiety the most. This study is supportive of other evidence that suggests that stress reduction means simply giving one an acceptable way of recovering from a stressful incident.

PHYSICAL ACTIVITIES FOR STRESSFUL SITUATIONS

Many occupations and professions produce various kinds of stressful conditions, and many of these occur in the immediate work environment. The foregoing discussion focused on the importance of physical activity in helping one deal with stress. The present discussion is concerned with a person's active behavior in a stressful situation. More specifically, what can one (executive, office worker, teacher, and others, such as a college student in the classroom) do in the way of physical activity to deal with a stressful situation in the immediate environment?

What then are some of the physical activities that one can engage in as a reaction to a stressful situation? Obviously, it would not be appropriate to engage in isotonics by dropping to the floor and start doing pushups or to break into a jog around the room. Isometrics are recommended for this purpose and they can be performed in a more or less subtle manner and not necessarily be noticed by others. The following are some possibilities, and certainly creative individuals will be able to think of others.

1. *Hand and Head Press.* Interweave fingers and place hands at the back of the head with elbows pointing out. Push the head backward on the hands while simultaneously pulling the head forward with the hands. Although this can be done while standing, it can also be done while sitting at a desk or table and is less conspicuous.
2. *Wall Press.* Stand with the back against the wall. Allow the arms to hang down at the sides. Turn hands toward the wall and press the wall with the palms, keeping the arms straight (a useful activity when the boss has your "back to the wall").
3. *Hand Pull.* Bend the right elbow and bring the right hand in with the palms up close to the front of the body. Put the left hand in the right hand. Try to curl the right arm upward while simultaneously resisting with the left hand. Repeat using the opposite pressure. This can be done while standing or sitting at a desk or table.
4. *Hand Push.* The hands are clasped with the palms together close to the chest with the elbows pointing out. Press the hands together firmly.
5. *Leg Press.* While sitting at a desk or table, cross the left ankle over the right ankle. The feet are on the floor and the legs are at about a right angle. Try to straighten the

right leg while resisting with the left leg. Repeat with the right ankle over the left ankle.

6. *The Gripper.* Place one hand in the other and grip hard. Another variation is to grip an object. While standing, this could be the back of a chair or, while sitting, it could be the arms of a chair or the seat.

7. *Chair Push.* While sitting at a desk or table with the hands on the armrests of the chair, push down hard with the hands. The entire buttocks can be raised from the chair seat. One or both feet can be lifted off the floor, or both can remain in contact with the floor.

8. *Hip Lifter.* While sitting at a desk or table, lift one buttock after the other from the chair seat. Try to keep the head from moving. The hands can be placed at the sides of the chair seat for balance.

9. *Heel and Toe.* From a standing position, rise on the toes. Come back down on the heels while raising both the toes and the balls of the feet.

10. *Fist Clencher.* Clench fists and then open the hands extending the fingers as far as possible.

This short list is comprised of representative examples of isometric exercises, and they actually can be referred to as *stress exercises*. These types of activities can be performed easily in most environments. Wherever they are performed it might be well to observe the following recommendations of the President's Council on Physical Fitness and Sports.

One hard six-to-eight second isometric contraction (or less if uncomfortable) per workout can, over a period of six months, produce a significant strength in a muscle. There is no set order for doing the isometric exercises - nor does a whole series have to be completed at one time. For each contraction, maintain tension for no more than eight seconds (or even less). Do little breathing during the contraction; breathe deeply between contractions. Start easily, and do not apply maximum effort in the beginning. For the first three of four weeks , you should exert only about one-half of what you think is your maximum force. Use the first three or four seconds to build up to this degree of force - and the remaining four or five seconds to hold it.

The isometric exercises recommended here have met with success with persons who have practiced them in any environment. You might wish to experiment with those that can be performed from a sitting position. It could be something to think about during an examination, or when a professor is delivering a lecture that stresses you because you feel that it is not worth the high tuition you are paying.

SUGGESTED ACTIVITIES

1. Conduct an interview with six or eight persons whom you know on campus. Ask the question, "What is physical fitness?" Tabulate your results and report to the class.

2. Hold a round table discussion on the topic, "Weak muscles effect personality."

3. Make a list of the characteristics you think a physically fit individual should possess. Discuss these with the class. How do you rate against the list?

4. Using the "stress" exercises in the chapter as a guide, make up one of you own and present it to the class.

5. Form a committee to make a survey of places in the community not already in use that could be made available for play and recreation. Think in terms of as many different activities as possible and look for areas suitable to them. Report your findings to the class.

Chapter 6

Body Restoration and Stress

To be effective in school, on the job, and in other pursuits and to enjoy leisure to the utmost, periodic recuperation is an essential ingredient in daily living patterns. Body restoration in the form of rest and sleep provide us with the means of revitalizing ourselves to meet the challenges of our responsibilities. It is no wonder that an Old Chinese proverb has it that: *Sleep is a priceless treasure and the more one has the better it is.*

1. What is the essential difference between acute and chronic fatigue?
2. What are some causes of fatigue?
3. How are rest and sleep alike and how are they different?
4. What are some theories of sleep?
5. What does sleep have to do with memory and brain function?
6. How does stress influence sleep?

FATIGUE

Any consideration given to body restoration should perhaps begin with a discussion of fatigue. In order to keep fatigue at a minimum and in its proper proportion in the cycle of everyday activities, nature has provided us with ways to help combat and reduce it. First, however, we should consider what fatigue is so that it may then be easier to cope with it.

There are two types of fatigue, *acute* and *chronic*. Acute fatigue is a natural outcome of sustained exertion, It is due to such physical factors as the accumulation of byproducts of muscular exertion in the blood and excessive "oxygen debt" -the inability of the body to take in as much oxygen as is being consumed by muscular work. Psychological considerations may also be important in acute fatigue. That is, an individual who becomes bored with what he or she is doing and who becomes preoccupied with the discomfort involved will become fatigued much sooner than if he or she is highly motivated to do the same thing, is not bored, and does not think about the discomfort.

Activity that brings on distressing acute fatigue in one individual may amount to mild, even pleasant, exertion for another. The difference in fatigue level is due essentially to the physical fitness; that is, training of the individual for particular activities under consideration. Thus, a good walker or dancer may soon become fatigued when running or swimming hard.

The key, then, to controlling acute fatigue is sufficient training in the activities to be engaged in to prevent premature and undue fatigue. Knowing one's limits at any given time is also important as a guide to avoiding excessively fatiguing exertion and to determining what preparatory training is necessary.

Chronic fatigue refers to fatigue that lasts over extended periods - in contrast to acute fatigue, which tends to be followed by a recovery phase and restoration to "normal" within a more or less brief period of time. Chronic fatigue may be due to any and a variety of medical conditions- ranging from disease to malnutrition (such conditions are the concern of the physician who, incidentally, should evaluate all cases of chronic fatigue to assure that a disease condition is not responsible). It may also be due to psychological factors such as extreme boredom and/or worry about having to do, over an extended period, what one does not wish to do.

Rest and sleep are essential to a good life, for they afford the body the chance to regain its vitality and efficiency in a positive way. Learning to utilize opportunities for rest and sleep may add years to our lives and zest to our years.

REST

In general, most people think of rest as just "taking it easy." A chief purpose of rest is to reduce tension so that the body may be better able to recover from fatigue. There is no overt activity involved, but neither is there loss of consciousness as in sleep. Since the need for rest is usually in direct proportion to the type of activity in which we engage, it follows naturally that the more strenuous the activity, the more frequent the rest periods should be. A busy day on a job or an outing may not be as noticeably active as a game of tennis, but it is the wise person who will let the body dictate when a rest period is required. Five or ten minutes of sitting in a chair with eyes closed may make the difference in the course of an active day. And for older people some recommendations suggest a half hour rest after meals and at other intervals during the day as needed. The real effectiveness of rest periods depends largely on the individual and his or her ability to let down and rest.

SLEEP

Sleep is a phenomenon that has never been clearly defined or understood but has aptly been named the "great restorer." An old Welsh proverb states that "disease and sleep are far apart." It is no wonder that authorities on the subject agree that sleep is essential to the vital functioning of the body and that natural sleep is the most satisfying form of recuperation from fatigue. It is during the hours of sleep that the body is given the opportunity to revitalize itself. All vital functions are slowed down so that the building of new cells, and the repair of tissues can take place without undue interruption. This does not mean that the body builds and regenerates tissue only during sleep, but it does mean that it is the time that nature has set aside to accomplish the task more easily. The body's metabolic rate is lowered, some waste products are eliminated, and energy is restored.

Despite the acknowledged need for sleep, a question of paramount importance concerns the amount of sleep necessary for the body to accomplish its recuperative task. There is no clear-cut answer to this query. Sleep is an individual matter, based on degree rather than kind. The usual recommendation for adults is eight hours of sleep out of every 24, but the basis for this could well be one of fallacy rather than fact. There are many persons who can function effectively on much less sleep, while others require more. No matter how many hours of sleep you get during the course of a 24-hour period, the best test of adequacy will depend largely on how you feel. If you are normally alert, feel healthy, and are in good humor, you are probably getting a sufficient amount of sleep. The rest that sleep normally brings to the body depends to a large extent upon a person's freedom from excessive emotional tension, and ability to relax. Unrelaxed sleep has little restorative value, but learning to relax is a skill that is not acquired in one night. (It is interesting to note that a report[1] in February 2002 proclaimed that contrary to popular belief, people who sleep six to seven hours a night live longer, and those who sleep eight hours or more die younger. This work quickly provoked a great deal of caution and criticism among experts on sleep, mainly because sleeplessness produces health consequences that this study failed to measure).

Is loss of sleep dangerous? This is a question that is pondered quite frequently. Again, the answer is not simple. To the normally healthy person with normal sleep habits, an occasional missing of the accustomed hours of sleep is not serious. On the other hand, repeated loss of sleep night after night, rather than at one time, apparently does the damage and results in the condition previously described as chronic fatigue. The general effects of loss of sleep are likely to result in poor general health, nervousness, irritability, inability to concentrate, lowered perseverance of effort, and serious fatigue. Studies have shown that a person can go for much longer periods of time without food than without sleep. In some instances successive loss of sleep for long periods have proven fatal. Under normal conditions, however, a night of lost sleep followed by a period of prolonged sleep will restore the individual to his or her normal self.

Theories of Sleep

Throughout the ages many theories about sleep have been advanced. The ancient Greeks believed that sleep was the result of the blood supply to the brain being reduced. A later idea about sleep was based on the research of the Russian scientist Ivan Pavlov. That is, that sleep was an aspect of the *conditioned reflex*. According to this theory the brain is "conditioned" to respond to any stimulus to become more active. And, the brain can develop the habit of reacting to certain stimuli with the slowing down of the activity. This means that when one is in an environment associated with sleep (bedroom) the brain gets a signal to start to slow down and finally one goes to sleep.

This theory was followed by one that suggested that chemical wastes accumulating in the body during waking hours tend to drug the higher centers of the brain, ultimately causing the slowing down of the brain and therefore sleep.

In more modern times scientists are of the opinion that sleep occurs in cycles and each of these cycles, which are one and one-half to two hours in length, a sleeper uses about three-fourths of this time in what is called S sleep. This is concerned with what are referred to as Delta brain waves in which one is in deep sleep. The second state is known as D sleep. At this time one may be in deep sleep but at the same time some parts of the nervous system are active and there is *rapid eye movements* (REM). The theory is that S sleep restores the body physically and D sleep restores it psychically. As we get older, there is an increase in the amount of REM and deep sleep decreases.

Memory, Brain Function and Sleep

With regard to *memory* and *brain function*, a survey[2] of more than 1,000 adults revealed that few understood the important role that sleep plays in maintaining normal daily brain functions, especially memory. Almost half were under the impression that sleep allows the brain to rest. Actually, some parts of the brain may be more active when one is sleeping. While asleep, the brain classifies and prioritizes all this accumulated information, and files it away so that it can be readily retrieved. This process begins with a retrospective review of the day's events, and traveling back in time, so that by morning, one may be immersed in childhood memories. In addition to memory, sleep is also critical in maintaining concentrating, learning and performance skills. The majority of those surveyed admitted that their mental capacities suffered when they did not sleep well. In those that said that lack of sleep affected them more mentally than physically, 40 percent cited increased stress as their greatest problem, and this was particularly true for women. Sleep has also been shown to improve the ability to learn repetitive tasks, like typing, or riding a bike.

When one does not get enough sleep, the ability to move information from short term memory to long term storage becomes impaired. For example, students who sleep several hours before cramming for an examination, retain much more information than those who do not. If one needs to resolve a problem, or make an important decision, "sleeping on it" is probably a good idea.

Sleep and the Heart

As far as sleep and the *heart* is concerned, many heart attack patients experience insomnia (inability to sleep) in the period immediately prior to the event. The quality and type of sleep may also be important, since certain sleep states have been found to be associated with severe disturbance in cardiac rhythm, as well as heart attacks. These are particularly apt to occur during the REM phase of sleep, which is associated with dreaming. REM sleep is most frequent in the period immediately before spontaneously awakening in the morning, and is accompanied by a rise in sympathetic nervous system activity and secretion of stress-related hormones, resulting in increased blood pressure, heart rate, platelet clumping, and clot formation. This is thought to explain why so many heart attacks occur between 6 and 11 a. m.

Sleep and Stress

As mentioned previously, millions of people suffer from some sort of sleep disorders. Millions also have periodic insomnia and this condition frequently is stress related. Sleep deprivation for many is due to excessively long work hours, rotating shifts, last minute preparation for meetings, unexpected events such as the loss of a close family member, and, of course, for college students, preparing for examinations.

Working parents may not get enough sleep because of the stress of hectic schedules, or the need to awaken frequently for child care duties.

Although most people require seven or eight hours sleep each night, my own studies reveal that probably one half of us get as much sleep as we need. This can lead us to problems with alertness and life satisfaction.

Stress is the leading cause of temporary insomnia, and chronic insomnia, is common in almost every patient with persistent depression, which is often stress related. Just as stress is a major cause of insomnia, lack of sleep is an important source of stress for many individuals. In addition to irritability and fatigue, chronic sleep deprivation can contribute to many disorders. These in turn generate additional stress that interferes with sleep.

Getting a Good Night's Sleep

There are various recommendations that could be made about getting a good night's sleep, and there are many conditions that tend to rob the body of restful slumber. Most certainly, mental anguish and worry play a very large part in holding sleep at bay. Some factors that influence the quality of sleep are hunger, cold, boredom, and excessive fatigue. In many instances these factors can be controlled. We need to think of this in two ways; that is, things *not* to do as well as things to do. Although hunger could be an influence on quality of sleep, at the same time overeating near bedtime can interfere with sleep. Being "too full" can possibly cause digestive problems and keep us awake. On the other hand, a little warm milk can often serve as a suitable tranquilizer.

It is generally recommended that one not have any food containing caffeine several hours before retiring. The same can be said for alcoholic beverages. Although it may make you feel drowsy, at the same time the quality of sleep is likely to be disturbed.

An important factor about getting a good night's repose is the sleep environment. This means that conditions should be comfortable for satisfying sleep. We often hear about "good sleeping weather," which really means having the room at a suitable temperature. A general recommendation is that the room temperature be between 65 and 68 degrees Fahrenheit. However, this is an individual matter and one can adjust to the temperature found to be the most suitable.

It has been found that a more or less specific routine should be practiced. For one thing, it is a good idea that the process be the same each night, and should begin at the same hour, leading to repose at about the same time. That is, if your bedtime is normally 10 o'clock, your preparation should perhaps begin as early as 9:30 and possibly by 9 o'clock. You might wish to break off what you are doing at least one-half hour before the fixed time to retire.

The importance of sleep as a goldmine of research is evidenced by the fact that there is an organization called the Association of Professional Sleep Societies, and there are some 150 accredited sleep centers throughout the country.

Understanding the complex nature of sleep may be the province of scientists and other qualified experts, but an understanding of the value of sleep is the responsibility of everyone.

SUGGESTED ACTIVITIES

1. Hold a round table discussion on the causes of fatigue.
2. Interview several students on campus with regard to their sleep habits. Present your findings to the class.
3. Hold a panel discussion on how stress is related to sleep.
4. Record your hours of sleep every night for a week. Make an honest appraisal of the way you felt following each night's sleep. Can you find any relationship between the amount of sleep that you had and the way you felt the next day? After keeping the schedule, do you think you should be able to tell how many hours of sleep you need each night in order to function the next day?

Chapter 7

SEXOLOGY AND STRESS

The addition of the suffix *ology* to the word *sex* gives us the term *sexology* which means the study of sex. This, of course, is a broad term and includes such factors as sexuality, gender differences, sexual discrimination, along with a host of others, all of which will be dealt with in this chapter with some reference as to how they relate to stress.

1. What are some components of sexuality?
2. What are some of the major gender differences between males and females?
3. What are some forms of sexual behavior?
4. What is the extent of sexual discrimination?
5. How do hormonal conditions account for gender differences?
6. What are some of the stressors of sexual activity?

The need to learn to think in new ways about old things has been accompanied by a new awareness of the range of ways in which human beings can behave - sexually and otherwise. It is hoped that this new awareness plus greater knowledge and understanding of human needs will lead, in time, to patterns of sexual behavior that will be conducive to greater human happiness and fulfillment.

By way of perspective, it is interesting to know that our American sexual behavior, our ideas of sexual morality, our laws and extramarital and marital customs, derive from two major sources, historically speaking. For the most part, our sexual morality and laws originated among the ancient Jews (recorded in the Old Testament, for example, Leviticus), were picked up almost entirely by the Christian church, and were transmitted northward through Europe, to England and thence to America. This is the historical background behind our strong feelings, and in some cases severe laws, concerning sexuality. Times have changed, but have we always changed with them? It was Albert Einstein who once said something to the effect that everything has changed in recent years except our ways of thinking about them.

Such is pretty much the case as far as sexology is concerned in modern times. That is, our ways of thinking about such things as dating, courtship, sex, and marriage tend automatically to follow along traditional lines in spite of the fact that modern circumstances are in many ways vastly different from what they were in the past. For example, it is still claimed by some that "the woman's place is in the home," But is this reasonable in a society which has discovered that educated women can do virtually everything that men can do in the world of work? Is this necessarily true in a society where girls receive the same education as boys and in many cases decide that their greatest hope for happiness and self-fulfillment lies in science, professions or in business - rather than tending to the chores of housekeeping and child rearing, for which domestic work they may very well receive no training at all? Not only have times changed but they are in the process of changing now, perhaps still more rapidly than ever before.

COMPONENTS OF SEXUALITY

The whole area of sexuality is so broad in scope that it simply cannot be dealt with only in terms of "the quality of being sexual, a standard dictionary definition of the term. Indeed, sexuality needs to be thought of in terms of comprehensiveness. In fact, my distinguished colleague at the University of Maryland, Jerrold S. Greenberg, writing in my series, *Stress in Modern Society*[1] identified four specific sexuality components as cultural, psychological, biological, and ethical.

The *cultural* component of sexuality includes historical influences, intimate relationships (dates, marriage partners, friends), and all the sexually related customs we learn from people in our environment. This component is the sum of cultural influences upon our sexual thoughts and actions. In our society, these cultural influences include radio, television, films, advertisements, and literature. One need only look at the shelves of bookstores or videotape rental shops, read magazines advertisements for liquor, tobacco, or automobiles, note the films playing in local theaters, or listen to popular music on the radio to realize how pervasive sexual cultural influences are in contemporary American society.

The *psychological* component of sexuality includes our thoughts and how comfortable we are with our sexual selves. Some of us learned that sexual topics were taboo, sexual behaviors immoral, and sexual fantasies perverse. Some of us learned this at a very early age, either explicitly or incidentally. For example, young children naturally explore their genitals; it feels good to them. Parents who find this behavior embarrassing or who believe it to be wrong will admonish the child for such behavior. The child learns that deriving behavior from his or her genitals is wrong. However, even more subtle learning about sexuality occurs. What do you think the message is when the family conversations include such a wide range of topics that the omission of sexual ones is evident? Or when a sister's beginning of menstruation is "hush hush?" Or when birth control is never discussed in a family with teenage children? That these topics are off limits conveys the message that sexual thoughts and actions are wrong and bad; and if you have any of these thoughts, you are bad too. Since nearly everyone has a sexual desire or sexual fantasy or has touched his or her genitals at some time, it can be readily seen that the potential exists for a lot of distressed people in our society.

The *biological* component is the one first thought of whenever sexuality is the topic. This component includes one's physiological response to sexual stimulation, the biology of reproduction, puberty, physical changes as a result of pregnancy, physical changes associated with aging that affect sexual function, and the like. Perceptions of sexuality, for example, anxiety associated with moral judgment regarding particular sexual behaviors can interfere with normal biological functioning.

The *ethical* component of sexuality involves our judgments of what is right and what is wrong, what is good and what is bad, about sexual topics. We are influenced by our moral judgments, by past experience, by important adults in our youth, and by our religious views. In a changing society such as ours, these moral judgments are often called into question. Is abortion moral? If so, under what circumstances? Is premarital or extramarital sex moral? Is the use of contraceptives right? Is the trend for mothers of young children to work outside the home good? When components of our society change, the lack of societal consensus on societal moral issues becomes stressful for us. Furthermore, these moral issues influence other components of our sexuality. Disagreements on moral issues can have a negative impact on our relationships with other people, can lead to guilt and shame, and can result in difficulty with normal sexual physiology.

GENDER DIFFERENCES

Gender-role stereotyping makes, it incumbent on us to examine the whole area of gender differences. These differences are not only anatomical and physiological, but cultural, psychological, and sociological as well.

A starting point in the recognition of gender differences is that of the male and female reproductive structures, and this is the subject of the following discussion.

Male Reproductive Structures and Their Functions

The male reproductive system is composed of the penis (the sensitive head of which is known as the glans); the urethra (the tube which extends from bladder to glans and through which urine and semen are passed); the seminal vesicles (semen storage place); (the vas deferens (tube extending from the testicles); the epididymus (where sperm are stored and mature); and the testicles (which produce both sperm and male sex hormones.)

When blood fills the spongy tissue of which the penis is composed, an erection occurs. The penis may become erect as a result of sexual excitation, a full bladder, irritation as from tight clothing, or even for no specific reason that the individual is aware of. Rhythmic movements of the penis within the vagina or comparable close-fitting structure gives rise simultaneously to orgasm (neurological climax) and ejaculation (discharge of semen). (Most boys experience ejaculation at about 12 or 13 years of age.) Orgasm and ejaculation may occur as a result of self-stimulation or during sleep. When it occurs during sleep, it is referred to as a nocturnal emission or a "wet dream."

Sperm are microscopic and are shaped like tadpoles. Their thrashing tails propel them about and are the means by which they move through the vagina and womb and into the Fallopian tubes where conception ordinarily takes place. Well over 250 million sperm cells may be present in a single ejaculation. The fluid which carries the sperm comes from the seminal vesicles and the prostate gland and is called semen.

The testicles or testes are carried outside the body in a sac, the scrotum; and they produce male sex hormones (androgen or testosterone) as well as sperm. It is this hormone which, as a result of stimulation of the testes by the "master" endocrine gland, the pituitary, gives rise to the appearance of the secondary sex characteristics at puberty.

A loose skin, the prepuce or foreskin surrounds the end of the penis. Sometimes this skin is removed ("circumcized") shortly after birth. Various reasons ranging from "health" to ritualistic tradition are given for this practice, but a vast majority of males in human history have survived without this operation.

Female Reproductive Structures and their Functions

The external sexual parts of the female are the lips or labia (the labia majora and within them the labia minora). Within the labia are located, from the top to bottom, the clitoris, the urinary opening and the vaginal opening, inside which lies the vaginal tract where the penis is inserted during intercourse and into which sperm is deposited. The cervix or lower end of the womb (uterus) projects into the vagina at its far end. Fallopian tubes (oviducts) lead from the uterus to the ovaries.

The female clitoris is the counterpart of the male penis. It is quite small (from less than one-fourth to one-half inch in length) but extremely sensitive to stimulation. Moreover, it has a glans, a foreskin and in some females is capable of erection. Its stimulation is an important aspect of female sexual excitation; but distension of the vagina by the penis is also an important aspect of sexual excitation, at least in some females.

To some females the orgasm is a climactic event very much like that of the male. Others seems to find no less satisfaction in a different, less violent and perhaps more prolonged climax. Still others, enjoy the sexual experience without ever identifying a climax or orgasm as such. It has been suggested that since it apparently does not exist in females of other species the female orgasm is a purely human invention - by no means experienced by all human females. This information is of importance because many females feel that they are somehow inadequate if they do not reach a certain kind of climax. Indications are that unlike males, females are capable of a considerable range of natural variability in this respect.

The uterus is a pear-shaped structure in which the embryo grows until birth. Its lining, the endometrium elaborates both the menstrual material and, if conception takes place, a portion of the placenta. The embryo is attached to the placenta by the umbilical cord; and the placenta serves as an organ of interchange between mother and embryo. That is, nutrients pass from mother to child and waste materials pass from child to mother for elimination. However, there is no intermingling of the blood of child and mother; nor are there nerve connections between the two.

The ovaries are the female sex glands and are analogous to the male testes. They produce eggs (ova) and also, like the testes, secrete hormones. The female sex hormone, estrogen, actually includes a number of closely related hormones, and is responsible for the typically feminine secondary sexual characteristics which tend to become prominent beginning at puberty. A second major hormone, progesterone, is produced by the ovaries if conception occurs. This hormone then brings about change in the body which adjust it for child bearing. For example, the uterus prepares to hold and nourish the embryo, the breasts make ready to produce milk, and menstruation and ovulation (the releasing of an egg from the ovary) cease, with the result that additional conception cannot take place during pregnancy.

The Menstrual Cycle

During the years between puberty and menopause, the female undergoes a monthly (plus or minus a few days) cycle of events which, in effect, represent repeated efforts of the body to ready itself for child bearing. The cycle can be described as beginning with a gradual building up by the uterine wall of a rich supply of blood. Presently, ovulation occurs (an ovary expels an egg); and an egg is propelled towards the uterus via a fallopian tube. If a sperm reaches and penetrates the egg on this journey, conception has thereby occurred; and the fertilized egg moves on into the uterus and lodges in the "built up" wall where it begins the process of growth into a child. If this occurs, the fertilized egg, like a seed sprouting roots, becomes attached to the wall of the uterus; and the medium of interchange between mother and embryo, the placenta, is formed. (Following birth, the placenta is discharged - the "afterbirth.") On the other hand, if conception does not occur, the egg disintegrates, and the lining of the wall of the uterus is discharged from the body as in the menstrual flow.

Menstruation begins approximately 14 days after ovulation, lasts for four to six days, and then a new build-up of the uterine wall begins. This 14-day period between ovulation and the coming menstruation tends to be relatively stable in females. However, the number of days between ovulation and the last menstruation tends to vary markedly, depending upon the number of days in the particular female's total cycle. Thus, if a female has a 28-day period between the ending of one menstrual period and the beginning of the next, ovulation can be expected in the middle of the period - 14 days after one menstrual period and the beginning of the next. However, if a female has a 34-day lapse between periods, since the 14 days between ovulation and the coming menstruation tends to be constant - 34 minus 14 or 20 represents the number of days from last menstruation and to the coming ovulation. Obviously, calculating when a female will be fertile (perhaps for a period of about 12 to 48 hours per month) requires an ability to predict with accuracy when the next coming menstruation will begin. Such knowledge of any female menstrual cycle cannot ordinarily be acquired without at least a year's careful logging of the onsets of menstruation. Some females are so irregular that accurate calculations of ovulation is not possible. Some cycles are so short that ovulation occurs during menstruation. At any rate, an accurate knowledge of the individual female's pattern of menstrual cycles is required for predicting when conception is possible, whether a "safe period" or pregancy is being sought. A number of additional points of interest are associated with the menstrual cycle. Following are several: (1) Cycles that are ordinarily regular may become irregular or periods may be skipped entirely due to emotional upset, illness, or no apparent reason: (2) Unlike lower animals, the human female does not tend to experience maximum sexuality (called estrus or "in heat" in animals) during ovulation. Rather her sexual interest is likely to be greatest just before or just after menstruation. (3) Females sometimes are irritable or nervous shortly before menstruation. They and their mates should certainly be aware of this fact. (4) Many females experience mild to severe pains (dysmenorrhea) before and/or during menstruation. Occasionally the cause is organic, but often it is unknown. Sometimes it is apparently due to psychological factors. (5) The female should not regard herself as an invalid during menstruation. In fact, most should continue to do what they are used to doing, including bathing and being physically active. However, they should avoid such things as exceptionally heavy exercise and going into unusually cold water.

A long negative tradition has tended to put the phenomenon of menstruation in an evil light. It is not commonly called the "curse" anymore. ("The curse of Eve.") Nor so often thought of as being "sick." Still, because of a lack of education and guidance, the onset of menstruation is a severely traumatic experience to an unreasonably large number of teenage girls. At best, it is regarded as a nuisance by most females. However, mature individuals are likely to view it as a necessary condition of being a female - a basic aspect of femininity and an important factor in self-understanding and self-acceptance as a woman.

Other Gender Differences

When entering the world, the male child comes in with some degree of fanfare - "IT'S A BOY!!!" The female more often than not is likely to get a more suppressed announcement - "You have a little girl." Expectations are likely to be much loftier for males - "Maybe he will grow up to be president." I have yet to hear this said of a baby girl.

Interestingly enough, immediately after they are born we seem to relegate girls to somewhere between second and third class citizenship by dressing them in "pink" and boys in "blue." If the reader will indulge me while I delve into the field of color psychology with a bit of wild speculation perhaps I can explain. In certain kinds of competition first place is designated by a blue ribbon, second place, by a red ribbon, and third place, by a white ribbon. Thus, do we automatically declare boy babies *winners* over girl babies at the outset by garbing them in blue and by placing girls somewhere between second and third place - pink being a combination of red and white?

In any case, from a growth and developmental point of view, while at birth the female is from one-half to one centimeter less in length than the male and around 300 grams less in weight, she is actually a much better developed organism. It is estimated that on average that at the time of entrance into school, the female is usually six to 12 months more physically mature than the male. As a result, girls tend to learn earlier how to perform such tasks of manual dexterity as buttoning their clothing. In one of my own observational studies of preschool children some years ago, it was found that little girls were able to perform the task of tying their shoe laces at a rate of almost four times that of little boys.

Due to certain hormonal conditions, boys tend to be more aggressive, restless, and impatient. In addition, the male has more rugged bone and muscular structure and, as a consequence, greater strength than that of the female at all ages. Because of this, males tend to display greater muscular reactivity which in turn expresses itself in a stronger tendency toward restlessness and vigorous activity. This condition is concerned with the greater oxygen consumption required to fulfill the male's need for increased energy production. The male organism might be compared to an engine which operates at higher levels of speed and intensity than the less energetic female organism. Over three decades ago my friend and contemporary, the late Dr. Franklin Henry of the University of California, found in his research that males have what might be termed an "active response set" whereas females might have a "reactive response set." This could be interpreted to mean that males confront the environment with an activity orientation while females have a response orientation.

Another factor to take into account is the difference in Basal Metabolic Rate (BMR) in young boys and girls. The BMR is indicative of the speed at which body fuel is changed into energy, as well as how fast this energy is used. BMR can be measured in terms of calories per meter of body surface with a calorie representing a unit measure of heat energy in food. It has been found that on average BMR rises from birth to about three years of age and then starts to decline until the ages of approximately 20 to 24. The BMR is higher for boys than for girls. Because of the higher BMR, boys will in turn have a higher amount of energy to expend. Because of differences in sex hormonal conditions and BMR, it appears logical to assume that these factors will influence the male in his behavior patterns.

Some studies have shown that as far as hyperactivity is concerned, boys may outnumber girls by a ratio of as much as nine to one. This may be the reason why teachers generally tend to rate young males as being so much more aggressive than females with the result that young boys are considered to be more negativistic and extroverted. Because of these characteristics, boys generally have poorer relationships with their teachers than do girls, and in terms of behavior problems and discipline in the age range from five to nine, boys account for twice as many disturbances as girls. The importance of this factor is borne out when it is considered that good teacher-pupil relationships tend to raise the achievement levels of both sexes.

Various studies have shown that girls generally receive higher grades than boys despite the fact that boys may achieve as well, and in some instances, better than girls. It is also clearly evident that boys in the early years fail twice as often as girls even when there is no significant differences between intelligence and achievement test scores of both sexes. This suggests that even though both sexes have the same intellectual tools, there are other factors that militate against learning as far as boys are concerned.

Although all of this may be true for preteen boys, the situation seems to change for girls after about 13 years of age. After that time many aspects of society become anxiety-provoking for girls. This may be especially true of the school environment. Research in recent years on this subject can be summarized as follows.

1. There is little encouragement for girls to pursue mathematics and science.
2. There are subtle teacher practices, such as calling on boys more often or gearing school activities more to the males.
3. Boys call out answers eight times more often than girls. When boys call out, teachers are more apt to listen.
4. When boys do not answer, teachers seem more likely to encourage them to give answers or opinions than they are to encourage girls.
5. Girls are at a disadvantage in taking tests because such tests may be geared to male performance. Taking this into account some standard intelligence tests now have a masculinity-femininity index.
6. Although there does not appear to be much difference in test anxiety between boys and girls, at the same time girls are prone to suffer more stress over report cards than do boys.
7. Teachers appear to encourage male students to work with laboratory equipment more so than they do girls.
8. Vocational education programs are often geared to boys in spite of the fact that a large percentage of the work force is female.
9. Stereotypical images still appear in textbooks, with an overwhelming number of male authors and role models studied in class.

Some school systems are attempting to correct some of these conditions by inaugurating *gender equity* programs.

A point that needs to be raised at this time is the susceptibility to stress between males and females. As we know, the condition of stress is a highly individualized, subjective perception. Nevertheless, one expert on the subject Helen Kearney[2] raised the question: "Is there a commonality of stressors which women are uniquely susceptible"?

To this, the consensus is affirmative, as is the judgment that such stressors have multiplied at a rate far in excess of those of their male counterparts. This is attributed in large measure to radical changes in societal norms which have attended women's suffrage, the feminist movement, dramatic rates of divorce, increased geographical mobility, discontinuity in extended family relationships, and a steady influx of women into occupations and professions, previously the proprietary interest of males.

Among the negative consequences of such radical cultural transformations in the role of women have been disturbing qualitative and quantitative changes in illness patterns and increased incidence of life-threatening diseases. In fact, I have found that stress is causing more women than ever to consult their doctors; 50 percent of female office visits are said to be stress-related, and twice as many women as men make such office visits.

For several years some writers have suggested that there are signs that women's vulnerability increases as fast at their independence.[3] It is contended that over a century ago, peptic ulcers were a women's ailment, by a ratio of 7 to 3. Then, as frontier rigors were replaced by industrial ones, life got easier for women, and harder for men, and, from 1929 to 1940, nine out of ten victims were male. But since mid-20th century the incidence of ulcers of women was again on the rise.

Almost three decades ago an interesting point of view was expressed by Marianne Frankenhaeuser[4] of the Experimental Psychology Research Unit of the Swedish Medical Research Council. She suggested that women do not have the same readiness as do men in responding to environmental demands by adrenaline release. She did not feel that this response was due to sex, but more to a behavior pattern, that is common to men in Western society.

A study of gender individual differences in stress reactivity among college students is one that was conducted by Joy Humphrey and George Everly.[5] They used a "State Measurement Scale" for the purpose of finding out from male and female college students how they generally felt while experiencing a stress response situation. In other words, the purpose was to investigate the perceptual dimensions of stress reactions in males and females.

The study showed that males and females "perceive" different stress reactions. Of greatest disparity between the perceptions of males and females was the emergence of *gastrointestinal sensitivities* (such as upset stomach) exclusively among males and the emergence of *an aversive affective sensitivity* (such as feeling "high strung") exclusively among females.

The investigators felt that it was impossible to attribute any significance to the appearance of gastrointestinal sensitivity among males and an aversive affective sensitivity among females. However, they did speculate that sociocultural factors may have been involved. The reason for this is that it may be socially acceptable for males to develop "executive ulcers." Regarding the aversive affective sensitivity, generally speaking, males are taught to repress emotion, and many males perceive such emotion to be a sign of weakness. Similarly, females have been traditionally taught that it is appropriate for them to demonstrate emotion. As the era of changing sex roles progresses it will be interesting to see if perceptions of stress responsiveness change as well. If cultural factors do indeed influence perceptions of responsiveness, one might be willing to speculate that, eventually there would be more homogeneous perceptions of stress reactions among males and females. (Incidentally, I replicated this study recently and found essentially the same results after more than two decades) Another point of view indicating that women could be more stressed out than men is based on their prescription drug consumption. Psychotic drug prescriptions for females are twice as high as those for males, but the reason for this is not clear. One possibility is that women with emotional problems may be much more likely to consult a physician and also much more apt to admit that they are suffering from such difficulties than men. On the other hand, epidemiologic studies suggest that members of the so-called "weaker sex" are indeed much more prone to anxiety and depressive disorders. Feminists counter that the reason for this is that women are exploited in society and are therefore bound to suffer greater stress, which is mistakenly assumed by the (often male) doctors to produce intrinsic nervous stability. If this were true, one would suspect the female doctors evaluating patients of their own sex would be more sympathetic and not reach for the prescription pad so easily.

It has been suggested that just the opposite may occur. Women with nervous symptoms are more likely to have hypnotic tranquilizers prescribed when they consult female physicians. There could be a reason for this. For example, because female physicians may be more sympathetic and understanding, they are able to diagnose anxiety states more accurately and frequently, and regard such drug therapy as appropriate treatment.[6]

SEXUAL DISCRIMINATION

Discrimination of any kind whether it is racial, ethnic, or sexual, can be a very stressful experience for those victimized by it.

From certain points of view, ours has been a "man's world" traditionally, although no one can say with great confidence whether on the average, men have been happier or have had greater satisfaction in life than women.

Although various theories have been set forth, we can only speculate as to the prehistoric factors that resulted in the dominance of men. Nevertheless, their physical superiority for various activities and freedom from the periodic restrictions of weakness imposed by femininity and motherhood in women were no doubt influential considerations. Simone de Beduvoir,[7] the French philosopher and feminist, once suggested that as man rose above the animal level and began to exercise control over nature by means of tools, woman continued to be more closely bound to her animal nature and her body because of the maternal function, and the biological and economic conditions of the primitive horde must have led to male superiority. In any event, throughout the ages the male of the species has continued to dominate the female.

Women have been discriminated against in many ways; in relation to men they have been placed in subordinate roles. For example, "woman" means the "wife of man" and the implication could be that there is no such thing as a woman separate from wifehood. During their reproductive years women were often pregnant and occupied in caring for children, and this simply meant that men have been in a position to work out social arrangements that fit masculine wishes and needs.

In the sexual field, throughout recorded history women have been more discriminated against than men. In years past in prostitution the legal penalties have typically been assessed against women. She has been the one prosecuted rather than the man. Under the double standard the female has been severely faulted for the same sexual behavior for which the male achieved recognition from other males. Generally, not nearly such strong demands for virginity have been placed on males. In many instances of rape cases the woman had to prove her sexual virtue, and if she had violated conventionality in any way, the man could go free. This approach is only now changing. Traditionally, the penalties for adultery have been much more severe for women than for men. Also a menstruating woman has been considered "unclean." Even in the New Testament this uncleanness existed for seven days after menstruation, and anything she touched sat on, or lay on became unclean. She was therefore essentially an outcast curing this period. If any man had intercourse with her, he was unclean for seven days also.

According to custom the female should be appropriately ignorant concerning sex. Her concern was in establishing a relationship; one of her main objectives was "to hook a man." Since women were supposed to be innocent and before marriage sexually uninitiated themselves, they often expressed the desire to marry a sexually experienced man. Males were expected to be interested in the genital aspect of sex and, through prior experience, would know what to do. In this way female naivete would be both appreciated and overcome at the same time, The double standard accepted this as a legitimate distinction between male and female behavior. For the men, however, it gave them freedom to experiment sexually without being severely criticized. Although many of these inequalities still exist, women are now protesting them - asserting, even demanding their rights. Once this is achieved it will surely be to the advantage of both sexes.

By any valid measure, society has been demonstrably biased against females. And no doubt it is little consolation for women to know that certain majestic and powerful things are identified by the female gender; ships at sea, even our country ("stand beside *her* and guide *her*"), and of course, "Mother Nature."

Although there are some who will never want to absolve women from the "sin" of Eve for "Adam's folly," many successful efforts to diminish sex discrimination have been made in relatively recent years. Indeed, a phenomenon of modern society is the vast changes in female behavior and the assertiveness of the female personality. One of the areas in which this is most pronounced is in the field of *education*.

Back in the days when women were supposed to be "barefoot and pregnant," it was believed that there was little need for them to be educated. This was pretty much typical of the thinking that women were somehow inferior to men.

In the early American Common Schools (elementary schools) there were scattered examples of *coeducation* in the late 17th century. But there was no great trend until the expansion of public education between 1830 and 1845 in the developing Western United States. The distance between schools in that region and the small number of pupils caused elementary schools to admit girls. The movement spread naturally to the secondary schools during the reorganization of public education after the Civil War.

The right to be freely admitted to a college or university of one's choice came slowly to females. Scholarships and grants have traditionally gone more readily to men. At one time the question arose as to what educational degree should be conferred upon women. The awarding of a bachelor's or master's degree did not seem appropriate, so for a time such degrees as "Laureate of Science," "Maid of Philosophy," or "Mistress of Polite Literature" were conferred.[8]

In modern times, according to the United States Department of Education, the percentage of female high school graduates enrolling in college is now larger than males. And at the present time female college students outnumber males by more than a million.

All of this has been accompanied by an increase of women in the professions. For example, the law profession, formerly male dominated, has been invaded by women in the last few years, and it is expected that before long half of the lawyers will be women. The same is true of the medical profession. In 1992 there were slightly more than 100,000 women practicing medicine which accounted for only 17 percent of the nation's doctors. However, the American Medical Association projects that by the year 2010, 30 percent of all doctors will be women.

STRESSORS OF SEXUAL ACTIVITY

It seems appropriate to begin the discussion of sexual activity with some comments about *masturbation* because the guilty feelings associated with this form of sexual activity can be extremely stressful for those who engage in it.

Masturbation, perhaps more accurately termed sexual self-stimulation, is a very common behavior among both males and females during the course of growing up. In spite of a long tradition of opinion to the contrary, there is no evidence that it is harmful, physiologically speaking. But psychologically, it can be devastating. This is because by various means, frequently unspoken, parents and others convey to the infant and child the impression that there is something profoundly wrong about so much as unnecessarily touching the genitals - let alone intentionally stimulating them. (When the genitals are touched, as in urinating one is admonished to scrub the hands carefully because this part of the body has come to be thought of as dirty and germ ridden in spite of frequent bathing. Of course, under modern circumstances of living the genital region may actually be one of the cleanest parts of the body, and the urine of healthy people is harmless,)

The pressure of long tradition which tends to put masturbation in the darkest possible light is not sufficient to prevent or stop masturbation in most healthy young people, but it is quite sufficient to give rise to severe guilt reactions in those who do it, which is to say most young people. Thus, as in the case of so many "symptoms" of childhood and youth, the problem gets its start not in the behavior itself but in the minds, words, facial expressions, and other responses of adults.

The major reason why masturbation has been given a "bum rap" is that misconceptions about it have developed over the centuries. It began with the story of Onan in the Book of Genesis in the Old Testament. The widow of Onan's brother had no male children and Onan's father instructed him to personally remedy that oversight. Onan objected by "wasting his seed." The Lord smote Onan for this indiscretion and masturbation came to be known as Onanism. Christian mores were influenced greatly by Jewish codes of behavior and, consequently, masturbation was condemned by Christian laws as well. Little wonder that the vestiges of this attitude are still with us (for example, the firing of Surgeon General Joucelyn Elders in 1994 for her "untimely" remarks on this subject).

The following discussions will take into account various aspects of sexual activity, particularly those that are of concern to women.

Although all women are not stressed in the same manner by sexual activity, there are certain generalities that can be reported in this regard.

Commenting in my series on *Stress in Modern Society,* M. Lawrence Furst and Donald R. Morse[9] assert that even with the so-called sexual revolution many women are still mired in the Victorian era in their sexual thinking and behavior. Although most mothers do not encourage premarital sexual relations for their daughters, premarital sex has increased greatly. Of the women born prior to 1900, three out of four were virgins before marriage. In the 1970s three out of four had had premarital sex.

A major stressor for a woman about to have sexual intercourse for the first time is the fear that it will be painful. Although this varies among women, even with an intact hymen, if time is allowed for the onset of adequate natural lubrication, penetration usually causes only slight pain and bleeding.

The feeling of guilt accompanying premarital sex is another potential stressor. Nevertheless, there is evidence that these feeling do not prevent most women from engaging in premarital sexual activities, and generally the guilt feelings lessen in time.

Another cause for stress is related to the time needed for some women to become sexually aroused. That is, some women can become stressed if sufficient foreplay is lacking. In the same frame of reference it can be stressful for women to have a male partner with the "Speedy Gonzalez" syndrome; that is, when the male partner is "done" before his female partner has "started." Such an experience can cause no end of stress for some women.

Although it is not a concern for all women, another potential stressor for some of them is the question of whether to engage in extramarital sex. At one time not too long ago the "sport" of "wife swapping" (swinging) was popular among some couples. Perhaps this was an attempt to legitimize extramarital sex. In any case, extramarital affairs are probably on the decline because of the fear of AIDS, genital herpes, and other sexually transmitted diseases.

STRESS AND PREGNANCY

Writing in my series on *Stress in Modern Society,* John Sullivan and Joyce Cameron Foster[10] suggested that human pregnancy is a unique state in which the phenomenon of stress may be examined. Pregnancy is a time-limited experience in which there are enormous physical and psychological adjustments and changes (stresses). As the fetus grows and puts an increasing physiological load on the pregnant woman, the pregnancy process constitutes a "natural stress experiment." In addition, there is the experiential response of the woman and her partner. The amount of psychological stress during the pregnancy experience is a function of many factors: (1) personal, family and cultural beliefs, perceptions, and expectations; (2) prior response patterns to stress and illness; (3) the extent of life stresses currently/recently experienced; (4) perceived and actual coping abilities; and (5) response to the physical/ physiological changes of pregnancy. The vulnerability of the human organism to symptoms/illness during the pregnancy process is probably related to the total load of both physical and psychological stress. At the very least, the quality of the pregnancy experience is affected.

In one extensive study[11], the theory was developed that stress interacted with several other variables but more prominently symptom proneness-resistance. Measures of stress, symptom proneness and minor pregnancy symptoms were developed to operationalize a model of the general theory on 1,315 pregnant women. Two models of stress were formulated: (1) stress as a pure motivational variable that energized latent behavior tendencies; and (2) stress with stimulus properties that elicited stress-related behaviors. The first theory predicted the symptoms of pregnant women in the first trimester, the second theory predicted the symptoms of the third trimester. It was concluded that as the adaptive range of the individual narrows, the increased load of stress acts as an elicitor. In the lower ranges of adaptability, stress acts with properties of a purely motivational variable. Path analyses were constructed for each month from the third to ninth month of pregnancy. Since the path weights changed during this period, descriptions of the process of pregnancy in terms of stress, symptom proneness, and psychological upset was provided as these related to minor pregnancy symptoms.

The earliest stressor of pregnancy for some women is the missed "first period." Depending upon the attitude toward pregnancy, this can bring forth either extreme joy or depression, Once pregnancy begins, "morning sickness" can be quite stressful.

Although increased levels of female hormones play a major role, pathological vomiting during pregnancy can be psychologically induced with pregnant women having several severe social stressors. Pregnancy gingivitis (swollen, inflamed gums) is also said to be related to pregnancy hormones and stress. Other potentially stressful early pregnancy manifestations are fatigue, sleepiness and excessive-urination. The major event of the second trimester is the gradually enlarging waistline. This can be stressful and may induce temporary depression for the new mother, especially if she always was concerned with her figure. The expanding figure is, of course, normal, but since some women eat when they are under stress, this practice can lead to obesity following childbirth. In the third trimester, stress can be related to the enlarging, painful breasts and the kicking infant. In addition, there can be back pains that interrupt sleep, and sexual activities are greatly interfered with. Other possible third trimester complications are toxemia and persistent elevated diastolic blood pressure, both of which may be stress related.

SEXUAL HARASSMENT

It is difficult to define, or even describe the term *sexual harassment.* Perhaps we could say that whether or not something is sexually harassing depends in a large measure upon degree, circumstances, environment and a host of other variables.

Sexual harassment is defined as a form of sex discrimination under Title VII of the Civil Rights Act of 1964. Harassment ranges from the blatant exchange or denial of promotion and raises based on sexual favors to a "hostile working environment," defined by the Supreme Court as one in which the harassment is "sufficiently severe or pervasive to alter the conditions of the victim's employment and create an abusive working environment."

The fact that this definition is not extensive enough is shown in comments by some writers on the subject. For example, my previously-mentioned collaborators M. Lawrence Furst and Donald R. Morse suggest that sexual harassment takes many forms. These include being directly asked to go to bed with a fellow employee or boss, being touched without one's consent, being given suggestions of physical intimacy by intonation or description, hearing vivid descriptions of one's anatomy by fellow employees or supervisors, being forced to listen to "off-color" remarks or jokes, being shown pornographic pictures or films, and being coerced into wearing "sexy" clothes (without previously being apprised of that condition of employment).

Under any circumstances sexual harassment can be a very threatening and stressful experience for many women - not only on the job but in other environments as well. As a result of some forms of sexual harassment, some women have been known to suffer from such problems as migraine headaches, gastrointestinal disorders, loss of self-esteem, fear, sense of helplessness, back and neck pains and depression.

Although sexual harassment is most often inflicted on women, men can also be victims (some women delight in seeing a "shy guy" blush).

As mentioned, sexual harassment can take place in other environments as well as on the job. For example, at social gatherings, public places (especially elevators), schools, and colleges and the military.

Colleges across the country are asking task forces to reexamine and restructure their sexual harassment policies. Most colleges' policies defining sexual harassment are similar to those of the Equal Employment Opportunity Commission, which covers everything from unwanted sexual solicitation, verbal harassment, comments about anatomy, dirty jokes and any unwanted, repeated communication of a sexual nature. Although faculty members are sometimes involved, in most cases the problem is student harassment; that is, most students who complain about sexual harassment are doing so because of other students. Nationally, college officials estimate that about 25 percent of female students are the victims of some type of sexual harassment - more often than not from other students.[12]

In an important decision in February 1992 the Supreme Court expanded protection against sex discrimination at the public school secondary level. For the first time, students who are victims of sexual harassment and other forms of sex discrimination have the right to be awarded money damages from schools who receive federal funds.

In the military, sexual harassment has been a serious problem. For example, the United States Navy has been involved in a series of highly publicized incidents of sexual harassment and abuse. In 1989 a female midshipman (woman) at the U. S. Naval Academy was chained to a urinal and photographed by male midshipman. Later in November 1991 an admiral was relieved from a prestigious job after he failed to act promptly on a complaint by a female aide that she was sexually harassed at a convention of naval aviators. Such episodes as these have caused the Navy to change its behavior standards as of March 1, 1992.

This Navy policy states that members of the Navy and Marine Corps will be fired outright "on the first substantial incident" involving the following circumstances:

1. Threats or attempts to influence another's career or job to obtain sexual favors.
2. Offering rewards in exchange for sexual favors.
3. Physical contact of a sexual nature which, if charged as a violation of the Uniform Code of Military Justice, could result in punitive discharge.

The specific circumstances that would call for automatic dismissal on a first offense state that: "An incident is substantiated if there has been a court-martial conviction or the commanding officer determines that sexual harassment has occurred." A service member would retain the legal right to contest his or her dismissal. Previously, commanders had the option of dismissing the most serious violators of anti-harassment rules, but dismissal was not required.

For years, efforts to decrease the incidence of sexual harassment, particularly of women victims, were modest, at best. The major reason for this has been due to the reluctance of women to come forward when sexual harassment occurred because of fear of reprisals against them. However, all of that changed radically in October 1991 when Anita Hill, an articulate Law Professor from the University of Oklahoma appeared at the confirmation hearings of Supreme Court nominee, Clarence Thomas. Miss Hill testified that Mr. Thomas had sexually harassed her when she worked for him at the Education Department and the Equal Employment Opportunity Commission. Mr. Thomas denied the allegations and it came down to a question of which person was more believable. Interestingly enough, a survey of 100 judges found that by a ratio of two to one, they found Miss Hill more believable than Mr. Thomas.

The testimony itself was somewhat overshadowed by the insensitive treatment of Miss Hill by some members of the Judiciary Committee. In fact, the hearing was characterized by Senator Barbara Mikulski of Maryland as an *inquisition*, one meaning of which is "an investigation conducted with little regard for individual rights."

A large majority of women in America were infuriated by the proceedings and the fallout of the event has been a tremendous increase in the number of formal complaints of sexual harassment against corporate employers. Also, as a result of these hearings many employers began harassment sensitivity training and seminars for their employees.

SEXUAL ABUSE

The two most serious forms of sexual abuse are *rape* and *incest*. The former is difficult to define because legal definitions of the term may vary from one state to another. For purposes here rape will be considered to be "forcing one to engage in sexual intercourse or other sexual activities against his or her will." A common definition of the term incest is "sexual intercourse between persons so closely related that they are forbidden to marry."

While sexual harassment may be embarrassing and humiliating, sexual abuse can be devastating and have a lifelong impact on the victim. In this regard a study[13] reported here shows evidence of how child sexual abuse can have a stressful influence on collage-age women.

The primary purpose of this study was to examine the relationship between daily stressors and physical symptoms in college-age women with a childhood history of sexual abuse and women without a history of childhood sexual abuse. It was hypothesized that women with a history of childhood sexual abuse would be particularly susceptible to the effects of daily stressors on physical symptoms, and would show more covariation between daily stressors and physical symptoms, compared to women without a history of childhood sexual abuse.

Four hundred and ninety one female college students were screened for histories of childhood (before age 15) and adulthood (after age 15) contact sexual abuse. Of these participants, 18 women with only a history of childhood sexual abuse were assigned to the stress abuse group, and 27 women with no history of childhood and adulthood sexual abuse were assigned to the nonabuse group. These women filled out self-report measures of daily hassles and physical symptoms for 28 consecutive days.

During the five days preceding a highly stressful day, women in the stress abuse group reported significantly more physical symptoms than during the five days preceding a day of low stress. For the nonabuse group, there were no significant differences in reported physical symptoms between high-and low-stress days.

The pattern of results for physical symptoms suggests that women with a history of childhood sexual abuse may be particularly susceptible to the effects of heightened daily stress, and may display this susceptibility in the report of physical symptoms.

SEX EDUCATION

Sex education has to do with the joyous appreciation of living; of oneself as a special person; and of relationships with other people in families, in school and with one's friends. It means learning respect for other persons as human beings and the importance of getting along with each other. It means understanding that all living things grow and reproduce, how mothers and fathers take care of their babies, that good health practices make for good health, how the human body functions, what changes to expect as one's body grows, and that some individuals grow differently or more slowly. It means learning to tell the difference between what is helpful and what is harmful to people, making responsible decisions about one's own behavior, and making the most of one's best capabilities as a human being.

Much education in sexual attitudes and values takes place at home, some good, some not so good, long before children come to school. Parents continue to be the most crucial educational force as long as children are under their influence. As children grow, more sex education is given by peers both in school and outside the classroom. The classroom provides the more formal setting for guided discussion of whatever content has approval of parents and teachers. The neighborhood, the community, the church, the social class and the culture in which children live all add their own special dimension.

The school deals with its part by first developing a sound sequential program that deals with basic understandings appropriate to the early grades. These basic understandings provide a foundation for more complex learnings in the later grades as children grow and develop. This program, unlike a mathematics curriculum, will be more readily accepted if it is developed by teachers and parent representatives together.

To develop such a program parents and teachers need to know first what children are learning from a variety of sources to which they are exposed. Second, they need to know what children *want* to know as the most effective teaching comes from this. Third, they should have identified what children may *need* to know for a good start toward health attitudes and behavior in the realm of sex and in the broader sense of human sexuality.

A program should be designed to follow children's interests and to answer their questions rather than to initiate them. This being the case, parents have the opportunity to respond to their children's questions before they come up at school.

Sex education in the schools can be a great experience for students, parents and teachers, but it needs to be thoroughly planned, reviewed by a group which is broadly representative of the community, approved by a majority of parents, and taught by qualified teachers. Such a program can help boys and girls understand themselves, become wholesome individuals, and mark another step toward maturity.

At the present time, antisex-education forces are not so vigorously at work as they used to be on a national scale, but they are far from inactive. Where sex education has been initiated or continued, school personnel can expect to meet challenges at any time. Also, whenever children and youth are involved in some publicized sexual episode such as the raping of a classmate, the antisex-education people tend to blame the event or situation on school sex education and its arousing effects on the students. This can occur even though it is well known that such things can always happen, whether or not there have been sex education programs in the schools.

The overall trend of the times is in the direction of greater openness about sex. Accurate information is increasingly available to virtually all who want it. The language taboo is not nearly so strong. Mass media are available to deal directly with many aspects of the subject and, even within families where there was the least talk about sex, there is now oftentimes reasonably comfortable discussion of some aspects of the subject.

Vulnerable as they are to public pressure, it is hard to imagine the schools not following the general trend toward greater objectivity, openness and direct dealing with new knowledge as is expected in all other subject areas.

SUGGESTED ACTIVITIES

1. Devise an inquiry form about sexual discrimination practices. Submit this to several fellow students, and report your findings to the class.
2. Hold a panel discussion on the subject of gender differences
3. Hold a round table discussion on the modern attitudes about sexual behavior.
4. Hold a round table discussion on the subject of sexual harassment.
5. Interview several students on campus regarding their feelings about sex education. Report your findings to the class.

Chapter 8

SUBSTANCE USE AND STRESS

In a recent analysis of some of the nation's largest metropolitan daily newspapers I found that more than ten percent of the print space was devoted to substance use in some form. Moreover, national polls consistently show that upwards of three-fourths of the population considers substance use as one of the country's most serious concerns.

In the discussions that follow about alcohol, tobacco, and drugs in general, it is taken for granted that you are aware of certain negative aspects of these widespread uses and abuses; and that you already have a set of notions and conditioned responses concerning them. Further, you have a certain amount of interest in thoughtful discussions of them that might be helpful to you in forming your opinions. (Alcohol, and nicotine in tobacco are considered as drugs but the heading "drugs" later in the chapter is more concerned with "hard drugs" such as heroin and cocaine).

1. How does alcohol consumption affect the nervous system?
2. How does alcohol affect the brain?
3. How is alcohol related to stress?
4. What is meant by passive smoking?
5. What are some of the diseases associated with smoking?
6. How is smoking related to sex?
7. What are some of the psychological factors related to drug use?

ALCOHOL

According to my surveys, beer is the most popular alcoholic beverage with college students who drink, followed by wine, with "hard liquor" a distant third.

Beer production like most alcoholic beverages started ages ago. Beers are formed when the starch in grains is converted to sugar, which is then fermented. Various primitive people learned to convert starchy foods into fermentable material by chewing them, thus allowing the amylase in their saliva to convert starch into sugar. Beers vary in strength of alcoholic content with most American beers in the four to five percent range.

Wine is probably the oldest type of alcoholic beverage. It was likely discovered independently at many points in time by prehistoric people as a result of ingesting wine produced by the accidental fermentation of sugar in berries, various plant juices, and honey. The concentration of alcohol in terms of volume varies with natural fruit wines having eight to 12 percent alcohol. However, many American wines are "fortified" with additional distilled alcohol to bring the alcohol content up to 12 to 14 percent.

The "hard liquors," whiskies, gin, vodka, rum, brandies, and liquors usually contain 40 percent alcohol (80 proof) to 50 percent (100 proof) by volume.

In the 13th century distilled alcohol came to be widely recognized as a substance that could produce special effects when consumed. By the 1400s a leading German physician, Hieronymus Brunschwig, reported that *aqua vitae,* as it was called, had the power to do all sorts of good things for people. Among them were: combating cold-related diseases; comforting the heart; healing sores; causing hair to grow on one's head; bestowing a good color to the skin; killing external parasites; protecting against deafness; relieving toothache; sweetening breath; healing canker sores; improving one's facility in speaking; freeing one of belches; easing dropsy, gout and jaundice; reducing painful, swollen breasts; curing urinary tract diseases, including the dissolving of kidney stones; serving as an ingredient in an antidote for food poising; restoring shrunken malfunctioning sinews; eliminating fevers; giving courage to youth; and improving memory. However, Brunschwig cautioned that this potent panacea was to be ingested only in the morning on an empty stomach, in a daily dose of five or six drops with a spoonful of wine.[1] It is most unlikely that people in today's society would subscribe to many of the above claims for alcohol.

The main point of interest about alcohol is that it is absorbed quickly into the bloodstream and is then available to affect the nervous system. Who you are, how much you drink, and how readily you metabolize alcohol determines the meaning that this has for you.

There are a few individuals who retain good judgment and bodily control after considerable drinking; however, there are many who only think that their judgment and control remain good. Some become angry and savage after drinking less than it takes to make others only sleepy or very talkative.

The point is that alcohol affects the brain, the central control, and thereby it affects the individual's perceptions and his or her ability to direct behavior. After a possibly stimulating effect initially, alcohol tends to have a depressing effect on the nervous system. Consequently, alcohol has been used as an analgesic because it can alter the perception of pain. It is sometimes recommended before meals: to sharpen the appetite and encourage pleasant relaxation.

Throughout much of history, humans have lightened, or endeavored to lighten, their burden with drink. On the other hand, as everyone knows, the coin has a reverse side. Alcohol may also mean deterioration of personality functioning. Beyond the point of easing tensions, it may give rise to loss of inhibitions related to speech and sensory and bodily control. Fans of Shakespeare may remember that Othello says, "God, that men should put an enemy in their mouths to steal away their brains."

The extent to which it is safe and justifiable to entrust behavior to a more or less narcotized upper brain is an extremely complex question that cannot be answered in general terms. At any rate, some people have concluded that alcohol has a place in good living and that responsible people are perfectly capable of using it wisely. Others feel that there is no place for drinking under any circumstances. They point to the matter of public record that alcohol is perhaps the most abused drug in our nation. Deaths attributed to its abuse number well over 100,000 per hear. Alcoholism costs our economy an estimated $125 billion a year in health-care expenses, lost wages, reduced productivity, and accidental damage; and it exacts a hidden cost from the individuals who suffer from alcoholism, and additional cost for those around them.

Drinking Behavior

Like so many other concerns of children and youth in modern society is the fact that the consumption of alcoholic beverages is starting earlier in life. It has even found its way into the elementary school. Recently, when I was discussing this matter with an elementary school teacher, she related the following anecdote. It seemed that one of her fourth grade boys had acquired the name of "Tequila Joe" from some of his classmates. With a little "detective work," it was discovered that Joe had been bringing a small container of the Mexican liquor to school several times a week and enticing his classmates to have a drink during recess. It is very unlikely that such behavior is standard practice; but at the same time it is extremely disturbing that such an event could actually take place.

There have been a number of studies about teenage drinking that have been conducted by various public and private agencies. In 1994 the National Council of Alcoholism and Drug Dependence computed the results of several such studies. Some of the findings revealed the following information:

1. Middle school, junior high, and senior high students drink 35 percent of all wine coolers sold in the United States.
2. About 18 percent of 10th grade students and 30 percent of 12th grade students in the United States report that they were drunk in the last month.
3. Among teenagers who do "binge drinking" (those who consume four or more drinks in a row on a single occasion), 39 percent said they drank alone, 58 percent when they are upset, 30 percent when they are bored, and 37 percent drink to "feel high."
4. It is estimated by researchers that alcohol use is implicated in up to two/thirds of date rapes and other sexual-assault cases among teenagers and college students.
5. Among sexually active teenagers, 16 percent use condoms less often after drinking.
6. Almost 80 percent of teenagers are not aware that a 12-ounce can of beer has the same amount of alcohol as one ounce of whiskey,
7. Fifty-five percent of teenagers are not aware that a five-ounce glass of wine has the same amount of alcohol content as a can of beer.

In a study[2] conducted at colleges where "binge drinking" is a common practice, researchers questioned 720 freshmen at 13 of these schools to see what happens to freshmen who enter the drinking culture. They found that 69 percent of the new students had binged by the end of their first semester, and 54 percent had done so during the first week of school. Among some of the other findings:

1. During the first semester, male and female freshmen binged almost equally.
2. Every freshmen questioned said alcohol was very easy to get on campus, and 96 percent said school drinking rules had no effect.

3. While 84 percent called alcohol a problem on campus, just over half considered it "appropriate" to get drunk at parties or with friends.

With regard to the results of the study, Henry Wechler of the Harvard University School of Public Health was quoted as saying, "We anticipated they would drink a lot, but these findings surprised even us. We found they start drinking early, and they do it often."

My own surveys of college student drinking have yielded the following information:

1. Sixty percent said they drank because there was drinking at home.
2. College students are more likely to be aware of the dangers of drinking than high school students.
3. Sixty five percent who drank said they dislike the taste of alcoholic drinks.
4. Males are likely to drink 20 percent more of the time than females.
5. Forty percent of females said they drank alcoholic beverages at least once a week.
6. About 50 percent of males said they drank alcoholic beverages at least once a week.
7. About 75 percent of all college students said that alcohol is "bad for the body."
8. About 35 percent of college students of both sexes said it was necessary to drink for social acceptance.
9. About three-fourths of drinkers came from "drinking families," while less than 15 percent came from "nondrinking families."

In a project with two of my colleagues a very disturbing finding revealed that over one-half of the college male athletes and about one-third of the female athletes regularly used alcoholic beverages as a means of coping with stress.[3] In this regard, studies show that drinking among college athletes as well as the general student population has increased dramatically in recent years. In fact, it has become one of the most challenging situations for college officials who try to deal with this increasing problem. In this connection, the following study[4] reported here about alcohol use by college students is of interest.

Alcohol use in response to stress by college students may be affected by the presence of symptoms of depression. This study focused on the methodological issues as possible sources of equivocal findings regarding the relationship between depressed mood and alcohol use in response to stress in a college student population.

Depressed mood and alcohol coping were assessed both cross-sectionally and repeatedly over time in 125 college students. Participants were assessed at baseline using a diagnostic self-report measure of depression as well as a measure of typical coping style. In addition, daily measures of stress, symptoms of depression, and coping were completed for 45 consecutive days.

Different relationships between depressed moods and alcohol coping were found when depressed individuals were analyzed separately from those who were not depressed. Although a significant correlation between the daily use of alcohol coping and daily depressed mood was found, there were no differences between depressed and nondepressed participants (as assessed at baseline) on daily alcohol coping.

These findings have implications for the relationships between mood and use of alcohol for coping; the findings suggest that cross-sectional measures of mood and alcohol use may obscure differences as assessed repeatedly over time. In addition, these findings support the utility of frequent assessment of depressive symptoms when implementing or evaluating programs that target coping skills in college students.

Questions College Students Most Frequently Ask About Drinking

For a period of several years I taught classes in *health* to all levels of students from junior high school through the college graduate level. One of the topical areas in these classes was concerned with alcohol consumption. The following discussion involves those questions college students most frequently ask about this subject. I have provided answers that I consider to be sensible, if not necessarily traditional

How much alcohol does it take to actually make a person drunk? Some people consider themselves drunk when they first notice alterations in their perceptions or any small difficulty with their speech. Many social drinkers consider this the time to stop because they dislike the feeling of losing control.

On the other hand, there are those who evaluate drunkenness by the old English drinking-house verse:

- He is not drunk who from the floor
- Can rise again and drink once more;
- But he is drunk who prostrate lies
- And cannot drink and cannot rise.

In other words, opinions vary greatly as to the meaning of the word *drunk*. Moreover, individuals vary greatly as to their reactions to a given amount of alcohol. For example, other things being equal, a big person can tolerate more alcohol than a small one. However, others things are seldom equal, and, as many people know, some small men drink rather copiously without showing marked effects; and many a small woman has embarrassed her much larger escort by her admirable staying power. It is believed that an individual's ability to produce larger amounts of liver enzyme involved in the metabolism of alcohol could be partly responsible for such a difference. A further factor determining the appearance of drunkenness is that up to a point many practiced drinkers learn not to show the usual symptoms.

Is it best not to drink at all? Certainly, it is best for some people not to drink. On the other hand, some of the most respected, productive, and basically responsible people have been known to "take a drink."

You can hardly have reached this stage in your life without having received at one time or another considerable information concerning the "evils of drink." Thus, there is no point in belaboring the evidence concerning the relationship of alcohol and various personal social pathologies. You are aware of it on a statistical if not personal basis already. But to make a point by analogy. Of the many normal, responsible, nonmurderous people who enjoy hunting and target shooting every year, a certain percentage invariably shoot themselves or someone else because they have been drinking.

This analogy with shooting makes considerable sense from several points of view. However, one of the characteristics of people under pressure is that they tend to do various things "too much" as part of their reaction to their problems. They may eat too much, stay up too late, talk too much, or smoke too much- and of course they may drink too much. Thus, the "moderate" drinker is likely to be tempted periodically to drink more heavily when frustrated, unhappy, or desperate. As with heavy smoking, heavy drinking may easily outlast its immediate cause. However, such a development is not inevitable. Most people have the good sense to make a practice of seeking the solutions to their problems where they are likely to be found - not in the bottle.

What makes some people who drink go out of their head?

Losses of muscle control are probably caused by a reduced flow of blood to the cerebellum (that part of the brain which controls muscle coordination). Also, mood shifts typical of drunkenness are perhaps linked to imbalance in the rate of metabolic activity in various parts of the brain cortex (the seat of conscious thinking).

In drunkenness experiments, brain scans have been made of volunteers who had consumed various amounts of alcohol. The heavy drinkers who had less oxygen reaching the cerebellum were unable to walk a straight line. Those who drank moderate amounts of alcohol could walk a straight line and at the same time had a normal flow of blood to this part of the brain.

As far as mood changes are concerned, those drinkers with positive changes (friendly and joyful) tend to show higher metabolic rates (more glucose use) than those with negative changes (anxiety and depression) who have an opposite metabolic pattern.

Is it true that drinking alcohol can actually be good for you? Alcohol has been used for centuries as a sedative and is still used for this purpose by some physicians under certain conditions. Some physicians may also recommend limited amounts of alcohol for some patients for relief from tension, and, perhaps, as appetite stimulation at the end of the day. Moreover, some physicians have even been known to recommend it for relief of the cardiac pain in some heart patients. Other physicians protest that there are better ways of relieving pain and tension and stimulating the appetite, and they recommend against drinking even small amounts of alcohol because of its possible habit-forming qualities. Perhaps the latter view may be less prominent than it was a few years ago because there are some who now feel that it is possible that alcohol taken moderately may not only be harmless to health, but beneficial. In fact, some studies have actually shown that persons who restrict their intake to one or two drinks daily are likely to live longer than those who do not drink at all. However, it should be noted that recently some physicians have cautioned that use of alcohol more than three times a week could be a factor in breast and colon cancer.

How can you tell when you have had enough to drink? Depending on how alcohol affects you, you may have had enough before you start. A difficulty with alcoholic drinks with some people is that sometimes they tend to "taste like more" in spite of the fact that the more you drink the less objectively you become in evaluating your behavior. After drinking you may be undisturbed by being what you would ordinarily consider a complete fool. Many people who enjoy social drinking but do not care to lose their realistic self-monitoring capabilities or see their control deteriorate, set an arbitrary limit on themselves - one, two, or three drinks, perhaps depending what they intend to do after the "party is over." The arbitrary-limit idea may seem somewhat unsporting, but in many cases it makes sense in that it helps one avoid having to make the decision of the basis of a subjective (and possibly hazy) appraisal of the situation. Incidentally, it is becoming popular for one person to act as the "designated driver" at occasions where alcoholic beverages are served.

As far as women are concerned, some scientists believe that men can drink more alcohol than women, and that women typically get drunk more quickly than men. It is felt that the difference is all in the stomach, where men make far higher amounts of an enzyme that breaks down alcohol before it gets into the bloodstream. The result is that men are not as likely to get as intoxicated as women on the same amount of alcohol.

Does drinking alcohol make you fat? Alcohol cannot be stored in the body and is metabolized more or less rapidly. Consequently, it may meet a certain of the body's energy and heat needs, thus making proportional amounts of carbohydrates and fat foods that would otherwise have been used available for storage in the body as fat.

Many people are under the impression that beer causes them to develop a "beer belly" and other unattractive fat deposits. Questioning usually reveals that they drink their beer with high energy foods such as peanuts and other snack foods which can create a "beer belly" without the help of beer.

Does alcohol increase sexuality? As far as alcohol and sexuality is concerned, it is believed that alcohol has an initial effect that might stimulate body functions in general. However, the important point seems to be that the effect of alcohol upon the brain is such that after relatively little drinking, inhibitions tend to be relaxed. At such times, awareness of taboos and social restraints, including those related to sex may tend to be lessened. Concern for consequences of one's behavior may also be diminished. On the other hand, after a certain amount of drinking, especially when fatigue builds up, some males could tend to become temporarily impotent.

Alcohol and the Heart

It was mentioned previously that some physicians have recommended alcohol for the relief of cardiac pain in some heart patients. In fact, it has been shown that moderate alcohol consumption is associated with a significantly decreased incidence of death due to coronary heart disease.[6]

A variety of explanations for this include:

1. Alcohol consumption seems to increase levels of high density lipoprotein (HDL), often referred to as "good cholesterol," since higher values are associated with lower coronary mortality.
2. Certain substances found in wine and beer markedly reduce platelet clumping, an important contributor to clot formation.
3. Biologically active compounds found in wine have potent antioxidant activity which block the action of free radicals. These unstable molecules can transform low density lipoprotein (LDL) into oxidized form, which hastens the development of atherosclerotic plaque.
4. Alcohol may act as a tranquilizer, diminishing the production of stress-related hormones which can cause cardiac damage.
5. Psychosocial factors associated with alcohol consumption, particularly in the companionship of family and friends may strengthen social support, which has been shown to provide powerful cardioprotective and stress reduction benefits.

Alcohol and Stress

There are numerous conflicting claims about stress and alcohol. Both also share many other common characteristics. Stress can be a killer, and so can alcohol. Conversely, a certain amount of stress increases productivity, and there are good stresses that promote health. Similarly, as mentioned previously, there is evidence that moderate alcohol consumption can reduce the risk of heart attack.

Some people drink because of stress, but many others enjoy a drink before their evening meal, or wine with their meals, when they are relaxed, and the cares of the day are behind them. Both drinking behavior and how we respond to stress are determined by a combination of genetic and environmental factors. These are currently being investigated to determine whether connections between how we respond to stress may provide clues to drinking behavior, and the development of chronic alcoholism.

As previously reported the response to stress is complicated and complex and involves activation of hormonal activities that have widespread metabolic and physiologic effects. These are further amplified by autonomic nervous system responses, all of which affect smooth muscle tone, the breakdown of carbohydrates, fat and protein stores, cardiovascular and gastrointestinal function, the kidneys, and many other organs and systems. Alcohol can also exert important influences on metabolism, the central nervous system, and other systems and organs of the body. When acute stress or alcohol intake is transient, the body is usually able to maintain homeostasis to prevent damage. Chronic stress and chronic alcoholism are much more insidious and harmful, and both can cause impairment in immune system function, growth, learning, and memory.

Some studies suggest that many people drink to cope with job stress, marital and personal problems, or financial worries. In general, the more severe the stressor, the greater the degree of alcohol consumption, and such drinking behaviors tend to be aggravated in individuals who have poor social support. It is also influenced by genetic factors, past experience, expectations about ability of alcohol to alleviate stress and the individual's perceived sense of control over the stressor. High levels of stress are most likely to result in abnormal alcohol intake in the absence of alternative resources, when alcohol is readily available, and the individual believes that alcohol can alleviate the problem.

All of this raises the question as to whether alcohol increases or reduces stress. It can probably do both. While alcohol is generally thought to interfere with cognitive processes, low doses might actually improve the ability to perform complex mental problem-solving tasks under stressful conditions. Alcohol can stimulate the hypothalamic-pituitary-adrenal responses to stress. At the same time chronic alcohol intake can increase adrenaline reactivity to stress. This may result in increased resistance to the harmful effects of subsequent stressors, much like the "stage of resistance" in Selye's General Adaptation Syndrome (discussed in Chapter 2) during which the body's defenses are maximized.

Although a clear association between stress and the development of chronic alcoholism has not been proven, both acute threatening and chronic life stresses are usually responsible for relapses in former drinkers. Of all the influences of stress on drinking behavior, the most significant appears to be its influence on the return to drinking after a period of abstinence. One study[6] followed men who had successfully completed an inpatient alcoholism treatment program, and monitored physical and mental health, stress levels, and behavioral patterns. It was found that those who subsequently relapsed, had experienced twice as many severe and prolonged stress before resuming drinking, compared to others who continued to abstain. This group also scored low on measures of coping skills, self-efficacy, and social support. A return to drinking was most apt to occur in men who expected that alcohol would relieve their stress, particularly those who relied on other drinkers for social support.

TOBACCO

Samuel Butler, the famous 19th century English author, once commented that St. Paul did not forbid smoking, but he probably would have if he had known about it. Be that as it may, we know that in modern times the spread of smoking has had to fight strong, sometimes indignant positions, almost every step of the way.

At any rate, one of the greatest milestones in the history of tobacco use was the May 1988 pronouncement by former Surgeon General C. Everett Koop that nicotine, the active ingredient in tobacco, is every bit as addictive as those headline-grabbing substances of abuse, heroin and cocaine. This meant that smoking passed from merely being habit forming to addictive. (In the first surgeon general's report in 1964, smoking was defined as habit forming and not as addictive)

As an addictive drug, nicotine may be one of the most powerful, with some scientists contending that it is ten times more so than heroin. There is no question that such addiction has a crippling effect. Therefore, it was somewhat alarming to find in my surveys of college students that almost one-fourth of them "reached for a cigarette" when under stress: especially so when there are so many more suitable stress coping techniques.

The American Cancer Society has reported that more than 3,000 United States teenagers become regular smokers daily. According to Dr. Douglas Jorensby of the University of Wisconsin Center for Tobacco Research and Intervention, this problem is complicated by the fact that "The tobacco industry has targeted young women as replacement smokers" for men who are quitting."[7]

Although some progress has been made in curbing smoking in recent years, perhaps upwards of 50 million Americans continue to smoke. No wonder that the tobacco industry continues to thrive. Millions of people in the United States are involved to a greater or lesser extent in the tobacco business. This number includes hundreds of thousands of stockholders. In addition, tobacco products are an important part of United States exports with hundreds of millions of dollars worth of cigarettes alone sold abroad each year. There are certain implications in these economic statistics. Nonetheless, society has to make choices between the livelihood of some and the greater good for all.

Finally, it appears that upwards of 2,000 scientific studies portray nicotine as (1) a mood-altering drug, (2) providing consistent and repetitive patterns of use, (3) continued use as leading to tolerance and need to increase the dosage, and (4) cessation leading to withdrawal symptoms, including irritability, poor concentration, or sleep disturbance.

Aside from all of this, male readers may be surprised to learn that impotency rates appear to be higher in men who smoke. In fact, one study[8] found the incidence of impotency in male smokers being treated for heart disease was 56 percent, compared to only 21 percent of nonsmokers, a 266 percent increase, and 70 percent of older men attending impotency clinics are smokers. The reason for this is that smoking inhibits the production of nitric oxide. The mechanism of penis erection has now been demonstrated to be due to the local release of this chemical messenger, which causes marked dilatation of blood vessels. Thus, smoking as a means of coping with stress could have a negative impact on one's sex life - certainly an inducement for giving up the "filthy weed."

On the basis of the data available, any sensible person must recommend against heavy smoking. In connection with moderate smoking, since it tends to lead into heavy smoking under the pressure of emotional stress or boredom, people are just as well off if they do not smoke at all. If they do, it would seem wise to find other outlets for their tensions.

Passive Smoking

Passive smoking is a term that has been used to describe smoke breathed in by nonsmokers, and this has become an important issue in recent times. That is, it is concerned with the rights of the nonsmoker, mainly in public places. Since it has been established that passive smoking can be injurious to health, various attempts are being made to try to compensate for this. Airlines do not permit smoking on all domestic flights, and many restaurants have designated nonsmoking areas. Many worksites are now being declared "smoke free." In addition, The American Lung Association has made certain suggestions that can improve environments for nonsmokers: (1) if smoke bothers you and if a person in your presence asks permission to smoke, you can indicate your preference by requesting that he or she not smoke; (2) the Association provides "Thank you for not smoking? signs; and (3) ask to be seated in nonsmoking sections where such an option is available.

In 1994 The American Heart Association released its first statement on passive smoking and children. It noted that "the initiating events that lead to coronary artery disease, certain forms of cancer, and chronic obstructive lung diseases occur in youth who use or are *exposed* to tobacco products."[9]

Why People Smoke

A question often asked is, Why do people continue to smoke since we now have so much information about its being a serious health problem? It would seem that people smoke for a variety of reasons, above and beyond the impression created by advertisers that doing so is essential as food and sleep. There is a suggestion from psychoanalysis that the cigarette may represent a source of oral gratification that is reassuring, a source of security - in short, a psychological nipple. The quite young sometimes look upon smoking as a way of appearing older, and the quite old sometimes look at it as a way of appearing younger. At one time Hollywood types associated their way of smoking with sophistication, toughness, and so on, and other smokers may by a process of association feel that some of these qualities rub off on them. Many smokers are inclined to give a variety of reasons (excuses) as to why they smoke. Many of them say they find it a relief from nervousness, and there is no question that it helps many people figure out what to do with their hands. Thus, smokers may rationalize that there are quite a few so-called rewards associated with smoking. (Recall that almost one-fourth of the college students in my surveys said they "reached for a cigarette" when under stress). Even hypnotists have often found it difficult to deal with even though the individual may have been urged to stop smoking for medical reasons. A smoker needs to ask: What does it do for me?

Smoking and Body Weight

Some estimates suggest that, on average, nonsmokers weigh about seven pounds more than smokers. It has been demonstrated that when people quit smoking they often gain weight. (Some of them give this as a reason for resuming their smoking habit.) There have been cases where smokers have gained as much as 50 pounds after quitting but the average gain is about seven pounds.

The precise reason why smokers gain weight after stopping is not entirely clear. However, it may be that after they have stopped smoking, smokers may turn to high-energy sweet foods. In the case of the smoker, nicotine seems to substitute for such foods.

Many studies show that after about a year's time, persons who have quit smoking have ceased to gain weight, perhaps the results of "kicking the habit." Presently, there are a number of smoking-cessation programs, and most of them ordinarily recommend exercise and serious attention to diet.

Diseases Associated with Smoking

There are all sorts of estimates about smoking as a world-wide killer, some as high as three million annually, or one person every three seconds. In the opinion of most experts, smoking causes about 90-percent of all lung cancer. A substantial body of evidence to support this view can be summarized as follows:

1. Lung cancer is rare among men and women who have never smoked.
2. Nearly all lung cancer patients report heavy smoking habits, whereas this is true only for a small portion of the general population.
3. There is a "dose-response" relationship between smoking and lung cancer; that is, the more one smokes, the more significant the increase in risk of developing lung cancern.
4. Smokers who break their habit significantly reduce their subsequent risk of developing lung cancer.
5. At least 15 chemical compounds isolated from tobacco have been shown to cause cancer in laboratory animals.
6. Precancerous changes in the lungs are evident among smokers long before they would be expected to develop cancer, in contrast, the lungs of nonsmokers are usually perfectly normal.

Although nearly all lung cancer patients are heavy smokers, all of the people who smoke do not in fact ever develop lung cancer. Although cigarette smoking is the primary cause of lung cancer, it is not the only cause. There is some evidence that heredity may play a role in some cases. Air pollution is certainly an important factor, especially among those exposed to very harsh atmospheric conditions.

A number of other serious diseases are also associated with smoking. Evidence from several countries confirms that cigarette smoking is one of the major risk factors contributing to the development of coronary heart disease. Cigarette smokers also have higher death rates from stroke than nonsmokers. Peripheral vascular disease, an extremely painful condition of the limbs, is also aggravated by smoking. This habit is the most important cause of chronic obstructive bronchlopulminary diseases such as emphysema and chronic bronchitis in the United States. In fact, clinical studies of high school students have demonstrated that abnormal lung function and symptoms are more common among smokers than nonsmokers even in their youthful years.

Although most everyone has probably heard about the association of smoking and lung cancer, the risk of other cancers are not so widely appreciated. Cancers of the larynx, mouth, lips, esophagus, pancreas, and urinary bladder are also significantly increased among smokers.

Smoking is also hazardous to the offspring of pregnant women. Infants of smoking mothers tend to be somewhat retarded in their weight and degree of maturity at birth. Miscarriages may also be increased among such women. In fact, recent data suggest that as many as eight percent of miscarriages are caused by smoking. Finally, the young person who contemplates smoking should also consider that peptic ulcer, tooth loss, and various allergies are significantly increased among cigarette smokers of all ages.

Smoking Behavior

The last half century has been one of extensive investigation of health and smoking. The number of articles and research reports has been in the thousands. Recognizing that prevention may be much less expensive and more effective than efforts to try to get adults to quit smoking, researchers have focused on prevention among teenagers. All manner of research has been undertaken and much of it has centered around socio-economic status, parental smoking, age, gender, as well as peer smoking. I have sifted through a large number of these studies and the following list of generalizations is concerned with behavior and consequences as well.

1. Older persons may cut down on their own smoking when they are involved in efforts to change smoking behavior of younger persons. (This is in keeping with experiments that show that volunteers benefit as much as those they try to help.)
2. Antismoking campaigns within the context of school curriculum can be affective in the smoking behavior of teenagers.
3. Half of 20-year olds will likely die from smoking if they began as teenagers.
4. Teenagers who smoke are more likely to commit suicide. (This does not mean that smoking causes suicide but that teenagers who are depressed are smokers.)
5. Those who reach age 21 without smoking daily remarkably improve their chances of not becoming addicted to smoking.
6. There are adverse physiological and metabolic changes in those who smoke.
7. From an ethnic point of view, seventh grade Hispanics show the highest rate of ever smoking, followed by Anglos, Blacks, and Asians.

8. Smokers who begin smoking at a younger age are more likely to become heavy smokers as adults.
9. Some younger smokers feel that they do not need to worry much about some diseases they might get 40 or 50 years from now as a result of smoking.
10. In recent years there has been a rise in smoking of college freshmen from nine percent to 12.5 percent.
11. On quitting:
    a. Seventy percent of those who smoke would like to quit completely,
    b. Over three-fourths of teenage girls who smoke have tried to quit.
    c. Young smokers are not likely to respond to health risk messages because they mistakenly think they can quit anytime they want.

DRUGS

Drug abuse can be considered as the chronic or habitual use of any chemical substance to alter states of body or mind for other than medically warranted purposes. Addiction can be specified in purely medical terms, while what constitutes abuse depends on a particular social context. An individual is said to be addicted only if he or she develops a physical dependence on a given drug. That is, when the drug does is increased or if the drug is discontinued altogether, the addict will experience a withdrawal syndrome, which often vomiting, muscle cramps, convulsions, and delirium.

Both physiological and psychological factors determine the effects that drugs have upon individuals. For example, people who have used prescribed Benzedrine inhalers to facilitate breathing have sometimes been surprised to find themselves unable to sleep. Since these individuals were ignorant of the stimulating qualities of the inhalant, the wakefulness could have been due to the physiological effect of the drug. On the other hand psychological factors may have a profound effect upon a drug's action.

In the case of "pep pills," as with tranquilizers, the need to use them under special circumstances is recognized. However, experience has shown that the fit and properly rested physical base of the personality is amply prepared to rise to the greatest majority of demands placed upon it. Its own built in boosters (for example, the adrenal gland) have seen the human race through its emergencies in the past and are probably still adequate for most of our needs.

On the matter of tranquilizers, a long list could be made of the reasons why people are not tranquil. The stresses of daily living, cultural changes that shake up traditional values, uneasiness as to just what the rules of the game are and just what one's role in the game is - these are among the things that can possibly threaten tranquility. Moreover, the mass media work systematically to shock, jolt, rattle, and otherwise stimulate the public with highlighted "news" on subjects ranging from the international situation to local violence and the anticipated weekend traffic death toll.

When a person needs a crutch to see him or her through the recovery of a broken leg, he or she should by all means be given a crutch. Using it when not needed, however, will so weaken the leg as to make the crutch necessary for walking. Similarly, in an emergency of a stressful kind a tranquilizer may be needed and medically prescribed by a physician. But beyond the emergency situation, artificial tranquilizing tends to reduce the individual's ability to deal with his or her world. As a crutch it encourages a kind of emotional flatness which is never the condition of a person who has gained "peace of mind" through thoughtful and realistic use of his or her own personality resources.

Generally speaking, it is sometimes rationalized that when "pep pills" are prescribed by physicians for normal people, they might be considered, rightly or wrongly, aids to handling life, in the one case to depress reactions to it or to avoid over-reacting, and in the other case to increase the ability to react beyond one's usual limits. Another class of drugs, such as heroin and cocaine, are taken for a basically different purpose than aid in adjusting to special pressures of life. These are aids in escaping from life by blotting out thought and sensation. In medical situations their use may mean escape from severe, even intolerable pain. In addiction it means escape from customary sensation arising from internal or external sources. (However, some drugged individuals are able to be aware of not being aware: that is, they are not able to describe what it "feels like" not to have feelings). A "shot," "puff," or pill is the vehicle needed for "floating in a blissful void," which when described, seems curiously similar to certain profound hypnotic states. At any rate, the drug addict appears to be actively troublesome only when deprived of the needed drug. The rest of the time, according to authorities who work with addicts, he or she does not seek stimulation such as happiness or physical activity but a world of peaceful, nonthinking, nonfeeling (nonbeing?) blankness.

Although some people have taken drugs regularly in small quantities for years as a quiet, occasional respite from life, in countries where their use is illegal, the user therefore may become preoccupied with the threat and actively involved in a desperate struggle to maintain a supply. It is at this point that drug addiction is likely to become the basis of a racket (to provide drugs at outrageous prices) and the cause of crime by the addict (at any price and in any way to pay for the needed drug). The extent to which the addict affects other people by nonparticipation in socioeconomic affairs or by the violence of the struggle to keep his or her life line open determines whether this addiction is a sociological problem. The personal health of the addict often suffers grievously because of his or her utter lack of concern or provision for it.

Addiction represents a turning away from life, It is obviously not compatible with intensive striving toward objectives such as those ordinarily sought by average citizens. The taking of habit-forming drugs is hazardous because experimenting with them can readily lead to addiction, particularly if the individual is confronted with problems, disappointments, frustrations, or failures, which invite a desire to escape.

Drug Behavior

Rise in drug use is attributed in part to fewer users seeing it as a risk, and as a result, fewer of them disapprove of its use. Following is a generalized list of recent findings:

1. About one-half of 17-year-olds see no risk in using marijuana, cocaine, or heroin.
2. If teenagers use marijuana there is an 85 percent chance they will use cocaine later.
3. Those who are not on drugs have three times a better chance of graduating from high school.
4. It is estimated that during the past year five million teenagers sniffed lighter fluid and other inhalants in order to get "high." This has become a concern that some people believe is as serious as the use of cocaine and heroin. My own surveys of college

students revealed that about one in ten resorted to drugs as a means of relieving stress.

They were about equally divided in the use of prescription and nonprescription drugs.

SUBSTANCE USE EDUCATION

Health educators are inclined to identify certain topical areas as *sensitive.* Along with sex education, alcohol, tobacco, and drug education fall into this category. These sensitive areas that are commonly included in health teaching have certain things in common. Most obvious, society is in a state of psychological conflict over them; when we tend to condemn and reject them, at the same time we are very likely to also praise and accept them. All are subjects of moral and religious conflict. All have important legal and political implications. Moreover, all tend to be more or less closely associated with each other in a *negative* way. That is, delinquent youth and crooked or deviant adults tend to be assumed to drink and take drugs. This is the stereotype, even though large numbers of the most respectable and productive members of society also drink and take various drugs. Another important thing that these sensitive areas have in common is an assumed ill effect upon health. However, this assumption is confronted with the fact that each has its advocates who claim beneficial health effects from it, (although it is just about impossible to make a prosmoking argument as far as health is concerned). The laws concerning each tend to reflect the general confusion and conflict as well as changing attitudes.

It seems necessary to raise a question as to how far the schools can hope to go in solving problems of substance abuse. These problems involve the entire society, and their solution would seem to require societal decisions and actions beyond what this one segment of society, the schools, can be expected to accomplish alone.

Still, the schools undoubtedly have an important role to play in substance use education when they provide objective presentations of facts and meaningful evaluations of their implications. In this context *meaningful* refers to such things as active discussions in which students are helped to use their cognitive capabilities to make rational decisions on their own. Some of these educational benefits may not be evident until today's school-aged children and youth are adults and parents capable of influencing societal decisions and actions. However, in terms of immediate benefits one has to be impressed by the large number of young people who, because of school substance use education, have evidently behaved more rationally concerning these substances than they might otherwise have done. Evidence to support this notion is seen in the success of many schools that have inaugurated what are called "Life Skills Courses." Almost half of the students who take such courses in junior high are less likely to experiment with alcohol and drugs when they get to high school.

Of course those students who usually respond best to substance use education have a feeling of being in control of their own behavior rather than being swept along by what others do; they see themselves as having a clear-cut choice to make for themselves. They have a feeling of really belonging in significant ways to a family or other social unit where individuals are respected and considered capable of rational decision-making.

SUGGESTED ACTIVITIES

1. Conduct a survey of fellow students about drinking habits. Present your findings to the class.
2. Conduct a survey of fellow students about smoking behavior. Present your findings to the class.
3. Hold a panel discussion concerning the use of tranquilizers to reduce stress.
4. Hold a round table discussion on the use and abuse of alcohol, tobacco, and drugs to control stress.
5. Invite a member of the college health service to speak to the class on the subject of substance abuse.

Chapter 9

STRESS IN CHILDHOOD

Although we tend to think of undesirable stress as being mainly concerned with adults, there is plenty of evidence to demonstrate that it can have a devastating effect on developing children. One of the problems of stress in children is that they are not likely to be able to cope with it as well as adults. The reason for this is that they do not have the readily available options that adults might have. In fact, many prominent child psychologists have made the following comparisons between the choices in coping with stress, open to children and adults:

1. An open display of anger is often considered unacceptable for children. For example, a teacher can be angry with a student, but children in turn may not have the same right to be angry with a teacher.
2. Adults can withdraw or walk out, but this option of freedom is not likely to be available to children.
3. An adult can get a prescription for "nerves" from a physician - another option that is not available for children.
4. More often than not, children may be punished for using some of the stress-coping techniques that are satisfactory for adults. Yet, some of these behaviors are considered unacceptable as far as children are concerned.

1. What are some of the causes of childhood stress?
2. How are children stressed during the process of development?
3. What are some of the family stresses that impact on children?
4. What are some of the factors in the stressfulness of school adjustment?
5. How can the 3Rs be stress inducing for children?
6. How does competition in the school environment cause childhood stress?
7. How can school tests be stressful for children?

CHILD DEVELOPMENT AND STRESS

Children face unending challenges and demands in the process of their development. It is up to adults who deal with children to help them adjust to these challenges and demands.

As children begin the various stages of development, many are beset with problems of stress. The very first stage of child development, the period from birth to about 15 months, is considered to be the "intake" stage, because, behavior and growth are characterized by *taking in*. This not only applies to food but to other things, such as sound, light, and the various forms of total care. At this early stage in the child's life *separation anxiety* can begin. Since the child is entirely dependent on the mother or other care-giver to meet its needs, separation may be seen as the being denied of these important needs. It is at this stage that the child's overseer - ordinarily the parent - should try to maintain a proper balance between meeting the child's needs and "overgratification." Many child development experts seem to agree that children who experience some stress from separation or from having to wait for a need to be fulfilled are gaining the opportunity to organize their psychological resources and adapt to stress. On the contrary, children who did not have this balance may tend to disorganize under stress.

During the stage from about 15 months to three years, children are said to develop autonomy. This can be described as the "I am what I can do" stage. Autonomy develops because most children can now move about rather easily. The child does not have to rely entirely on a caregiver to meet every single need. Autonomy also results from the development of mental processes, because the child can think about things and put language to use.

It is during this stage that the process of toilet training can be a major stressor. Children are not always given the needed opportunity to express autonomy during this process. It can be a difficult time for the child, because he or she is ordinarily expected to cooperate with, and gain the approval of the principal caregiver. If the child cooperates and uses the toilet, approval is forthcoming; however, some autonomy is lost. If the child does not cooperate, disapproval may result. If this conflict is not resolved satisfactorily, some clinical psychologists believe it will emerge during adulthood in the form of highly anxious and compulsive behaviors.

The next stage from three to five years, can be described as "I am what I think I am." Skills of body movement are being used in a more purposeful way. Children develop the ability to daydream and make believe, and these are used to manifest some of their behaviors. Pretending allows them to be what they want to be - anything from astronauts to zebras. It is possible, however, that resorting to too much fantasy may result in stress, because the children may become scared of their own fantasies.

Unquestionably, children at all the early age levels, beginning at birth (and possibly before as well) are likely to encounter a considerable amount of stress in our complex modern society. The objectives of those adults who deal with children should be to help them reduce stress by making a change in the environment and/or making a change in the children themselves.

SOME GENERAL CAUSES OF STRESS IN CHILDREN

As mentioned in Chapter 2 during the last several years, various researchers have studied certain life events as causes of stress. They have attempted to find out what kinds of health problems are associated with various events that occur to people either in the normal course of events, or as a result of some sort of misfortune. It will probably be recalled that this took the form of life events and daily hassles. As far as life events stressors for children are concerned the following appear to be the most prevalent:

1. The death of a parent
2. The death of a sibling
3. Divorce of parents
4. Marital separation of parents
5. The death of a grandparent
6. Hospitalization of a parent
7. Remarriage of a parent
8. Birth of a sibling
9. Hospitalization of a sibling
10. Loss of a job by mother or father

In the area of daily hassles in my own studies of childhood stress, I have collected data on daily stressors of children in four different age ranges. Listed below are the five most common daily hassles of children at these ages.

Ages 5-6
- Fighting with my brother
- Not knowing what I should do
- Starting school
- When I have to go to bed early
- Having to eat stuff I don't like

Ages 7-8
- When my parents don't trust me
- When my mother blames me for something I didn't do
- Afraid I will fail
- Kids who don't like me
- Having to do homework

Ages 9-10
- When I can't watch TV
- When teachers don't treat me like a person
- When I don't get credit for something I did
- Unfair punishment
- Parents who think they know everything

Ages 11-12
- Teachers who think they know it all
- Not being as strong as I would like to be
- Girls who think they are smart
- Kids who make fun of me
- Wearing my older brother's clothes

Obviously, most of these daily hassles can be dealt with in a suitable manner by alert adults. These are general causes of stress and more specific cause will emerge in the following discussions.

HOME AND FAMILY STRESS

The magnitude of home and family stress on children is well documented. For example, of the life events that are most stressful for children, well over half of them of them are concerned with home and family. Without question, changes in society with consequent changes in conditions in some homes are likely to make child adjustment a difficult problem.

Such factors as changes in standards of female behavior, larger percentages of households with both parents working, economic conditions, mass media such as television, as well as numerous others can complicate the life of the modern-day child.

Some psychiatrists are convinced that some home conditions can have an extremely negative influence on the personality and mental health of some children, not only at their present state of growth and development, but in the future as well. In fact, studies show that the interaction of stress factors is especially important. Most of these studies tend to identify the following factors to be strongly associated with childhood (and possibly later) psychiatric disorders: (1) severe marital discord, (2) low social status, (3) overcrowding or large family size, (4) paternal criminality, (5) maternal psychiatric disorder, and (6) admission into the care of local authorities.

With only one of the above conditions present, a child is no more likely to develop psychiatric problems than any other child. However, when two of the conditions occur the child's psychiatric risk increases fourfold.

Dimensions of stressful events can be discussed in terms of entrances and exits in life events, affect and stress, and multiple stressors. The theory and research on families and children is drawn from different disciplines, thus making a coherent theory difficult. Much of theorizing has been done by family sociologists and family systems psychiatrists who have concentrated on the entire family system while neglecting the individual adaptation. In contrast, the psychological literature has largely dealt with the adaptation of individuals to stress. Psychological studies have dealt with self-reports and direct observation, although there seems to be a renewed interest in old methods - such as parental interviews -being used in new ways. Two notable psychological forces have broadened contemporary perspectives on stress and coping; the lifespan movement and the ecological movement. The research suggests that most children can cope and adapt to the short-term crisis, such as divorce, within a few years. However, if the stress is compounded by other stresses and continued ad-versity, developmental disturbances may occur. Responses to stress are modified by such variables as temperament and personality, developmental status, sex, and support systems.

The Stress of Child Abuse

Obviously, child abuse can be a serious stressor for some children and a review of the research on this factors can be summarized as follows:

1.   Social stressors associated with child abuse include unemployment, lack of social support, stressful life events, and high levels of confusion.
2.   Sociological and maternal characteristics are inextricably intertwined in mutual causal relationships in child abuse.
3.   Early separation during the post-partum period (failure of bond formation) is also associated with abuse and neglect of mothers.
4.   Both situational stress and strength of social networks are significant predictors of abuse.
5.   Mothers living in highly stressful situations who report strong social networks are less likely to be abusers than mothers living in high stress situations who report weak social networks.
6.   Abusive mothers fail to regulate their behavior in relation to the performance of their children and such a response style is more likely to occur in the context of situationally induced stress.

As mentioned in Chapter 7, a serious form of child abuse concerns those who are sexually abused. According to a report[1] from the National Institutes of Mental Health, abuse in childhood can have significant long-term biological consequences and "changes in the brain's stress response system." A seven-year study followed 170 girls ages 6-15 years, half of whom had been sexually abused. Endocrine and immune system function was compared to a control group with no history of such trauma, The abused girls had abnormally high levels of stress hormones which have been shown to cause damage to brain cells crucial for thinking and mental capabilities. In addition, they also demonstrated higher levels of antibodies associated with impairment of immune system function.

Divorce and Marital Dissolution

During the past several years the number of children who have experienced parental divorce has tripled. In fact, about half of all marriages end in divorce. Millions of children are living with a divorced parent, and one-third of all children have experienced parental divorce during childhood and adolescence.

Depression, anger, self-blame, anxiety and low self-esteem frequently occur after divorce. In addition, social interaction problems, non-compliance, aggression and school difficulties occur more frequently among children of divorce than children from intact families. For some children, divorce produces mild or transient behavior problems, but for many others, this transition in family structure leads to enduring emotional and behavioral difficulties. Various aspects of divorce and stress have been studied and several important results can be identified as follows:

1.   Approaching it from a child's perspective much of the confusion in studying the impact of divorce on children has been a result of a failure to view divorce as a process involving a series of events and changes in life circumstances, rather than a single event.
2.   At different points in this sequence children are confronted with different adaptive tasks, and will use different coping strategies.

3. In understanding the child's adjustment to divorce it is important to look not only at changes in family structure but also at changes in family functioning and at stresses and support systems in the child's extrafamilial social environment.

4. Personal distress and child rearing attitudes are rarely influenced by age, number of children, or length of marriage.

Life Changes

Although some children seem to take any kind of change in their lives in stride, many others tend to suffer serious distress as a result of it. Oftentimes there can be certain psychological consequences because of these life chances.

One study conducted several years ago[2] involved family relocation and examined the effects that moving and separation have on families and suggested a role for mental health agencies in easing these stressful life events. Knowledge of family separation, father's entry and re-entry into the family, and mobility in general originates from studies of military families showing that those best able to adapt to the frequent arrivals and departures experience low levels of rootlessness. Families that experience heightened alienation experience greater problems. Children whose fathers are frequently absent are reported to experience greater dependency needs and more academic problems and to have higher referral rates for emotional problems. Literature on stress in the corporate family closely parallels findings on military families. A move consists of four stages: (1) preparation, (2) migration, (3) overcompensation, and (4) decompensation. Approaches used to strengthen family functioning during relocation include: (1) education, (2) competency promotion, (3) community organization, and (4) natural caregiving. Four factors of corporation assistance is recommended and include the establishment of relocation officers to oversee operations, a site visit by the family, educational seminars for employees and spouses, and publications about moving. It was concluded that community care and information can ease the stress of moving families and help them to cope with new circumstances.

Sibling Stress

The fear that some children have of the prospect of being "replaced by" or at the least, "taking a back seat to" a new arrival can be stress inducing. Since the average American family has two-plus children, this is a problem that most families will need to deal with. Some researchers have attempted to shed light on the problem and the following summary of findings seems warranted:

1. During the first month post birth mothers are sometimes viewed as less warm, supportive, and protective toward the firstborn and less consistent when disciplining.

2. Firstborns sometimes show an increase in sleep and eating problems and physical ill health.

3. Negative behavior in the social-emotional area increases, especially in the case of females.

4. Factors which appear to influence stressfulness include the m
    aware of potential difficulties in advance of the availability of
    the family, the reaction of the firstborn, the mother's physical he
    behavior in relation to mother and firstborn.
5. By three months postbirth changes in the behavior of parents a
    generally positive direction.
6. By six months postbirth, mothers experience highest levels of personal stress and
    conflict in the marital relationship and physical ill health on the part of the firstborns
    seem highest at this time.
7. The reduction of stress within the family following birth of a child is viewed as an
    important goal for families to try to attain.

SCHOOL STRESS

There are a number of conditions existing in many school situations that can cause much
stress for children. These conditions prevail at all levels - possibly in different ways - from
the time a child enters school until graduation from college. The child or adolescent who is
facing a set of demands with insufficient resources may respond in many ways that are
harmful or maladaptive.

Miscoping responses can include behavioral and environmental responses such as social
withdrawal, alcohol or drug abuse, and truancy. In the cognitive area, an imbalance of
demands and resources could result in feelings of low self-esteem and beliefs about being a
failure. Related to these is the possible evolution of "learned helplessness," the belief that
one's actions essentially are unrelated to the consequences that are experienced.

Stress and the Child in the Educative Process

School anxiety as a child stressor is a phenomenon with which educators, particularly
teachers and counselors, frequently find themselves confronted in dealing with children.
Various theories have been advanced to explain this phenomenon and relate it to other
character traits and emotional dispositions. Literature on the subject reveals the following
characteristics of anxiety as a stress-inducing factor in the educative process:

1. Anxiety is considered a learnable reaction that has the properties of a response, a cue
    of danger, and a drive.
2. Anxiety is internalized fear aroused by the memory of painful past experiences
    associated with punishment for the gratification of an impulse.
3. Anxiety in the classroom interferes with learning, and whatever can be done to
    reduce it should serve as a spur to learning.
4. Test anxiety is a near universal experience, especially in this country, which is a test-
    giving and test-conscious culture.
5. Evidence from clinical studies points clearly and consistently to the disruptive and
    distracting power of anxiety effects over most kinds of thinking.

It would seem that causes of anxiety change with age, as do perceptions of stressful situations. Care should be taken in assessing the total life space of the child - background, home life, school life, age, sex, - in order to minimize the anxiety experienced in the school. It seems obvious that school anxiety, although manifested in the school environment, may often be caused by unrelated factors outside the school.

The Stressfulness of School Adjustment

One of the most stressful life events for some young children is "beginning the first grade." One of the reasons for this may possibly be that older childhood friends, siblings and even some unthinking parents admonish the child with "wait until you get to school - you're going to get it." This kind of negative attitude is likely to increase any "separation anxiety" that the child already has.

It was mentioned previously that such separation anxiety begins in the first stage of a child's development, from birth to 15 months. It can reach a peak at the latter part of the developmental stage from three to five years, because it is the first attempt to become a part of the outer world -the school. For many children this is the first task of enforced separation. For those who do not have a well-developed sense of continuity, the separation might be easily equated with the loss of the life-sustaining mother. The stress associated with such a disaster could be overwhelming for such a child. Learning to tolerate the stress of separation is one of the central concerns of preschoolers; adults would be alert to signs and seek to lessen the impact. Compromises should be worked out, not necessarily to remove the stress, but to help the child gradually build a tolerance for separation.

In extreme cases of the separation problem, a child's reaction typically may include temper tantrums, crying, screaming, and downright refusal to go to school. Or, in some instances, suspiciously sudden aches and pains might serve to keep the "sick" child home. What the child is reacting against is not the school, but separation from the mother. The stress associated with this event may be seen by the child as a devastating loss equated with being abandoned. The child's behavior in dealing with the stress can be so extreme as to demand special treatment on the part of the significant adults in his or her life.

The aim in such cases should always be to ease the transition into school. It is important to keep in mind that the separation is a two-way street. Assuring parents of the competence of the school staff and the physical safety of their child may go a long way toward helping to lessen the stress. If adults act responsibly and with consistency, the child should be able to make an adequate adjustment to this daily separation from family and, in the process, learn an important lesson in meeting reality demands.

Stress and Competition in the School Environment

In a study conducted with 200 fifth-and sixth-grade children one of the questions I asked was "What is the one thing that worries you most in school?" As might be expected, there was a variety of responses. However, the one general characteristic that tended to emerge was the emphasis placed on *competition* in so many school situations. Although students did not state this specifically, the nature of their responses clearly seemed along these lines.

Most of the literature on competition for children has focused on sports activities; however, there are many situations that exist in some classrooms that can cause *classroom stress*. An example is the antiquated "Spelling Bee" which still exists in some schools, and in fact, continues to be recognized in an annual national competition. Perhaps the first few children "spelled down" are likely to be the ones who need spelling practice the most. And, to say the least, it can be embarrassing in front of others to fail in any school task.

It is interesting to note that the terms *cooperation* and *competition* are antonymous; therefore, the reconciliation of children's competitive needs and cooperative needs is not any easy matter. In a sense we are confronted with an ambivalent condition which, if not carefully handled, could place children in a state of conflict, thus causing them to suffer distress.

In generalizing on the basis of my own experience and examination of the available evidence with regard to the subject of competition, it seems justifiable to formulate the following concepts:

1. Very young children in general are not very competitive, but become more so as they grow older.
2. There is a wide variety in competition among children; that is, some are violently competitive, while others are mildly competitive, and still others are not competitive at all.
3. In general, boys tend to be more competitive than girls.
4. Competition should be adjusted so that there is not a preponderant number of winners over losers.
5. Competition and rivalry produce results in effort and speed of accomplishment.

Those who deal with children at the various educational levels might well be guided by the above concepts. It might be kept in mind that competition should not necessarily be restrained. On the other hand, it should be kept under control, so that competitive needs of children are met in a satisfactory and wholesome manner.

How the 3Rs Can Stress Children

Various school subjects could be considered as stressful for many children - males and females alike. Prominent among school subjects that have a reputation for being more stress inducing than others are those concerned with the basic 3Rs. For many boys and girls attending school daily and performing poorly is a source of considerable and prolonged stress. If children overreact to environmental stresses in terms of increased muscular tension, this may interfere easily with the fluid movement required in handwriting tasks, decreasing their performance and further increasing environmental stresses Many educators have seen children squeeze pencils tightly, press hard on the paper, purse their lips, and tighten their bodies, using an inordinate amount of energy and concentration to write while performing at a very low level.

Reading is another school activity loaded with potential anxiety, stress and frustration for many children. One of the levels of reading recognized by reading specialists is called the "frustration level." In behavioral observation terms, this can be described as the level in which children evidence tension, excessive or erratic body movements, nervousness, and distraction.

This frustration level is said to be a sign of emotional tension or stress with breakdowns in fluency and a significant increase in reading errors.

The subject that seems to stress the greatest majority of students is mathematics. This condition prevails from the study of arithmetic on entering school through the required courses in mathematics in college. Mathematics has become such a problem in recent years that an area of study called "math anxiety" is receiving increasing attention.

As a result of stressful experiences in school mathematics classes, there seems to be what could be called "math-anxious" and "math avoiding" people; they tend not to trust their problem-solving abilities and experience a high level of stress when asked to use them.

Teachers who make an effort to reduce the number of stressful situations in mathematics programs will not only be helping their students to become better mathematics learners but at the same time will be helping them as future adults to be more confident and capable performers in mathematics tasks. The same could be said for reading and writing tasks.

THE STRESS OF SCHOOL TESTS

In more than 40 years as a teacher - which included all levels from elementary school through the university graduate level - I have observed many students who were seriously stressed by "testphobia," or what has now become known more commonly as *test anxiety*.

Perceived stress appears to depend on psychological sets and responses that individuals are likely to bring to the testing situation than to manufacture on the spot. Students respond to tests and testing situations with learned patterns of stress reactivity. The patterns may vary among individuals and may reflect differences in autonomic nervous system conditioning, feelings of threat or worry regarding the symbolic meaning of the test or testing situation, and coping skills that govern the management of complexity, frustration, information load, symbolic manipulation, and mobilization of resources. There are also individual patterns of maladaptive behavior such as anxiety, a sustained level of autonomic activity after exposure to a stressor, and the use of a variety of such defense mechanism as learned helplessness and avoidance behavior.

Perceived stress also depends upon the nature of the task to be performed. As tasks get more complex and require greater degrees of coordination and integration of the nervous system, a given stressor level will affect task performance as if it were a stronger stressor.

What then, does the nature of test anxiety imply for educational goals and practice? Perhaps there should be continuing opportunity for all school personnel and parents to report on their experiences with the tests that have been used. This feedback should also place a great deal of emphasis on the students' reactions to their testing experience. It is essential that the reactions of children that give evidence to emotional disturbance in relation to tests be carefully considered, especially when test results are interpreted and used for instructional, guidance and administrative purposes.

Finally, it is important to take a positive attitude when considering test results. That is, emphasis should be placed on the number of answers that were correct. For example, the child will be more likely to be encouraged if you say, "You got seven right," rather than, "You missed three." This approach can help minimize stress in future test taking.

HELPING CHILDREN UNDERSTAND THEMSELVES

There is no question that children face unending challenges and demands in the process of their development. It is up to adults who deal with children to help them adjust to these challenges and demands.

Children themselves have numerous concerns about their place and function in modern society, or what can be termed *self-concerns that induce stress in children.* The following descriptive list of such factors is presented to alert the reader to these child concerns, to facilitate an understanding of some of the things that need to be done in order to assist children in dealing with stress.

1. *Self-concerns associated with the meeting of personal goals.* Stress can result if adults set goals too difficult for children to accomplish. For example, goals may be much higher than a particular home or school environment will permit children to achieve. On the other hand, when goals are set too low, children may develop the feeling that they are not doing as much for themselves as they should. This aspect of stress is also concerned with the fear children have that they will not reach their goals in life. It is interesting to note that with some children this can happen early in life.

2. *Self-concerns that involve self-esteem.* This involves the way a child feels about himself or herself. Self-esteem can often be highly related to the fulfillment of certain *ego needs.* Some children may feel that there are not enough opportunities offered in modern society for them to succeed. This is perhaps more true of children who are in a low socio-economic environment.

3. *Self-concerns related to changing values.* It is frustrating for some children when they do not understand the value system imposed on them by some adults. They may develop the feeling that adults are not inclined to place a value on those factors that children believe are important to them personally at their various stages of growth and development.

4. *Self-concerns that center on social standards.* In some cases, children get confused with the difference in social standards required at the different levels of development. It is sometimes difficult for them to understand that what was socially acceptable at one age level is not necessarily so at another.

5. *Self-concerns involving personal competence and ability.* This might well be the self-concern that frustrates children the most. Certainly, lack of confidence in one's ability can be devastating to the morale of a child. Many children are becoming increasingly concerned with their ability, or lack thereof, to cope with problems such as expectations of parents and keeping up with schoolwork.

6. *Self-concerns about their own traits and characteristics* Not the least of concerns among children are those factors that are likely to make them different from the so-called average or normal child. This has to do with the social need for *mutuality,* which means their wanting to be like their peers. When children deviate radically from others in certain traits and characteristics, it can be a serious stress-inducing factor.

It should be mentioned that not all of these self-concerns are characteristic of all children, particularly because of the individual differences among them. That is, what may be a serious self-concern for one child may be a minimal concern for another. Nonetheless, these self-concerns can serve as guidelines for adults in some of their dealings with children In closing this chapter, it is emphasized again that childhood stress can have s serious impact at a later time in life. In this regard, a recent study[3] examined the etiology of suicidal behavior from cognitive and developmental perspectives in a sample of 181 suicidal and nonsuicidal college students. It was hypothesized that cognitive functioning would serve as a mediator between early life events and suicidal behavior. The study examined child maltreatment, family instability, and poor family environment as early negative life events, and examined self-esteem, hopelessness, and problem-solving deficits as cognitive factors. In addition, individuals perceived social support before age 18 and current social support and life stress were also examined in relation to the preceding variables. Findings indicated that early negative life events have a mild impact on suicidal behavior, but a stronger impact on cognitive deficits, which in turn have a strong impact on suicidal behavior.

SUGGESTED ACTIVITIES

1. Conduct a round table discussion on child development and stress.
2. Seek permission at a local elementary school to survey children on what worries them most in school. Present your findings to the class.
3. Interview a teacher in a local elementary school to find how the school environment can be stressful for children. Present your findings to the class.
4. Hold a panel discussion on the subject of test anxiety.

Chapter 10

STRESS AMONG OLDER ADULTS

Whatever is the world coming to? Eighty-year-olds are running the Marathon. Stationery stores are selling birthday greeting cards for 100-year-olds. A physician asks his octogenarian patient if his parents are still living. There is an increasing number of grandchildren who are upwards of 50 years of age. And on...and on...and on.

These days when a statistic regarding life expectancy is announced it becomes obsolete almost immediately. The oldest of the old are not only here to stay, but in increasingly larger numbers. In fact, the United States Bureau of the Census predicts that the number of persons 100 years of age and older will increase from 66,000 in the year 2000 to 285,000 in the year 2050.

Will it ever end? Not likely very soon with some predictions suggesting that human beings will eventually live for a century and a half.

As we move further into the 21st century the aging population will make it incumbent upon us to reconsider social, economic, political and other factors that could impact upon the world's future. When we examine the behaviors, needs, and interests of those in the upper age ranges, we also need to take into account the problems of stress they might encounter and how they can deal with them.

1. What are some theories of aging?
2. What are the effects of aging?
3. How do older adults perceive stress?
4. How do older men and women differ in their response to stress?
5. What are some of the fears and worries of older adults?
6. How do older adults deal with stress?

Labeling individuals for one thing or another has become so commonplace in modern society that practically everyone has some sort of identification that distinguishes him or her from others. Such is the case with the various age ranges. Generally speaking, a person proceeds through the classifications of infant, child, adolescent, young adult and adult. Then, too, there are the traditional age milestones. Sweet 16 and never been kissed, If younger, don't trust anyone over 30. Life begins at 40. And, of course, the biblical reference to "three-score and ten."

After reaching adulthood there does not seem to be much agreement on how to refer to one in a certain age range. Most standard dictionaries define middle age as the period of life from about 40 to 60. After so-called middle age there is no consensus on how to refer to one in a certain age range. Just to mention a few appellations, one can be referred to by any of the following: oldster, senior citizen, old fogey, old geezer, old bat, old bag, and so on. And finally, there is just plain old, and eventually old, old. In general, persons over 65 are considered *elderly,* those over 75 as old, and traditionally those over 35 have been described as old, old. But in very recent times another range has been added; that is, those in their late 90s and early 100s are said to be the *oldest old.*

In any case, there is a great deal of difficulty determining just what old is. Barnard Baruch, the famous financier and government adviser who lived to be 94, once said that he considered a person old who was 15 years older than he. Certainly, this could be a valid criterion for one who is 70 and would like to feel "young."

CONCEPTS OF AGING

People who do not understand the process of aging sometimes feel that something unnatural is happening to them. Others who adhere to old wives' tales think that there is a certain stereotype to which they must conform. Unfortunately, there is an old concept of aging that is still held by some persons. This is that aging and disease are intertwined. To be old has been equated with being diseased. Moreover, the aging process has been perceived by some as an inevitable declining. By narrowly defining aging in this manner, a perplexing problem arises. According to this perspective, older persons are by definition "less healthy" than younger adults since their life expectancy is less.

Unfortunately, even some members of Congress have tended to impose stereotypical classifications upon older persons. For example, a content analysis of published congressional speeches found that most Congress members used stereotypes when describing older people. Interestingly enough, both negative and positive themes occurred, such as perceiving older persons in poor health, as unable to change, as living in institutions, to be financially well off, to make friends easily, and to be good listeners. Stereotypes were used by advocates who were promoting funding for older people as well as by. those in favor of decreasing funding for them.[1] It will be the intent of the following discussions to provide the reader with information that should dispel these outmoded notions.

The United States Bureau of Census describes its concept of aging as follows. Aging marks the inexorable running out of the biological time clock for the individual, given the limited life span of possibly 100 years for the human species. Although the aging process goes on steadily throughout life, aging most commonly refers to changes in later life, following the reproductive period. Aging proceeds at different rates for different individuals if it is defined in physiological, psychological, behavioral, or sociological terms rather than chronological terms. Physiologists will look for the signs of aging in the loss of functional efficiency of various bodily organs. Psychologists will look for signs of aging in the decline of neuromuscular skills, learning ability, judgment, memory, and sensory acuity. Behavioral scientists and sociologists will look for signs of aging in the individual's disengagement from social roles and growing inability to live independently. For some, the signs of physiological deterioration or the ability not to function independently come earlier than for others, but they inevitably appear for all as time passes.

Demographically, aging is defined essentially in terms of chronological age. A demographic approach can be justified on the assumption that, for large populations, the aging process, functional age, and physiological age follow chronological age closely. This approach avoids the problem of fixing the "onset" of aging in the individual case, a task faced by the biological and behavioral sciences and beset with grave difficulties. Moreover, the demographic approach can take advantage of statistical tabulations made from censuses and population surveys for conventional age groups.[2]

Various private and public organizations and agencies periodically provide demographic data about older people. With such rapid changes in the status of the older population, it is obvious that such material can quickly become out of date. With this in mind, the following information generalized from a number of recent sources is provided for reader interest.

1. Persons 65 years or older represent about 16 percent of the United States population.
2. There is a gender ratio of about 150 older women to 100 older men.
3. Since 1900 the percentage of Americans over 65 years of age has more than tripled.
4. The older population is getting older. The age group 65-74 is more than eight times larger than in 1900, the 75-84 age group more than 14 times larger and the 85 and over age group, more than 28 times larger.
5. The number of persons celebrating their 65th birthday increased by more and 1,000 per day since 1900.
6. Persons aged 65 and older are expected to represent 20 percent of the population by the year...2030.
7. In the 40 years span from 1990 to 2030 persons aged 65 or older will have more than doubled.
8. More than half of the older women aged 65 and older are widows. They outnumber widowers by five to one.
9. The average income for persons 65 and older is slightly more than $15,000 for men and nearly $9,000 for women.
10. Women 65 years and older have about twice the poverty rate of men.
11. About 30 percent of persons 65 years and older view their general health as fair to poor. This compares to about eight percent of those under age 65.

THEORIES OF AGING

The precise reason as to why people age is a complicated and complex one, and it is not entirely understood. In fact, Steven Austad[3] the notable gerontologist has indicated that some 330 different theories have been advanced to explain what happens. Of course, many of these theories have long since been disproven, and gerontology researchers continue to seek answers to why we cannot keep healing ourselves and why we inevitably decay as we grow older.

Of all of the theories of aging, two have emerged as prominent: (1) that our cells are programmed from birth to begin the aging process, and (2) that a complex combination of hormone, nervous-system, and immune-system actions tell our bodies when to begin to age.

Some students of aging suggest that the aging process can be more easily understood if one views it from the perspective of the body replacing used up cells throughout life. As time passes, the rate of cell replacement is gradually but constantly receding. This process can begin at about the time the body has reached full growth.

Contrary to some popular thought, the body part that tends to age the least is the brain, and this may be the reason for the old saying, "The brain is willing but the body is not." Indeed, we all must eventually "come to grips" with the fact that things wear out Cars wear out. Clothes wear out. Welcomes wear out. And bodies eventually wear out, if one lives long enough.

Finally, the aging process may be speeded up by the kind of life one lives. Failing to abide by personal health practices and allowing oneself to succumb to emotional stress can take its toll.

EFFECTS OF AGING

As has been previously stated, determining exactly when an individual is old is not an easy matter. We have all known older persons who were "spry for their age." At the same time, others appear old when they are in high school. Nevertheless, as one ages there are certain bodily changes that ordinarily occur. The following brief general discussion will take a few of these changes into account, but it should be clearly understood that we are referring to the so-called "average" person and that all such changes should be tempered by individual differences that exist among all of us. Thus, the following should be read with this general frame of reference in mind.

In the process of aging, one's body may not have as much strength and endurance. In addition, there may be a decrease in reaction time and speed of movement. Reaction time is the time elapsing between a sensory stimulus and the response to it. Speed of movement is concerned with how long it takes to move the body or one of its segments from one place to another. A case in point is applying the brakes of a car. One reacts and it takes a certain amount of time to respond, and then it takes time to get the foot from the accelerator-to the brake.

The lowering of basal metabolism, the rate at which energy is produced, causes one to tire sooner as well as to be more sensitive to changes in weather conditions. For women, child-bearing capacity ends, of course, with menopause, but there are cases on record where men have fathered children at an advanced age.

Vision and hearing may become less functional, but this can be compensated for with various aids. As far as hearing is concerned, although lower tones may be heard well by older persons, sometimes they have difficulty with higher tones. In this general connection, perhaps a distinction should be made between hearing and listening. Although hearing is the instrument for listening, the latter is concerned with auditory perception - the mental interpretation of what a person hears. This is to say that one may be hearing something but at the same time not listening to it. Such a reaction by an older person could possibly be misinterpreted as failure to hear.

There can be a slowing in tissue repair, and the same is true for cell growth and division. This is probably a reason that older persons are likely to "bruise easily."

HEALTH AND DISEASE AND AGING

With the advent of the science of gerontology (study of aging), much has been learned about health and disease and aging. We now have come to recognize that the health *needs* and *interests* of the older population do not differ appreciably from that of other ages levels. In a sense this is to say that old age is not necessarily accompanied by illness. In other words, disease is not a significant concomitant to old age.

The fact that older persons are not necessarily afflicted by ill health is shown in my surveys, which indicate that although some may admit to "slowing down," less than 15 percent of persons over 65 are operating on a limited basis. The means that over 85 percent of older persons enjoy reasonably good health. In addition, my surveys show that the large majority of older people consider themselves to be in a healthful state. Conversely, very few actually believe that they could classify themselves as ill.

It may well be that being an older person might have certain advantages with regard to health. As an example, although older persons are likely to acquire more chronic conditions than the general population, it also appears that they may not acquire infectious diseases at the same rate as younger adults. Then too, they have built up immunity to some diseases that they have previously had. Not only this, but they can acquire immunity to other infectious diseases as well. This may be the reason why older persons, on average, tend to have fewer cases of the common cold than younger segments of the population.

Although it may be true that some diseases are more prevalent during old age, this does not necessarily mean that such diseases are due to old age. That is, some conditions such as arthritis and cataracts that are associated with old age, are not necessarily caused by it. For example, in many cases a disease could get its start at anytime during one's life. Incidentally, it may not be common knowledge that there are various incidences of children suffering from arthritis. All of this should point up the importance of periodic medical and health appraisal for the purpose of uncovering unsuspected conditions. Such a practice can partially assure that a potentially debilitating condition, if not arrested, can at least be properly controlled. This is what is known as preventive health measures, and they provide some degree of protection for some of the diseases ordinarily associated with old age.

MENTAL FUNCTIONING AND AGING

It has already been mentioned that the brain appears to be the one body part that ages the least. This can be considered one of the good features of old age because one can continue to engage in interesting intellectual pursuits even after the body slows down physically. In fact, most gerontologists believe that exercise should include the mind as well as the body.

By and large, aging has little influence on mental functioning, unless of course, older persons allow this to happen. Sometimes older persons are depicted as having a poor memory or losing it altogether, and as a consequence some of them accept it to be true. However, as far as memory and forgetfulness of older people are concerned, if an 80-year-old were asked what he or she was doing on December 7, 1941, almost without exception there would be accurate recall because this date is identified as one of the most tragic in American history - the bombing of Pearl Harbor. The reason for this is that although the memory of some older persons tends to decline for things that have happened recently, this is not necessarily true for things that have happened in the past. Important events are likely to be stored in one's memory bank almost indefinitely.

Gerontologists tend to agree when there is lack of memory of recent events it is perhaps due mainly to lack of interest and attention instead of a lack of ability to remember. It is also felt by some that if there is a change in the memory of older persons, it may be in the direction of greater accuracy. Although older people may not always learn new things or "catch on" as quickly as some younger persons, it also seems to be true that when something is learned older people may remember it better and possibly more accurately. It should be pointed out that problems of memory are not necessarily unique to older persons. I have known younger extremely intelligent individuals who have had poor memories. Actually, there appears to be little or no correlation between memory and intelligence. (As an aside, those of us in my profession have the luxury of being forgiven for memory lapses and forgetfulness because we can retreat to the safe haven of the "absent-minded professor" syndrome.) Also it is interesting to note that some research indicates that older persons may be more practical in their orientation to problem-solving than younger adults. Rather than thinking idealistically, they may be more likely to consider the impact that a decision will have on others.

Among the various agencies that are studying aging and memory are the Memory Assessments Clinics, a private research group based in Bethesda, Maryland, and the Laboratory of Neuroscience, a part of the National Institute of Aging. The researchers tend to agree on such points as: (1) only about five percent of people over 65 suffer from acute memory disorders, (2) some older persons may have more trouble recalling isolated facts like names; and (3) the brain's processes for storing and retrieving information may slow down over time. As far as the latter is concerned, it is believed that incoming data in the form of electrical impulses cause transmitters and receivers to branch out from the brain's nerve cells (neurons) to form electrical circuits with nearby neurons. The transmitters and receivers relay information across the cell junctions, and chemicals called *neurotransmitters* are produced at the junction to speed the electrical impulse along. One theory for why slowdown occurs suggests that as the brain ages, it produces fewer of these transmitters.

There appears to be agreement in the scientific community that other mental capabilities begin to decline before memory. Fortunately, these other (reasoning and spatial skills, processing speed and working memory, dual task attention) can easily be compensated for. To remain as sharp as possible in one's later years, it is good to anticipate and rehearse solutions to spatial tasks. This tactic includes devising methods or devices that would help one remember where the car is parked, avoid being rushed, and familiarizing oneself with new places or destinations before important meetings or appointments at unfamiliar sites. Working memory can be augmented through anxiety management, putting in extra effort, working closely with others and, if necessary, professional assistance.

In another frame of reference, history is replete with cases where individuals have made significant intellectual and cultural contributions to society in their later years. For instance, Grandma Moses did not begin work on her famous paintings until she was 78. Similarly, Clara Barton founded the Red Cross when she was over 60 and served as its president until age 84. In more modern times the legendary song writer, Irving Berlin, who composed some of America's most beloved music of the 20th century, died in September 1989 at the age of 101. And, the late George Burns, the popular comedian, was still entertaining appreciative audiences in his 100th year. The late Claude Pepper, in his late 80s, was the recognized champion of the elderly and made many impassioned pleas in their behalf on the floor of the United States House of Representatives.

In one of my interviews with an 82-year-old woman, she commented, "I have had a full and satisfactory life, but now I am - for the first time - afraid; not of death but of the approach of 'senility.'" How unfortunate that anyone in modern times would be led to subscribe to this outmoded idea. It is true that at one time it was thought 'senility' caused physical deterioration of the brain. It is now believed that if such deterioration occurs it is likely to be caused by illness or an injury, not by aging. Although the term *senility* was once used to describe the condition of physical and/or mental infirmity of old age, the term has fallen into disrepute among gerontologists and many members of the medical profession. Among some gerontologists the term *senile* has been replaced by the term *dementia,* the general trend being to define a disease factor related to this codition such as Alzheimer's disease.

LONGEVITY

Simply stated, longevity means length of life, or the number of years left of life expectancy. For obvious reasons most of us are interested in length of life as well as how much longer we can expect to live.

It is interesting to consider life expectancy in the past as compared to the present. At about the time of Christ, average life expectancy was less than 25 years. By the 1850s this had risen to about 35 years, and by the 1960s to a bit over 65 years. And due to modern medical advances and technology, life expectancy continues upward at a tremendous rate. As soon as a prediction is made it is almost out of date. Incidentally, one estimate indicates that presently there have been more than 50,000 persons who have reached 100 years of age, and this number is supposed to increase to 1,000,000 by the year 2040.

With many persons living much longer than in the past, the sciences of *gerontology* and *geriatrics* have almost become household words. As mentioned previously, the former is concerned with the study of aging, while geriatrics is a branch of medicine that deals with diseases of old age.

It is recognized that heredity plays a part in the life length of some persons. For example, other things being equal, people who have had parents and grandparents who lived long lives tend to have a long life span themselves. However true, we are not able to select our ancestors. Nonetheless, at least some of us are in a position to have some control over the kind of environment in which we must function. This means that we should give serious consideration to such concerns as periodic health and medical examinations, practicing good nutrition, getting sufficient rest, and engaging in wholesome physical activity and exercise. Although there is no particular formula that will guarantee that one will live to a "ripe old age," it is quite possible that we may eventually learn how to manipulate the aging process and postpone aging by many years. This might be accomplished by engaging in health and fitness practices as well as becoming involved in certain forms of hormone therapy.

WHAT STRESS MEANS TO OLDER ADULTS

In studying how older adults perceive stress, the same procedure was used as that for college students reported in Chapter 1. Older adult's concepts of stress focused on the number of times certain *key* words emerged in the responses. The following list gives the percentage of key words.

Key Word	Per Cent
Emotion	23
Strain	16
Tension	16
Worry	16
Pressure	10
Anxiety	10
Adjustment	6
Frustration	3

These data were collected with one of the items of the Humphrey Stress Inquiry Form which was submetted to more than 600 adults in the 65-85 year age range. Slightly more than 500 older adults answered this item. The following is a sampling of these responses. Stress is:

- severe emotional and/or physical strain usually caused by conditions beyond our immediately control.
- environmental conditions that produce internal disturbance in the attempt to adjust.
- the impact of emotional and physical occurrences over which one seems to have no control.
- the inability to handle daily problems without too much mental strain.
- tension build up due to factors that are unknown causes.
- pressure and anxiety.
- mental and physical worry.
- emotional problems and health.
- anticipating fear and anxiety.
- the inability to handle problems without too much mental strain.
- when you are upset emotionally and you have trouble relaxing.
- worrying about things that you can't do anything about.
- mental or physical tension or strain.
- emotions in distress.
- mental tension of being uptight.
- emotions effected by unpleasant incidents.
- a feeling of anxiety over family.
- problems that people worry about.
- inability to adjust.
- worry and grief.

- pressure from physical and mental strain.
- nervousness and tension.
- the impact of emotions.
- mainly mental anguish and tension.
- pressure from everyday activities.

STRESS GENDER DIFFERENCES IN OLDER ADULTS

As far as gender differences in stress in older adults is concerned, some interesting information is available. For example, in my interviews with older adults a question often raised was: "Who suffers more from stress, older men or older women?"

A serious stressor among some older women in my surveys was one of *financial worries*. About twice as many women as men cited this to be a source of stress for them. Moreover, this was the case of so-called well-to-do women as well as those with low and average incomes. They were concerned as to whether or not they would have enough money to "see them through."

In this general connection the following interesting information was reported at a meeting of the Older Women's League:

1. Despite the myth of the "wealthy elderly," the nation's women age 65 and older fare worse economically than their male counterparts.
2. In general, older women are poorer, those who work have worse jobs, are paid less, have worse pensions and worse medical coverage and are more obligated to care for family members who are ill or disabled.
3. Older women are less likely to reap the economic benefits from a lifetime of work and they are more likely to live in poverty and isolation.
4. Rather than being cared for, they are likely to continue to sacrifice their health and their livelihood to care for others.
5. About 15 percent of older women fall below the government's official poverty line. The figure for older men is less than half as high.
6. On the average, if women become widowed, divorced or separated in old age or if they are already single, they lack resources and health and pension benefits equal to those of men.
7. As one example of financial income, a typical male in the age range of 65 to 69 averages more than 27 percent in social security benefits than do women in the same age range. As far as pension benefits are concerned males average over 45 percent more monthly than do women. Generally speaking, according to this report there is ample reason for the average older woman to consider financial problems as a serious source of stress.

EMOTIONAL RESPONSES OF OLDER ADULTS

Like any other population, older adults engage in various aspects of emotional reactivity. In my interviews and surveys of older adults a great many forms of *fear* emerged. Following are the ten most prominent of these. Fear:

- of growing older and "senility."
- of inability to accept change,
- of having an accident,
- of what the evening news will bring,
- of where our country is headed,
- of lonesomeness
- of being harmed,
- of not being accepted,
- of not getting enough rest.

Controlling *worry* is a difficult problem for those older adults who have problems adjusting. In my surveys of older adults the following were the six most prominent worries. Worry:

- about health.
- about family members.
- about adult children.
- about lack of accomplishment.
- about lack of money.
- about time pressure.

It is interesting to note that there are a variety of factors that induce *anger* in older adults. Some of these factors that were the cause of anger in the older adults in my surveys were:

1. Mediocrity in others.
2. Complaints of contemporaries.
3. Arguments.
4. Poor drivers on the road.
5. Waiting in line.
6. People trying to tell me what to do.
7. Unpleasant odors (smoke, paint).
8. Gossip.
9. That I can't drive.
10. Rock and roll music.

HOW SOME OLDER ADULTS ARE DEALING WITH STRESS

One dimension of my surveys of stress among older adults was concerned with what measures they were taking in dealing with stress. This information is summarized in the following discussion.

Almost four-fifths of the respondents used *recreational activities* as a coping measure with about half of these citing reading as the favorite activity.

Although about one-half of the respondents said they engaged in the use of alcohol for "social drinking" purposes, slightly over one-fourth said they used an alcoholic beverage to relieve stress. As one 83-year-old man put it, "When I feel stressed I take a drink which relaxes me."

Only about six percent said they used tranquilizers for the purpose of relieving stress and they were about equally divided between prescription and nonprescription drugs.

Slightly more than ten percent engaged in meditation as a stress reducing technique. All of these respondents reported great success with the technique and recommended it for everyone. In other populations that I have studied only about five percent used meditation. One exception to this is psychiatrists with 20 percent of them using the technique.

About 40 percent said they tried to use some sort of muscular relaxation to reduce stress and many of these were members of retirement residences where this activity was a part of an organized stress management program. This was also true of the practice of meditation.

Slightly more than one-half said they were able to reduce stress by resorting to divine guidance such as praying and reading the Bible. Almost 90 percent of these were women.

In this regard, a study by Catherine Ross[4] is of interest. Using a representative sample of 401 18 to 83 year old Illinois residents and controlling for sociodemographics and willingness to express feelings, her telephone survey found that the stronger a person's religious belief, the lower the level of psychological distress. Protestants had the lowest distress levels, followed by Catholics, Jews, and others. Differences in belief systems, however, especially a belief in the American Protestant ethic, did not explain differences in distress among religious groups.

It was gratifying to learn that more than 70 percent used physical exercise as a method of coping, the most popular activity being walking with well over two-thirds engaging in this form of exercise. On questioning, however, walking was in the nature of "strolling" and not "brisk" walking which would ordinarily be recommended. A large proportion of the respondents professed a need for more knowledge about exercise.

It has been my experience that for older adults a well-designed training program not only increases life satisfaction, but also augments maximum oxygen intake by at least 20 percent, with associated increases in muscle strength and joint flexibility, dispersal of accumulated fat, and halting of bone mineral loss. There is a considerable amount of objective evidence to support the idea that physical exercise can be most beneficial for older adults.

The fact that exercise can improve the *cognitive abilities* of older adults is shown in one interesting study.[5] The subjects were 62 men and women ages 55-88 who exercised vigorously and 62 sedentary individuals in the same age range. Variables such as education and medical condition were taken into consideration. The experimental group performed significantly better on measures of reasoning, working memory and reaction time - all of which reflect brain functions. It was concluded that exercise may help forestall degenerative changes in the brain associated with normal aging.

Some older adults suffering from *depression* have benefited from exercise and two studies are reported here.

In a study[6] of older adults between the ages of 60 and 80 years, 70 percent of those who exercised for an hour twice a week for nine months showed reductions in depression as measured by Zung's Depression Inventory Scale. In contrast, 40 percent of age-matched individuals who belonged to clubs for retired persons showed increases in depression. No explanation for the increase in depression was given other than it was "a fact which gives an idea of the rapid deterioration of those persons." The supervised exercise program included warm-ups, flexibility and abdominal strength exercises, and a slowly paced ten-minute run. Exercisers also improved on measures of neuroticism and reported decreases in the number of psychosomatic complaints and doctor visits.

In another study[7] of exercise and depression the effects of exercise on 38 elderly nursing home residents and senior community center participants were evaluated. Subjects were three males and 35 females between the ages of 50 and 98 years. The program included only balance and flexibility activities. Exercisers who showed signs of clinical depression as measured by the Zung Self-Rating Depression Scale reported significantly less depression at the end of the eight-week exercise sessions. Many older adults complain of "being stiff in the joints." This pertains to *flexibility* - range of motion in a joint. Some of the research on flexibility in older adults and exercise is reported here.

One study[8] was conducted to see whether or not significant improvement in flexibility could be demonstrated by older adults who participated in a fitness program. Fifteen women from ages 71 to 90 exercised for 30 minutes twice weekly for about seven months. There was significant improvement for ankle flexion and lower back flexion.

In another study[9] effects of exercise on flexibility measures was examined with a group of 18 people 60 years old or older. They met three times a week for 30 minutes for a total of 29 sessions. Results showed significant improvement in the shoulder-hip-knee flexibility.

In a final study[10] reported here the effects of an exercise program on finger joint resistance (stiffness) among 20 older men 63 to 88 years, and 20 males 15 to 18 were examined. The right index finger was exercised by lifting weights attached to a pulley for a total of 18 sessions over six weeks. In the beginning the older men had significantly greater joint stiffness than the younger men, although the older men had the same significant improvements in flexibility as the younger men. This study demonstrated that joint stiffness is also reversible , and young and old reacted in the same manner to the training.

Sometimes *self-esteem* decreases in older adults due to a variety of factors. For instance, lower self-esteem can be generated by negative attitudes that some younger people have toward older adults. Other factors are concerned with a decline in social interaction and the power and control some older adults have over their environment. Situations that place a value on abilities of older adults, as well as to respect their right to make decisions go a long way in increasing self-esteem.

There has been some research in this area and one representative example is reported here. Twenty three persons in the 60-69 year age range participated in an aerobic exercise program. There was a control group of 19 persons ranging from 60-78 years of age. Those in the experimental group exercised three times weekly for 14 weeks while the control group continued their normal lifestyle. The study revealed significant increases in self-concept for the experimental group.

SUGGESTED ACTIVITIES

1. Invite a local physician who practices geriatric medicine to speak to the class on how he/she advises older patients to cope with stress.
2. Invite a social director of a local retirement resort to speak to the class on how social activities are planned to help residents cope with stress.
3. Visit a local retirement resort and interview several residents about the subject of stress. Report your findings to the class.
4. Conduct a round table discussion about stress and exercise for older adults.
5. Hold a panel discussion on the subject of gender differences in stress responses of older adults.

Chapter 11

JOB STRESS

Innumerable authoritative sources have proclaimed that job stress is now one of the nation's leading adult health problems. According to the United States Bureau of Labor Statistics, stress at the worksite is affecting an astonishing number of people. It is estimated that well over one-fourth of the American workforce is afflicted in some way by job stress. Because of this, costs to employers can run into hundreds of billions of dollars annually in absenteeism, reduced output, and poor workmanship. Added to this is the fact that job stress can be the cause of a large number of health-related matters.

The problem of job stress is not restricted to the United States; there is no question that it has reached global epidemic proportions. This concern has been demonstrated by the fact that the International Labor Office issued a 275-page publication on the subject. This comprehensive report titled *Preventing Stress at Work* examined the problem of job stress in numerous occupational pursuits throughout the world.

1. What are some of the ways in which bosses cause stress for workers?
2. What are some of the conditions that cause stress among blue collar workers?
3. What is technostress?
4. What are some of the stress inducing factors for physicians and nurses?
5. What are some of the factors that cause stress among teachers?

AN OVERVIEW OF JOB STRESS

There are many stress-related conditions connected with one's job, and it is well known that some kinds of employment are highly stressful, while others are considered relatively stress free. Various studies comparing such groups have indicated that those in highly stressful occupations tend to have a higher incidence of serious diseases, possibly resulting from stressful conditions on the job.

Perhaps the secret lies in attempting to obtain a position of employment where one can deal with stress levels required of that position. The late President Harry Truman characterized this situation with his often-quoted statement, "If you can't stand the heat, stay out of the kitchen." In this particular regard, it has been shown that persons with low confidence in their competencies are likely to seek relatively secure and undemanding occupations, while those with high self-confidence are more likely to seek more demanding occupations.

There seems to be no question that job stress has reached worldwide epidemic proportions, and various surveys bear out the fact that job pressures represent a leading source of stress for adult Americans, and that the problem has escalated progressively over the past several years. Similar problems exist all over the world to such an extent that it is now considered to be a worldwide problem. No particular occupation appears exempt. Waitresses in Sweden, teachers in Japan, postal workers in America, bus drivers, in Europe; and assembly line workers everywhere are showing increasing signs of job stress.

The nature of job stress varies with different occupations, but affects workers at all levels. Following are some of the major sources.

1. Inadequate time to complete a job to one's satisfaction.
2. Lack of a clear job description or chain of command.
3. Little recognition or reward for good job performance.
4. Inability or lack of opportunity to voice complaints.
5. Lots of responsibility, but little authority.
6. Inability to work with superiors, co-workers, or subordinates because of basic differences in goals and values.
7. Lack of control or pride over the finished product.
8. Insecurity caused by pressures from within or without due to the possibility of takeover or merger.
9. Prejudice because of age, gender, race, or religion.

MANAGEMENT STYLE AND STRESS

It should be mentioned that among the sources of job stress listed above, many of them apply to management style. By and large a higher level of job satisfaction is likely to prevail when there is a management style that involves human relations rather than one that is autocratic in nature. This is borne out by a number of studies, some of which are reported here.

A Northwestern National Life Insurance study[1] recommends several suggestions for decreasing employees' stress to reduce the incidence of stress-related illness, disability, burnout, or resignation. Companies are advised to facilitate communication among employees and between management and employees; minimize personal conflicts on the job; let employees have adequate control over how they do their work; ensure adequate staffing and expense budgets; support employees' efforts; give employees competitive personal leave and vacation benefits; reduce the amount of red tape that employees must deal with; and recognize and reward employees' contributions.

The effect of participatory action research (PAR) was examined by Catherine Heaney and her associates[2] in two plants with divergent management styles, one cooperative and the other using top-down, traditional, hierarchical management (PAR) involves researchers, management, and union representatives in joint problem solving). It was found that PAR involvement improved employee participation in decision making in both contexts, increasing co-worker support and decreasing strain in the traditional plant, and improving employee perceptions of management's openness to suggestions in the cooperative plant. R. Karasek and T. Theorell[3] found that the importance of extending the individual decision latitude component, together with the need to reorient existing production systems, are ways to counteract occupational stress. They recommend that companies decentralize authority and involve workers in decision making, since they believe the only real solution to stress is a participatory redesign of work.

In closing this section of the chapter it seems important to reexamine the traditional concept of the *boss* as conceived by Henry Sims and Charles Manz[4] in their book, *Business Without Bosses: How Self-Management Teams are Producing High Performing Companies.* These authors maintain that organizations of the 21st century will rely on self-managing teams and that such teams are coming to the forefront as a critical factor in survival. They assert that a few years ago only 250 manufacturing plants in the United States were using such teams. In terms of percentages that number is low and more recent estimates would probably indicate the number of companies using teams to be nearing 50 percent.

While the team approach displaces bosses, it does not eliminate the need for leaders, but these leaders are determined by the teams rather than having a supervisor thrust upon them. It could be that employees do not need bosses continuously staring over their shoulders, telling them what to do, and chewing them out for what they have done wrong. By organizing people into teams and equipping them with what they need to do the job themselves, companies can do business without bosses.

In order for those self-managing teams to be effective the concept must be embraced by executives who are interested in being competitive. And the executives must fine tune the concept to make it work for their organization.

Although one may support the team concept, it should also be recognized that there are challenges in bringing self-management teams into existence. But once in place they seem to be very effective. In fact, it is likely that productivity can be 30 to 50 percent better than that of traditional work-groups. Therefore, it seems logical to assume that such an organizational practice could go a long way in reducing stress among corporate employees.

WORKERS' COMPENSATION CLAIMS DUE TO STRESS

The growing number of job stress problems has resulted in a large increase in workers' compensation awards for these conditions. Rulings vary from state to state on mental-physical, physical-mental claims. All agree that if a physical injury on the job results in an emotional disorder then it is work related. Many states also recognize the opposite possibility, such as a heart attack due to a mental trauma or a stressful relationship with a supervisor. However, it is the third type of stress case, the mental-mental type, that is increasing. In such instances, the worker claims that a mental disorder like depression or anxiety is due to some stressful job problem or even fear of unemployment. In one recent two-year period, 11 percent of all occupational disease claims, reported in 13 representative states, were mental disorders related to stress. This reflected an increase of more than 300 percent over a two-year period.

One of the fastest growing segments of workers' compensation claims for job stress is what is known as *repetitive stress injuries.* They are manifested by complaints of soreness and tenderness of the wrists and fingers due to repetitive trauma, especially in computer operators, whose performance may be unknowingly monitored by superiors. One such ailment, *carpal tunnel syndrome,* is characterized by numbness and weakness of the hand due to prolonged pressure on the palm from keeping the wrist in a cocked position from constant typing.

Unions are increasingly educating members about their rights to compensation for job stress. In addition, physicians, legislators, attorneys, and judges are becoming more familiar with relationships between stress and illness.

The following is a small sampling of situations concerned with various aspects of workers' compensation claims that are related to job stress.

1. In New York City the relationship between job stress and heart attack is so well acknowledged that any police officer who suffers a heart attack on or off the job is assumed to have a work-related disability and is compensated accordingly.
2. Several years ago the Missouri State Division of Employment Security awarded benefits to a former automobile assembly line worker who quit his job simply because of "assembly line blues."
3. Courts in at least six states have ruled that emotionally ill employees deserve compensation for "stress accumulated gradually on the job."
4. In Michigan a secretary became hysterical when her boss constantly criticized her for going to the bathroom too often. She received $7,000 and her attorney appealed to get a larger amount.
5. A Maine state trooper, whose duties involved cruising around a quiet rural area, became severely depressed because he was on call 24 hours a day. He claimed that his sex life deteriorated because he never knew when the phone would ring. The case was settled out of court for $5,000.
6. In a recent Federal Employee Liability Act decision the jury awarded more than $300,000 to an employee who claimed that fear of contracting asbestos-related disease caused him severe stress and anxiety.
7. In California over a 10-year period there was a 700 percent increase in workers' compensation claims for mental stress. Even a judge received an award by claiming that he suffered a stroke from overwork because of an increased caseload of workers' compensation claims.

This problem has become so serious that one could be tempted to speculate that the phenomenal escalation of workers' compensation awards for job stress could possibly threaten to bankrupt the system in some states.

MEASURING AND EVALUATING JOB STRESS

Increasing concerns about the adverse health effects of job stress have mandated the need to develop scientific methods to measure and evaluate this complex problem. Various questionnaires and rating scales have been developed to study stress in specific occupations, particularly health care work environments. General measures are often used to rate such things as depression, anxiety, and expression of anger. *The Maslach Burnout Inventory* measures perceptions of professional-client interactions in terms of emotional exhaustion, depersonalization, and personal accomplishments. Attempts to measure job stress and strain in physicians and nurses have resulted in the development of the *Work Related Strain Inventory.* This originally consisted of 45 statements designed to reflect stress-related symptoms reported in health professionals. This was based on a combination of other measures such as the *Physician Stress Inventory, Self-Rating Depression Scale, Social Support Measures,* and *Social Desirability Scale.* It has been refined into an 18-item questionnaire with the assigned items being accorded relative weights of significance, utilizing both reverse or positive scoring. Finally, there is may own *Humphrey Stress Inquiry Form* that can be adapted for use in any specific situation. This instrument which has a reliability coefficient of .90, has been used to collect significant portions of the data reported in this chapter.

STRESS IN BUSINESS AND INDUSTRY

Stress in business and industry encompasses all manner of individuals from blue collar workers to corporate chief executive officers. None are immune to the potential ravages of stress, with stressors abounding at all levels of the work force.

Over a period of years I have studied stress-inducing factors at all levels including blue collar workers, office personnel, managers, and the highest level of corporate executives.

In the discussions that follow, I will report some of my findings about stress-inducing factors encountered on the job in business and industry. These result include a combination of many different populations of workers and included among them are office workers, business executives, various kinds of draftmen, civil servants, and blue collar workers. I have separated the stressors into four classifications: (1) conditions concerned with facilities, equipment, and supplies, (2) conditions concerned with time factors, (3) conconcerned with general organizational factors, and (4) conditions concerned with superiors (boss types).

Conditions Concerned With Facilities, Equipment, and Supplies

Slightly more than one-fourth of those surveyed identified stress-inducing factors in this classification. In the present context, *facilities* are considered to be all of those things that, in one way or another, involve the physical plant and surrounding areas. *Equipment* refers to those kinds of materials that are not as permanent as facilities such as various kinds of machinery. *Supplies* are those materials used almost daily, and are expended over a relatively short period of time. These include an enormously large range of materials such as paper, pencils, and the like.

About 65 percent of the respondents considered deficiencies in equipment as stress inducing. Twenty percent identified physical conditions, such as lack of repairs, poor lighting, poor room temperature, and unkempt facilities, as causes of stress. Thirteen percent referred to lack of facilities as a cause of stressful conditions.

Conditions Concerned With Time Factors

More than one-fourth-of the respondents found that various factors relating to time were a serious cause of stress. Of this number more than one-half said they were put under stress because of insufficient time for planning. About one-third of the workers who identified the time factor as stress inducing simply said there was just not enough time in the day for them to do the kind of job expected of them. Because of this, it became necessary for them to take work home. Interruptions for various reasons were consider by 18 percent to be an un-necessary infringement on their time. Those in this category also complained that it took a great deal of time to get things back on an even keel because of such interruptions.

Conditions Concerned With General Organizational Factors

Responses of almost one-half of those surveyed were directed to stress-inducing factors in this general classification. Forty-four percent of this total considered *record keeping* practices to be an important cause of stress. Included among record keeping chores were too many forms and too much red tape, unnecessary paper work, and other assorted tasks that could be placed in the general classification of "busy work."

Eighteen percent felt that *unreasonable deadlines* were a cause of stress, and they felt that they were victims of the "get it in yesterday" syndrome. Fifteen percent considered *excess meetings* as stress inducing mainly because such meetings were often poorly organized and rarely served any constructive purpose. The remaining respondents who identified stress-inducing factors in this general classification named as stressful such concerns as being asked to perform duties unrelated to the job. (secretaries who are required to make and serve coffee.)

Actions of "Boss Types" that Induce Stress

Boss types are considered to be those who are an employee's immediate superior, such as supervisor, foreman, department head, or administrator. The responses were subclassified into the three broad areas of *administrative practices, administrative incompetence,* and *personality conflicts.*

About 40 percent of the respondents felt that administrative practices were a serious cause of stress. Eighteen percent believed that some of the reports they were asked to prepare for their superiors were so much busy work and did not serve the purpose for which they were allegedly intended. Twelve percent cited faulty evaluation procedures used by superiors as putting them under undue stress. They identified such practices as unfair evaluation, lack of recognition of qualified workers, failure on the part of superiors to "weed out" poor workers, and, in general, evaluation procedures that were seriously lacking in validity. The remaining 10 percent considered autocratic tactics of an administrator as stress inducing and generally expressed this in terms of "the boss whose ideas are the only ones." In this particular regard and as mentioned previously, studies have shown that authoritarian approaches produce more stressful situations for employees than do human-relations strategies for leadership.

For 29 percent of the respondents administrator incompetence was a serious stress inducing factor. The most noteworthy concerns of employees were expressed in the following ways:

The boss who:
- controls rather than helps.
- is of little help with most problems.
- does not understand the working situation.
- has never worked at the job himself.
- lacks an understanding of the demands of the job.

Almost one-third of the employees considered certain personality conflicts as stress inducing. Chief among these was inability to communicate with the boss. This was closely followed by complaints such as:

- The boss has a bad feeling toward me.
- There is an incompatible relationship because of petty demands.
- The boss interferes too much.
- The boss is unfair in his dealings with employees.
- The boss who is out to get the workers.

(Later in the chapter I will discuss stress- inducing factors for bosses.)

Stress Among Blue Collar Workers

One might think that the so-called blue collar worker does not suffer much stress because he or she does not have the same degree of responsibility as superiors. However, this is not necessarily the case and a number of studies and authoritative pronouncements bear out this contention.

My own studies of how blue collar workers cope with stress are of interest. A relatively small number engaged in organized *physical exercise* to cope with stress. For the most part they felt that they received enough strenuous physical activity on the job. However, about one-half of them engaged in *recreational activities,* the most popular of which was bowling.

In about 20 percent of the cases they *discussed their problems with others* as a means of coping with stress. Included among those with whom problems were discussed were workmates, boy/girl friends, spouses, and other relatives.

About 15 percent: resorted to *drugs and various forms of medication.* They were about equally divided in the use of prescription and nonprescription drugs.

One popular coping technique was the use of alcohol with about 65 percent engaging in this practice. Many said that "lifting a few" went a long way in helping them relax and thus reduce stress.

Stress Among "Boss Types"

As mentioned before boss types are considered to be those individuals who are an employee's immediate superior. This could include all manner of managers up to those who hold high level executive positions.

While employees identified numerous actions of bosses that induce stress, bosses, in turn, named many anxiety-provoking stimuli. One of the greatest stressors for bosses was incompetent workers. Other stress-inducing factors for them were not too unlike those identified by those they supervise. They felt plagued by a multitude of daily interruptions that deterred completing tasks that had been started. Another stressful condition was one that prevented them from being able to block out time to plan or execute an intended plan because of unexpected circumstances arising. Many found it stressful when they had to reorganize priorities almost daily. Also inducing stress were too many meetings and too many matters to coordinate.

Technostress

Technostress is another new and growing problem. This term refers to anxiety, depression, frustration, and dehumanization increasingly being seen in people who work in a high-tech environment. A variety of employee activities is now under surveillance, including number and length of restroom breaks, number of computer keystrokes per minute, and speed in processing or replying to telephone requests for information. These and other "big brother" intrusions are expanding to affect millions of workers in airline offices, government agencies, insurance companies, mail-order houses, and telephone companies, giving the workers the feeling that they are laboring in electronic sweatshops. Computers are frequently programmed for high-achievement goals, and employees are pushed to work faster and faster to meet them, much as when manufacturers speed up assembly lines. Through the telephones and computer terminals they use, their performance can be analyzed in *microchip detail.*

However, since computers measure quantity better than quality, the fastest operators are more apt to be rewarded than those who actually do the best work. In addition, supervisors often make judgments about workers based on eavesdropping without employees' knowledge or any opportunity to defend themselves.

Technostress also stems from the information overload that has resulted from the accelerated speed of data acquisition and communication enhancements. Computers, fax machines, cellular phones, call forwarding, call waiting, conference calls, remote-access answering machines and services, beepers, express mail, same-day courier service, and so on, now make it feasible to contact anyone, anywhere, at any time. Consequently, human contact and personal relationships have steadily disintegrated. In some offices, workers only a few feet apart seldom speak to each other, communicating primarily through their computer terminals. A few become so enchanted with or accustomed to the consistent speed and accuracy of their computer activities that this spills over into their personal lives; they expect or demand the same rapid and flawless responses from family and friends.

In closing this section of the chapter, it should be noted that the discussion has been confined pretty much to the private sector. Although there is some overlapping of stressors, there is no question that those in public service can also become seriously stress ridden. For example, it is well known that many policemen and firemen place their lives *on the line* daily.

STRESS IN THE PROFESSIONS

The term profession as defined by most standard dictionaries is a "calling requiring specialized knowledge and often long and intensive preparation." Included among the professions are health care providers (physicians, dentists, and nurses) teachers, and lawyers. My own studies of stress among professional personnel have focused upon health care providers, (especially physicians and nurses), and teachers. Thus, a major portion of this section of the chapter will be directed to these areas.

Health Care Providers

Physicians, dentists, and nurses are not the only health care providers who are likely to suffer from stress. For example, it may well be that emergency medical personnel witness the most stressful side of life. They see victims of shooting and stabbing, children who are burned or beaten, accident victims, and every conceivable acute cardiac emergency and serious illness. It has been well established that exposure to a single traumatic event, so-called critical incident stress, can result in depression and suicide and other symptoms quite similar to those seen in Vietnam veterans with Post Traumatic Stress Disorder. However, emergency medical personnel are constantly exposed to situations that are often even more traumatic and horrible than those seen during war. Their biggest source of stress, however, is that they must often wait up to eight hours or more after they bring their patients to an emergency room before being released to a physician or hospital representative. Often this service is abused by nonurgent cases, and frustration becomes intolerable as they listen to other legitimate and desperate calls for help to which they cannot respond.

Physicians

Stress has become a major problem for some physicians. Alcoholism, substance abuse, suicide, depression, and divorce are significantly higher compared to other professional groups. Physician stress seems to have intensified in the past several years and it could get worse due to increasing control over practice habits by fiscal intermediaries, regulatory practices, and various hospital committees. Growing patient dissatisfaction, diminished public stature and respect, and rising malpractice insurance rates and suits are threatening to the average physician. The problems associated with physician stress are much greater than most people realize, with increasing numbers of doctors opting for early retirement while still in their 50s.

My own studies of stress among physicians included an interview/survey of more than 800 doctors in the Washington, DC area. Most of the major specialties were represented. The average age of the physicians was 48 years and the average number of years in practice was 16. Eighty-four percent were male and 16 percent were female.

The respondents were asked to list three factors that caused them the greatest amount of stress on the job. This mass of information was arbitrarily separated into five general classifications: (1) concerns with patients, (2) workload, (3) professional matters, (4) administrative functions, and (5) personal matters.

Those situations that involved *dealings and relationships with patients* were by far the most stress inducing; more than 80 percent of them reported such factors. Two general categories of patient relationships that caused stress were identified as *condition* of patients and *complaints*. In the former category, all respondents indicated a variety of factors that induced stress. Of these factors, the following were considered the most serious stressors:

1. Patients not responding well to treatment.
2. Emotional demands of patients.
3. Patients resorting to drugs and alcohol.
4. Unrealistic expectations of patients.
5. Emergent crisis situations.

As far as complaints were concerned, slightly more than 20 percent were stressed by angry patients, patients not satisfied with treatment, and angry families of patients.

The second most stressful situation for physicians could be placed in the general classification of *workload*. Almost 60 percent of the respondents reported overwork as stress inducing; however, most of them said that the heavy workload was pretty much their own doing. Contributing most to stress as a result of overwork were the overscheduling of patients, too many demands, uneven periods of overload, and insufficient time to complete priority tasks.

About 45 percent reported stress-inducing factors concerned with *professional matters*. The most stressful concern here focused on negative feelings toward colleagues and associates, with more than half reporting this as a serious stressor. Cited as stress inducing were disputes with colleagues, annoying coworkers, and uninformed colleagues. Almost two-thirds were stressed by fear of being sued for malpractice. Ten percent said they lacked faith in their professional ability and suffered anxiety about self-doubt regarding adequacy of the services rendered their patients.

Certain *administrative functions* were found to be stressful for almost 40 percent of the respondents. By far the most common stress-inducing factor in this category was worry about finances caused by the threat of being underemployed as a result of too few patients.

Nurses

When nurses were first labeled "angels of mercy," they were suitably portrayed. In my own personal experience in teaching courses to undergraduate, graduate, and nurses in service at the University of Maryland School of Nursing and Walter Read Army Hospital, I found that the one characteristic that most of them had in common was *dedication and caring*. This remains despite the fact that for the most part they are overworked, underpaid, and, in too many instances, downright "put upon" in one way or another. In modern times there is a phenomenal shortage of nurses, and this is due largely to the two factors of low salary and stress on the job.

The following is a report of my extensive survey of nurses in which I selected a 10 percent sample from 40,000 nurses in the State of Maryland, the District of Columbia, and Northern Virginia. The *Humphrey Stress Inquiry Form* (modified for nurses) was sent to each of the nurses in the sample. The responses were anonymous and of a self-reporting nature. Interest in the study was demonstrated by 2,290 returns, or 73 percent of usable forms.

The ranges of ages of the nurses was 22 to 67 years with the average age being 39 years. Years of experience ranged from one to 46 years for an average of 14 years. More than 25 nursing specialties were represented from *Ambulatory Care* to *Women's Health.*

I was able to obtain firsthand from nurses themselves those factors that induced the most stress. This was accomplished by simply requesting that they identify those factors connected with their job that were most stressful for them. Obviously, this resulted in a huge mass of data. It seemed appropriate to sort out the stressors and place them in what appeared the most appropriate classifications.

The difficulty encountered in attempting to devise a foolproof system for the classification of nurses' stressors should be obvious. The reason for this lies in the fact that it is practically impossible to fit a given stressor into one exclusive classification because of the possibility of overlapping. However, an attempt was made to do so, and it should be made clear that the classification on my part was purely arbitrary. Others might wish to use different classifications than those used here, and in the absence of anything resembling standardization, it would be their prerogative to do so. With this idea in mind, the following classifications of nurses' stressors were finally chosen.

1. Patients
2. Understaffing
3. Administration
4. Coworkers
5. Time
6. Physicians
7. Compensation
8. Supplies and equipment

Patients. It is not surprising that patients are a source of stress for nurses (64 percent). The following wide range of comments made by nurses about patients give some indication of stress that nurses are under when dealing with them.

- Super demanding patients.
- When a patient is going from bad to worse.
- Unstable patients not responding to treatment.
- Attempting to help patients when they have no desire to gain health.
- Lack of respect and compassion from patients.
- Too many patients to care for.

Understaffing. I have arbitrarily used understaffing to identify this classification of nursing stressors. It has also been described as: work pressure, work overload, unexpected urgent situations, not having enough time and resources to do the job, and having dual lines of authority to both medical and administrative staff. This classification is a significant source of stress for nurses, and about half of the nurses identified it as such. Some of the stressors that my nurse respondents cited in this classification follow.

- Shorthanded and always need more help.
- Too large a patient-nurse ratio in the hospital.
- People lined up at the door with multiple problems.
- Unstable work environment due to constant change in staff.
- Concern of losing staff members due to rapid changes taking place in nursing.

Administration. Forty-four percent identified certain aspects of administration as stressful. Some typical administration-induced stressors included the following responses.

- Displaced attitudes such as paper work over patient care.
- Too little support from hospital administration.
- Administration's attitude toward nursing department.
- Having little power in terms of administration.
- Mismanagement of administration.

Co-workers. Thirty percent of the nurses indicated that they were stressed in some way by their colleagues and co-workers. Following are some example of how nurses were stressed by these individuals.

- Uncooperative colleagues who are late and do not assume responsibilities.
- Ancillary help inconsistent and not dependable.
- Incompetence of peer and other employees.
- High demands placed on me by coworkers.

Time. In most studies on job stress well over one-fourth of the respondents cite various factors related to time as serious causes of stress. My study of nurses was no exception with 30 percent citing stressors in this classification. Some responses follow.

- Pressure to deliver more than I am able.
- Two or three things that need to be done at once.
- Getting behind in nursing care.
- Long hours.
- Being rushed; too many things to do in a certain time period.

Physicians. Almost one-fourth of the nurses indicated that physicians were a cause of stress. Following are some comments that were made in this regard.

- The doctor's anxiety level.
- Chauvinistic doctors who think they are God.
- Fear of permitting physicians to make poor choices in care.

- Lack of recognition from physicians.
- Irrational and unreasonable doctors.

Compensation. Although low salary is a chief cause of nurses leaving the profession, only 12 percent of my nurse respondents found this to be stressful. Most of these were younger nurses who were in the profession for a relatively short period of time.

Supplies and Equipment. Ten percent of the nurses were stressed because of the problem of supplies and equipment. Some of them commented as follows.

- Getting proper supplies and equipment.
- Malfunctioning supplies and equipment.
- Fighting with auxiliary department like dietary and pharmacy for things you need.

Teachers

The profession of teaching can be characterized by its uniqueness, and there are numerous factors that make this so. Teachers themselves in years past have been considered a unique breed. Although teachers may be thought of as *human beings* in modern times, at one time they were considered to be somewhat unlike their fellow man, a "third sex" so to speak. This stereotype has changed appreciably for the better, but nonetheless still persists in certain cases. Although some have designated teaching as the "greatest calling," others subscribe to George Bernard Shaw's "He who can, does, and he who cannot teaches."

Teachers typically make hundreds of decisions daily. They dispense acceptance, rejection, praise, and reproof on a wholesale basis. It is doubtful that many occupations can lay claim to such a "distinction." It is sobering to think that any one of these many decisions might have either a short- or long-range positive or negative influence upon a given student.

There are few professions as open to such intense public scrutiny. Perhaps one of the reasons for this is the constant flow of information from students in schools to their parents. In spite of efforts to counteract it, adults perceive the quality as declining.

My own extensive studies of stress among teachers began in 1980 and have been replicated as three-year intervals through 2001. The following discussion includes data from these studies.

I have classified teacher stress factors as (1) general school working conditions, (2) actions of administrators, (3) actions of colleagues, (4) actions of parents, and (5) student behaviors. The reader should understand that such classification is difficult and that some degree of overlapping occurs. There are instances when one certain stress-inducing factor could be placed under more than one classification. In such cases I have arbitrarily placed the item where I considered it to be best suited.

General School Working Conditions That Induce Stress. The whole area of school working conditions that induce stress has been subclassified into conditions concerned with (1) facilities, equipment, and supplies, (2) time factors, and (3) general organization factors.

Twenty-three percent of the teachers identified stress-inducing factors concerned with *facilities, equipment, and supplies.* Although teachers did not mention it as a stress-inducing factor, they tend to spend inordinate amounts of their own money for supplies. Some teachers said they did this for the purpose of alleviating stress brought about by insufficient supplies.

Sixty-five percent considered deficiencies in school equipment as stress inducing. Twenty percent identified certain school conditions, such as lack of repairs, poor lighting, poor room temperature, and unkempt facilities, as a cause of stress. Of this number 53 percent said they were put under stress because of insufficient *time* for planning. As might be expected, this condition was much more prevalent at the elementary school level where in some instances teachers are with the students all day long with little or no time at all for any kind of planning. This is, of course, due to the differences in organizational structure of the elementary school as compared to the secondary school.

Twenty-nine percent of the teachers who identified the time factor as stress inducing simply said that there was just not enough time in the day to do the job expected of them. Class interruptions for various reasons were considered by 18 percent of the respondents to be an unnecessary infringement on the time of teachers. Those in this category also complained that it took a great deal of time to get lessons back on an even keel because of such interruptions.

General Organization Factors. Responses of 49 percent of the teachers were directed to stress-inducing factors in this general classification. Forty percent of this total considered *record keeping* practices to be an important cause of stress. Included among record keeping chores were grading papers, clerical activities, too many forms, and too much red tape, unnecessary paper work and other assorted tasks.

Eighteen percent felt that *unreasonable deadlines* were a cause of stress. Fifteen percent saw abnormal *class size* as stressful, and most of these felt this involved additional stress concerned with attempting to meet individual needs of students. An equal 15 percent considered *excess meetings* as inducing stress, mainly because such meetings were poorly organized and rarely served a constructive purpose. Eight percent named as stressful such concerns as extracurricular responsibilities, paraprofessional duties, and other non-teaching duties, and insufficient inservice training.

Actions of Administrators That Induce Stress. For the most part, stress-inducing factors concerning actions of administrators were those involving the school principal. This, of course, is to be expected because it is this administrative officer with whom teachers are most likely to come in direct contact. Responses of teachers could be readily subclassified into the three broad areas of (1) administrative practices, (2) administrator incompetence, and (3) personality conflicts.

About 40 percent of the teachers felt that *administrative practices* were a serious cause of stress. Eighteen percent believed that preparation of lesson plans for the principal was busy work and did not serve the purpose for which they were allegedly intended. Twelve percent saw faculty evaluation procedures used by the principal as evaluation by inspection, unfair evaluation, lack of recognition for good teachers, failure on the part of the principal to weed out poor teachers, and in general, evaluation practices that were seriously lacking in validity.

Ten percent considered autocratic practices of the principal as stress inducing and generally expressed this in terms of "the principal whose ideas are the only ones." In this particular regard there appears to be little solid evidence to support one type of school administrative tactic over another. However, as mentioned previously, some studies in industry have shown that authoritarian approaches produced more stressful situations for employees than did human-relations strategies of leadership.

About 29 percent identified stressful conditions in the classification of *administrator incompetence*. The most noteworthy concerns of teachers were expressed in the following ways.

The principal who:

- calls himself a resources person but is not resourceful.
- knows nothing about the reading process.
- controls rather than helps.
- is of little help with problem children.
- does not understand the classroom situation.
- has not been in the classroom for ten years.
- lacks an understanding of the demands of the job.
- in general is an incompetent, uncooperative, poor administrator.
- avoids major problems so that he can attend to minor one.

About 31 percent of the teachers considered certain *personality conflicts* with the administrator as stress inducing. Chief among these was an inability to communicate with the principal. Following were some of the complaints.

- The principal has a bad feeling toward me.
- There is an incompatible relationship because of petty demands.
- The principal interferes too much.
- The principal is unfair in dealings with teachers.
- The principal is out to get the teachers.

Actions of Colleagues That Induce Stress. Teachers identified far fewer actions of colleagues that induce stress than they did in other classifications. This is to be expected because at least some degree of *esprit de corps* should prevail among those working toward a common cause. Nonetheless, there were a variety of stress-inducing factors in this classification. Many teachers felt that the teachers' lounge was a place to be avoided because it was used by colleagues to complain about the administration and school conditions in general. Some were stressed by the *free loader* condition that protected less than dedicated colleagues who are not carrying their share of the responsibility. The following were other factors that induced stress.

- Lack of responsibility of some teachers for discipline problems, thus placing this burden on others.
- Weak teachers being assigned few discipline problems so that this responsibility was shifted to more competent teachers.
- Peers unwilling to work with others.
- Indifference of some teachers toward students.

Actions of Parents That Induce Stress. Actions of parents that induce stress in teachers can be classified into the three areas of (1) lack of concern of parents for their children, (2) parental interference, and (3) lack of parental support for teachers.

In 45 percent of the cases *lack of parental concern for children* was stressful for teachers. They cited such things as parents not caring when a student does poorly, parents not being willing to help their children with school work, a lack of home discipline, and the difficult time they had in getting parents to conferences.

Thirty-two percent indicated that *parental interference* is a serious stressor. Such interference was often a result of parents having expectations that were too. high for their children. This, in turn, results in parental pressure on children, particularly for grades, possibly one of the most serious conditions in our schools today. Incidentally, in this general connection, it is interesting to note that attitudes acquired during childhood and youth can affect the way an individual reacts to stress as an adult. This may be significant in the case of persons whose families have emphasized performance and achievement to the exclusion of all other characteristics.

It has been suggested that the pressure exerted by parents for grades could be a contributing cause in the suicide rate among students. Moreover, it could be that parents are literally "driving their children to drink" because of the increase in alcohol consumption by the school age population, possibly due to the "grade pressure" syndrome.

The third classification of parental actions causing stress for teachers was that of *lack of parental support,* and 23 percent identified stress-inducing factors here. They were stressed by such factors as not being backed by parents and a generally poor attitude of parents toward teachers.

Student Behaviors That Induce Stress. Of all of the stress-inducing factors with which teacher must cope, those that involve student behaviors appear to be the most serious. These behaviors can be classified into the areas of student control and discipline and students with negative attitudes.

It is no small wonder that 65 percent of the teachers who identified factors in this general area say student control and discipline is a serious stress-inducing factor. This is not surprising because discipline has headed the list of major problems facing our nation's schools over several years of Gallup Education Polls.

Among the many stress-inducing factors identified by teachers under this classification are the following range of representative, examples.

Students who argue over test answers.
Restlessness of students.
Cheating by students.
Student insolence.
Student disobedience.

Lawyers

Traditionally, as a group, lawyers have had a severe image problem with the general public. Derogatory jokes about lawyers have abounded to the extent that complete books have been devoted to this subject. Individually, however, most people seem to place a great deal of faith in their own personal lawyer. Although there is not a great deal of data about stress among lawyers, they are, nonetheless, subject to certain stressors. It is interesting to note that a study[5] by the Washington State Bar Association found decreased satisfaction among lawyers with their job. The survey found that 55 percent of all lawyers in private practice reported not having enough time for themselves and 45 percent said they did not have enough time for their families. This has also been borne out in casual interviews with several lawyers who identified the time element as their greatest stressor. This, in turn, is closely related to heavy workload with insufficient time to accomplish all tasks. The second greatest stressor for lawyers is that of client relationships. They cited such things as unreasonable demands by clients, unrealistic expectations, and lack of confidence of clients. Various other miscellaneous stressors included the following responses.

- Risk of losing cases.
- Arbitrary behavior of judges.
- Judges unfamiliar with the law.
- Lack of respect from the bench.
- Lack of courtesy of opponents.

SUGGESTED ACTIVITIES

1. Survey some fellow students who have part-time jobs to find out how they are stressed on the job. Present your findings to the class.
2. Visit several local business establishments and ask the proprietor about the factors that are most stressful to them. Report your findings to the class.
3. Invite a nurse from the college health service to speak to the class about stress among nurses.
4. Conduct a round table discussion on the subject of stress in the teaching profession.

Chapter 12

REDUCING STRESS THROUGH RELAXATION

RELAX!!! I How many times have your heard this expression? Although it has frequent usage as a means of telling a person to "take it easy," or "cool it," more often than not those using the expression are not aware of its real meaning. Most of us need some form of relaxation in order to relieve the tensions encountered in daily living. The purpose of this chapter is to explore various facets of relaxation, along with those kinds of conditions that tend to produce a relaxed state. There are many procedures that can help improve a person's ability to relax, and thus reduce stress. It should be borne in mind that what may be satisfactory for one person may not necessarily be so for another.

1. What is the difference between relaxation and recreation?
2. Why does one need to experience tension in order to learn to relax?
3. What is the theory of Progressive Relaxation?
4. What is meant by mental practice and imagery in relaxation?
5. What is meant by the "game format" for practicing relaxation?
6. What is meant by creative relaxation?
7. What is the purpose of the "relaxation response?"
8. What is meant by the "Quieting Reflex?"

THE MEANING OF RELAXATION AND RELATED TERMS

In general, there are two types of relaxation - passive relaxation and deep muscle relaxation. Passive relaxation involves such activities as reading and listening to music. In deep muscle relaxation the reality of muscle fibers is that they have a response repertoire of one. All they can do is contract and this is the response they make to the electrochemical stimulation of impulses carried via the motor nerves. Relaxation is the removal of this stimulation.

The term *relaxation response* was introduced by Herbert Benson[1] of Harvard University and it involves a number of bodily changes that occur in the organism when one experiences deep muscle relaxation. There is a response against "overstress" which brings on these bodily changes and brings the body back into what is a healthier balance. Thus, the purpose of any kind of relaxation should be to induce a relaxation response.

It should be mentioned here that the following two chapters will take into account the stress reduction techniques of *meditation* and *biofeedback,* both of which can indeed be considered as relaxation techniques. Therefore, it seems important at this point that attention be give to the theory underlying these techniques, all of which are concerned with mind-body interactions, and all of which are designed to induce the relaxation response. In *progressive relaxation,* it is theorized that if the muscles of the body are relaxed, the mind in turn will be quieted. The theory involved in *meditation* is that if the mind is quieted, then other systems of the body will tend to become more readily stabilized. In the practice of *biofeedback,* the theoretical basis tends to involve some sort of integration of progressive relaxation and meditation. It is believed that the brain has the potential for voluntary control over all the systems it monitors, and is affected by all of these systems. Thus, it is the intimacy of interaction between mind and body that has provided the mechanism through which one can learn voluntary control over biological activity.

From the point of view of the physiologist, relaxation is sometimes considered as "zero activity," or as nearly zero as one can manage in the neuromuscular system. That is, it is a neuromuscular accomplishment that results in reduction, or possible complete absence of muscle tone in a part of, or in the entire body. A primary value of relaxation lies in the lowering of brain and spinal cord activity, resulting from a reduction of nerve impulses arising in muscle spindles and other sense endings in muscles, tendons, and joint structures.

The terms *relaxation, refreshment* and *recreation* are often confused in their meaning. While all of these factors are important to the well-being of the human organism, they should not be used interchangeably to mean the same thing. *Refreshment* is the result of an improved blood supply to the brain for "refreshment" from central fatigue and the muscles for the disposition of their waste products. This explains in part why mild muscular activity is good for overcoming the fatigue of sitting quietly (seventh inning stretch) and for hastening recovery after strenuous exercise (an athlete continuing running for a short distance slowly after a race).

Recreation may be described as the experience from which a person emerges with the feeling of being "re-created." No single activity is sure to bring this experience to all members of a group, nor is there assurance that an activity will provide recreation again for a given person because it did so the last time. These are more the marks of a psychological experience, an important essential requirement for a recreational activity is that it completely engrosses the individual; that is, it must engage his or her entire undivided attention. It is really escape from the disintegrating effects of distraction to the healing effect of totally inte-grated activity. Experiences that produce this effect may range from a hard game of tennis to the reading of a comic strip.

Some individuals consider recreation and relaxation to be one and the same thing, which is not the case. Recreation can be considered a type of mental diversion that can be helpful in relieving tension. While mental and muscular tensions are interrelated, it is in the muscle that the tension state is manifested.

For many years, recommendations have been made with regard to procedures individuals might apply in an effort to relax. Examples of some of these procedures are submitted in the ensuing discussions. In consideration of any technique designed to accomplish relaxation, one very important factor needs to be taken into account and that is that learning to relax is a skill. It is a skill based on the kinesthetic awareness of feelings of *tonus* (the normal degree of con-traction present in most muscles, which keeps them always ready to function when needed).

Unfortunately, it is a skill that very few of us practice - probably because we have little awareness of how to go about it.

One of the first steps in learning to relax is to experience tension. That is, one should be sensitive to tensions that exist in his or her body. This can be accomplished by voluntarily contracting a given muscle group, first very strongly and then less and less. Emphasis should be placed on detecting the signal of tension as the first step in "letting go" - (relaxing).

You might wish to try the traditional experiment used to demonstrate this phenomenon. Raise one arm so that the palm of the hand is facing outward away from your face. Now, bend the wrist backward and try to point the fingers back toward your face and down toward the forearm. You should feel some *strain* at the wrist joint. You should also feel something else in the muscle and this is tension, which is due to the muscle contracting the hand backward. Now, flop the hand forward with the fingers pointing downward and you will have accomplished a *tension-relaxation* cycle.

As in the case of any muscular skill, learning how to relax takes time and one should not expect to achieve complete satisfaction immediately. After one has identified a relaxation technique that he or she feels comfortable with, increased practice should eventually achieve satisfactory results.

PROGRESSIVE RELAXATION

The technique of progressive relaxation was developed by Edmund Jacobson many years ago.[2] It is still the technique most often referred to in the literature and probably the one that has had the most widespread application. In this technique, the person concentrates on progressively relaxing one muscle group after another. The technique is based on the procedure of comparing differences between tension and relaxation. As previously mentioned, one senses the feeling of tension in order to get the feeling of relaxation.

Learning to relax is a skill that you can develop in applying the principles of progressive relaxation. One of the first steps is to be able to identify the various, muscle groups and how to tense them so that tension and relaxation can be experienced. However, before making suggestions on how to tense and relax the various muscle groups there are certain preliminary measures that need to be taken into account.

1. You must understand that this procedure takes time and like anything else, the more you practice the more proficient you should become with the skills.
2. Progressive relaxation is not the kind of thing to be done spontaneously, and you should be prepared to spend from 20 to 30 minutes at a time in tensing-relaxing activities.
3. The particular time of day is important and this is pretty much an individual matter. Some recommendations suggest that progressive relaxation be practiced daily; sometime during the day and again in the evening before retiring. For many people this would be difficult unless one time period was set aside before going to school or to the job in the morning. This might be a good possibility and might help a person to start the day relaxed.

4. It is important to find a suitable place to practice the tensing-relaxing activities. Again this is an individual matter with some preferring a bed or couch and others a comfortable chair.

5. Consideration should be given to the amount of time a given muscle is tensed. You should be sure that you are able to feel the difference between tension and relaxation. This means that tension should be maintained from about four to not more than eight seconds.

6. Breathing is an important part in tensing and relaxing muscles. To begin with, it is suggested that three or more deep breaths be taken and held for about five seconds. This will tend to make for better rhythm in breathing. Controlled breathing makes it easier to relax and is most effective when it is done deeply and slowly. It is ordinarily recommended that one should inhale deeply when the muscles are tensed and exhale slowly when "letting go."

How to Tense and Relax Various Muscles

Muscle groups may be identified in different ways. The classification given here consists of four different groups: (1) muscles of the head, face, tongue, and neck, (2) muscles of the trunk, (3) muscles of the upper extremities, and (4) muscles of the lower extremities.

Muscles of the Head, Face, Tongue, and Neck

There are two chief muscles of the head, the one covering the back of the head and the one covering the front of the skull. There are about 30 muscles of the face including muscles of the orbit and eyelids, mastication, lips, tongue, and neck. Incidentally, it has been estimated that it takes 26 facial muscles to frown and a proportionately much smaller number to smile.

Muscles of this group may be tensed and relaxed as follows (relaxation is accomplished by "letting go" after tensing):

1. Raise your right eyebrows by opening the eyes as wide as possible. You might wish to look into a mirror to see of you have formed wrinkles on the forehead.
2. Tense the muscles on either side of your nose like you were going to sneeze.
3. Dilate or flare out your nostrils.
4. Force an extended smile from "ear to ear" at the same time clenching your teeth.
5. Pull one corner of your mouth up and then the other up as in a "villainous sneer."
6. Draw your chin up as close to your chest as possible.
7. Do the opposite of the above trying to draw your head back as close to your back as possible.

Muscles of the Trunk

Included in this group are the muscles of the back, chest, abdomen, and pelvis. Here are some ways you can tense some of these muscles.

1. Bring your chest forward and at the same time put your shoulders back with emphasis on bringing your shoulder blades as close together as possible.
2. Try to round your shoulders and bring your shoulder blades far apart. This is pretty much the opposite of the above.
3. Give your shoulders a shrug trying to bring them up to your ears at the same time as you try to bring your neck downward.
4. Breathe deeply and hold it momentarily and then blow out the air from your lungs rapidly.
5. Draw in your stomach so that your chest is out beyond your stomach. Exert your stomach muscles by forcing out to make it look like you are fatter in that area than you are.

Muscles of the Upper Extremities

This group includes muscles of the hands, forearms, upper arms, and shoulders. A number of muscles situated in the trunk may be grouped with the muscles of the upper extremities, their function being to attach the upper limbs to the trunk and move the shoulders and arms. In view of this there is some overlapping in muscle groups *two* and *three*. Following are some ways to tense some of these muscles.

1. Clench the fist and then open the hand, extending the fingers as far as possible.
2. Raise one arm shoulder high and parallel to the floor. Bend at the elbow and bring the hand in toward the shoulder, Try to touch your shoulders while attempting to move the shoulder away from the hand. Flex your opposite biceps in the same manner.
3. Stretch one arm out to the side of the body and try to point the fingers backward toward the body. Do the same with the other arm.
4. Hold the arm out the same way as above but this time have the palm facing up and point the fingers inward toward the body. Do the same with the other arm.
5. Stretch one arm out to the side, clench the fist and roll the wrist around slowly. Do the same with the other arm.

Muscles of the Lower Extremities

This groups includes muscles of the hips, thighs, legs, feet, and buttocks. Following are ways to tense some of these muscles.

1. Hold one leg out straight and point your toes as far forward as you can. Do the same with the other leg.
2. Do the same as above but point your toes as far backward as you can.
3. Turn each foot outward as far as you can and release. Do just the opposite by turning the foot inward as far as you can.
4. Try to draw the thigh muscles up so that you can see the form of the muscles.

5. Make your buttocks tense by pushing down if you are sitting in a chair. If you are lying down try to draw the muscles of the buttocks in close by attempting to force the cheeks together.

The above suggestions include several possibilities for tensing various muscles of the body. As you practice some of these, you will also discover other ways to tense and then let go. A word of caution might be that, in the early stages, you should be alert to the possibility of cramping certain muscles. This can happen particularly with those muscles that are not frequently used. This means that at the beginning you should proceed carefully. It might be a good idea to keep a record or diary of your sessions so that you can refer back to these experiences if this might be necessary. This will also help you get into each new session by reviewing your experiences in previous sessions.

CREATIVE RELAXATION

The approach to creative relaxation presented here was developed for the purpose of reducing stress in young children. However, it has gone far beyond this original purpose, since there has been successful application of it with various adult groups.

The creative relaxation approach suggested here combines a form of imagery and tensing and releasing. One person or a group creates a movement(s) designed to tense and relax individual muscles, muscle groups, or the entire body.

Creative relaxation simply means that there are contrasting creative movements that give the effect of tensing and letting go. An illustration is provided here for a better understanding of the concept.

This example shows the contrast (tensing and letting go) of the muscles in an upper extremity (arm). The leader could start by raising a question such as the following: "What would you say is the main difference between a ball bat and a jump rope?"

This question is then discussed and will no doubt lead to the major difference being that a ball bat is hard and stiff and that a jump rope is soft and limp. The leader might then proceed as follows: "Let's see if we can all make one of our arms be like a ball bat." (this movement is created) "Now, quickly, can you make your arm like a jump rope?" (the movement is created by releasing the tensed arm).

The experience can be evaluated by using these questions: "How did your arm feel when you made it like a bat? How did your arm feel when you made it like a jump rope?"

The creative person can produce a discussion that will increase an understanding of the relaxation phenomenon. This is but one example and one is limited only by his or her own imagination in developing others.

THE GAME FORMAT FOR PRACTICING RELAXATION

A game format can be used as a means of providing satisfactory relaxation. One advantage of this is that it can become more of a fun-oriented situation in case of boredom when using structured procedures. An example of the successful use of the game format is in the tensing and releasing phase with the game *Simon Says*. Each muscle group to be tensed and then relaxed is prefaced by "Simon says"; that is, "Simon says to close your eyes...Simon says to make your eyebrows touch your hair...Simon says to let go and feel your eyes relax." A five-second tensing of any muscle is followed by a 15-second relaxing of the muscle. The sequence for relaxing the muscles prefaced by "Simon says" is as follows:

1. Head
    a. Try to make your eyebrows touch your hair,
    b. Squeeze your eyes shut,
    c. Wrinkle your nose.
    d. Press your lips together.
    e. Press your tongue against the roof of your mouth.

2. Shoulders and Back
    a. Lift your shoulders and try to touch your ears,
    b. Bring your shoulders as far back as they will go.

3. Hands and Arms
    a. Make your fist as tight as you can
    b. Show me your arm muscles.

4. Stomach
    a. Make your stomach as hard as you can; pull it way in.

5. Upper Legs
    a. Lift your legs and feet off the floor,
    b. Press your knees together.

6. Lower Legs and Feet
    a. Press your ankles together.
    b. Press your feet together against the floor.

(Note: The game *Simon Says* is played as follows. One or more players face the person who plays Simon. Every time Simon says to do something, the players do it. However, if a command is given without the prefix "Simon says," the players remain motionless. For example, when the leader issues the command, "Simon says press your ankles together," everyone does this; but if the person playing Simon says, "Press your knees together," the players do not execute the command. The original purpose of this format was for use with children; however experience has shown that it can be equally successful with adults.)

MENTAL PRACTICE AND IMAGERY IN RELAXATION

Mental practice is a symbolized rehearsal of a physical activity in the absence of any gross muscular movement. This means that a person imagines in his or her own mind the way to perform a given activity. *Imagery* is concerned with the development of a mental image that may aid one in the performance of an activity. In mental practice, the person thinks through what he or she is going to do, and with imagery may suggest or another may suggest a condition and he or she then tries to effect a mental image of the condition.

The use of mental practice in performing motor skills is not new. In fact, research in this general area has been going on for well over half a century. This research has revealed that imagining a movement will likely produce recordable electric action potentials emanating from the muscle groups that would be called up if the movement were to be actually carried out. In addition, most mental activity is accompanied by general rises in muscular tension.

One procedure in the use of mental practice for relaxation is that of making suggestions to one's self. For the most part, in early childhood, we first learn to act on the basis of verbal instructions from others. Later we begin to guide and direct our own behavior on the basis of our own language activities - we literally talk to ourselves, giving ourselves instructions. This point of view has long been supported by research that postulates that speech as a form of communication between children and adults later becomes a means of organizing the child's own behavior. That is, the function that was previously divided between two people - child and adult - becomes an internal function of human behavior. Following is an example of this approach.

I am going to relax completely. First, I will relax my forehead and scalp. I will let all of the muscles of my forehead and scalp relax and become completely at rest. All of the wrinkles will come out of my forehead and that part of my body will relax completely. Now, I will relax the muscles of my face, (continue the procedure from head to toe) A way imagery can be used to promote a relaxed state is by making *comparative* statements such as "float like a feather," or "melt like ice." Creative persons (like yourself) will be able to think of many such comparative statements to assist in producing a relaxed state.

A good bit of research supports the use of imagery as an aspect of relaxation. For example, it has been found useful in self-instructional training with hyperactive children; also, it has been successful when used in the development of self-control programs in training disruptive children to have better control. (This will be discussed later in more detail).

THE QUIETING REFLEX

The Quieting Reflex Concept (QR) was discovered by the late Charles F. Stroebel when he was Director of Research, Institute of Living and Professor of Psychiatry, University of Connecticut Medical School, Hartford, Connecticut. This was an outgrowth of his work using biofeedback to treat stress disorders in a clinic population ranging from age seven to seventy.

Initially, the six-second QR was designed to help adults not "just relax," but to automatically adjust their body tensions up and down to meet the actual stress at hand. After six months' practice, QR remarkably increased their ability to avoid and eliminate stress illnesses.

QR is designed to teach people an important life skill, namely, the Quieting Reflex. It can help them live more productive, less stressful lives, while at the same time, enhancing their healthiness and their potentials by reducing the negative effects of inappropriately perceived stress. Thus, the purpose of the QR program is to help both children and adults approach the unavoidable demands of life in a way in which they can feel better about themselves and others and to live appropriately stressful lives.

The fight or flight response, which was discussed previously, is similar to a gear in a car. The passing gear is a wonderful emergency safety mechanism. When you get into a tight spot, you can push the accelerator to the floor and zoom out of the problem. At the same time, if you drive your car in passing gear all the time, it will wear out. Obviously, this is not a very effective way to use an automobile. The same is true for our bodies. We should not stay in passing gear unnecessarily.

The problem with many people is that they learn how to overuse the passing gear; and eventually they do not know how to get out of passing gear. Simply telling a person "not to worry" or "just take it easy" is not satisfactory because most people do not understand what it means to "just relax," nor do they know how to "not worry."

For the most part, stressful concerns require mental rather than physical caveman type of response, yet people use their fight or flight reaction in the absence of immediate physical threat. Inappropriate use of the fight or flight emergency response lessens the mental alertness people need to solve whatever problem is causing stress. This overuse of the fight or flight response is clearly inappropriate or maladaptive.

Many individuals inadvertently learn to activate the emergency response at the slightest sign and, therefore, repeatedly use this mechanism inappropriately. This panic reaction may then prevent them from performing appropriately, and from responding to their true potentials. In other words, the stress reaction acts as a block to learning and other life pursuits (actual laboratory body measurements of persons indicate that most of them have a quick panic reaction, lasting from six to ten seconds, and this reduces their ability to perform optimally).

Many people develop or maintain a high level of arousal much more frequently and for a much longer period than they should. Bodies of healthy people should quickly recover normal balance after their initial reaction to stress. This is the body's inherent quieting reaction, or Quieting Reflex. However, many children and adults have unconsciously taught their bodies to override their own natural quieting responses until constant tension, anxiety, and tightness begin to seem normal to them.

What the QR program is all about is a contrary response to the passing gear or emergency reaction. This contrary response is called the Quieting Reflex. It begins in early training phases as a response to things that get on people's nerves, that annoy them, or that get them frustrated or angry. With progressive practice, individuals can acquire a virtually reflexive ability to produce a set of behaviors that are actually contrary to the inappropriate use of the passing gear. The two obviously cannot happen simultaneously, so there has now been produced a new adaptive state where individuals do not have to get their bodies upset when it is not appropriate.

The emergency reaction involves approximately five steps. The first is increased vigilance or paying attention to what is potentially harmful in the environment; that is, to whatever is feared. Frequently, almost simultaneously with this, there is a blush reaction, a wetness of hands, or a tendency towards perspiration. Almost simultaneously comes a perking of attention and a tension of the musculature of the face. The face becomes grim. At about three seconds into this passing gear emergency response, there is a catching or holding of the breath or there is shallow quick breathing, almost panting. The next change is frequently a drop in hand temperature. The hands and often the feet become cold and clammy. And finally, the jaw is clenched much like a dog going into battle. These changes can be easily measured by laboratory instrumentation.

The Quieting Reflex is a reversal of these steps. The first thing that happens in the Quieting Reflex is that the person becomes aware that something is annoying him, making him tense or anxious. He learns how to monitor the body to determine what cues trigger off this emergency response, and then he learns a systematic way to reverse the emergency reaction by eliciting the Quieting Reflex. Thus, instead of being dependent upon tranquilizers or other drugs, young people and adults can use the six-second technique as a way of keeping their bodies calm when they really do not have to stand their ground and fight or run away.

It has been found that QR training helps people regain the capacity they had as younger children to recover quickly from excessive stress. In the course of training, young people learn to recognize when they are over-reacting to stress and learn specific techniques to bring their bodies back to a healthy level of activity. Later in training, they learn to apply these skills consciously in day to day school or job situations. Eventually, through repeated practice, the quieting techniques become the body's automatic and unconscious response to stressful situations. When an emergency response is inappropriate, the body automatically responds with a QR.

The great majority of individuals, as they become proficient in evoking the Quieting Reflex, gain a new sense of freedom. They recognize that many of the problems that have disturbed them in the past are not beyond their voluntary control. Their new sense of mastery with QR leads to enhanced self-concept and an ability to use their full potential in ways that were previously thought to be impossible.

USING RELAXATION WITH CHILDREN

Until relatively recent years, the use of relaxation to reduce stress has been pretty much reserved for adults only. However, in more modern times relaxation procedures have been found to be very effective with children.

Relaxation training has frequently been applied to problems involving cross-situational, overt motor behaviors of children, such as impulsivity, aggressiveness, and overactivity. The clearest applications have been made with hyperactive children, but relaxation training has also been applied to general aggression and learning problems.

The studies using relaxation training with hyperactive children have generally indicated that following training there is a reduction in muscle tension, and ratings of behavior by parents improve when compared to hyperactive controls. On the surface, this would suggest that such training may be an effective treatment for hyperactivity. However, relaxation training has not yet been proven to be superior to other treatment alternatives. Conclusions regarding the findings in this area are limited by methodological and design flaws, including non-homogeneous population sampling, inadequate numbers of subjects, and lack of adequate or appropriate control groups or conditions. Some factor or factors during relaxation produce changes in behavior of hyperactive children. However, the research to date does not appear to clearly indicate what these factors are.

Similar to the rationale for hyperactivity, relaxation training has been used to treat various learning and aggression problems. It is assumed that children who are tense or upset and who lack self-control have difficulty attending to learning tasks, and may be more likely to respond with aggression toward others when frustrated or provoked than non-tense children with better self-control. Children taught to relax are believed to become much more amenable to learning alternative behaviors or new information.

The results of the application of relaxation training with learning problems and aggressive behavior are mixed. Some studies demonstrate positive effects over controls, while others show no difference between trained subjects and controls. In no instance does relaxation training result in behavior that was worse than that of a control group, so the application of relaxation training to these problem areas does not seem to represent a risk to subjects. In these studies, multiple sessions of relaxation training are used, strengthening the contention in the adult literature that repeated training is necessary for acquisition of the relaxation skill and generalization of the skill to the academic environment.

As far as relaxation and avoidance behavior is concerned, the constructs of anxiety and fear can best be seen as physiological, cognitive, or behavioral arousal which functions to have the person avoid engaging in an aversive activity or coming into contact with an aversive stimulus. Relaxation training has long been applied to these problems under the assumption that relaxation serves as a competing response to the undesired arousal. In addition, relaxation may also facilitate the performance of a more adaptive behavior in a stressful situation.

The literature on using relaxation to reduce avoidance behavior is fairly consistent. Motor behavior is clearly reduced following relaxation training, but consistent cognitive and physiological changes are not always found. Studies which include multiple relaxation procedures affect multiple arousal dimensions. Those that are muscle relaxation only demonstrate clear, consistent effects with overt behavioral measures. Those mechanisms that are responsible for these differences are not yet identifiable, due to the lack of multiple, convergent measurement and comparisons of different relaxation training components.

In the area of medical applications relaxation training has been increasingly applied to medical problems that are thought to be the result of or maintained by specific tension or physiological arousal. As such, relaxation is considered a primary treatment used to target a specific kind of medical problem. Similar to the way a medication is used to target a particular physical symptom, relaxation training focuses on a particular response and the subject is taught to use the skill when the antecedent conditions related to the specific problems occur.

In general, application of relaxation training to medical problems of children seems promising. With few exceptions, the results in this area indicate that relaxation training results in symptom improvement for asthma, headaches, seizures, and insomnia, although the clinical significance of these improvements is unclear. Once again, the issue of how different training procedures impact different physiological, cognitive, and behavioral systems is noted. It is quite possible that different training procedures may be needed to impact the different problems presented in a medical setting.

SUGGESTED ACTIVITIES

1. Create an imaginary scene for relaxation and share it with the class.
2. Using the experiment for a "tensing-relaxing cycle" in the chapter as a guide, devise one of your own. Share it with the class.
3. Develop a creative relaxation movement to use with an adult group. Try it out with a classmate and share it with the rest of the class.
4. Using the information in the chapter as a guide (Simon Says), develop a game format for use in practicing relaxation.

Chapter 13

REDUCING STRESS THROUGH MEDITATION

The art of meditation dates back more than 2,000 years. Until relatively recent years, this ancient art has been encumbered with religious as well as cultural connotations. In the 1960s, countercultures began using it as a route to a more natural means of living and relaxing. Today, people from all walks of life can be counted among those who practice and realize the positive effects that meditation can have upon the human mind and body.

It is difficult to determine precisely how many people practice meditation. My own studies show that, in most populations, about four or five percent use meditation as a stress-reducing technique. One exception to this is its use among psychiatrists with about 20 percent of them reporting that they engage in meditation to reduce stress. It should not be surprising that physicians who specialize in "disorders of the mind" would themselves practice this technique at a much higher rate than others. As has already been mentioned the theory of meditation is that if the mind is quieted, then other systems of the body will tend to be stabilized more readily.

1. How should meditation be defined?
2. In general, what is meditation purported to do for a person?
3. Why is concentration important in meditation?
4. How would you compare sleep and meditation?
5. How are some of the bodily functions involved in meditation?
6. How did transcendental meditation (TM) get its name?
7. What is a mantra and how is it used?
8. In general, what does research show about meditation?

It has been asserted by Kenneth Pelletier[1] that meditation should be defined as an experimental exercise involving an individual's actual attention, not belief systems or other cognitive processes, and that it should not be confused with prolonged, self-induced lethargy. The nervous system needs intensity and variety of external stimulation to maintain proper functioning.

Robert Woolfolk and Frank Richardson[2] another authoritative source, suggest that at the very least meditation can give the mind a rest - a brief vacation from stress and worry, one that requires neither a travel agent nor days free from the responsibility of work or family. It is almost as though meditation allows us to temporarily shut down those information-processing mechanisms of the brain that are ultimately responsible for producing stress. In addition, giving us a more balanced outlook and increased energy for dealing with whatever difficulties face us.

Although there are many meditation techniques, *concentration* is an important factor contributing to success in most of them. The mind's natural flow from one idea to another is quieted by the individual's concentration. Lowering mental activity may be an easy task, but almost total elimination of scattered thoughts takes a great deal of time and practice on the part of the meditator.

The question sometimes raised is, Are sleep and meditation the same thing? Sleep has been likened to meditation, as both are hypometabolic states; that is, restful states where the body experiences decreased metabolism. But meditation is not a form of sleep. Although some similar psychological changes have been found in sleep and meditation, they are not the same and one is not a substitute for the other. In this regard, it is interesting to note that various studies have shown that meditation may restore more energy than sleep.

There have been countless positive pronouncements about meditation from some of the most notable scientists of modern times, who spend a good proportion of their time studying about stress. However, it has been in relatively recent years only that the scientific community has uncovered many of the positive effects that the repeated practice of meditation has upon those who are stress ridden. Various scientific studies have shown that meditation can actually decrease the possibilities of an individual contracting stress-related disorders, and that meditators have a much faster recovery rate when exposed to a stressful situation than non-meditators. Specifically, from a physiological point of view, meditation decreases the body's metabolic rate, with the following decreases in bodily function involved: (1) oxygen consumption, (2) breathing rate, (3) heart rate and blood pressure, (4) sympathetic nervous system activity, and (5) blood lac-tate (a chemical produced in the body during stressful encounters) . Also, meditation tends to increase the psychological ability of those who practice it, as well as to reduce anxiety. Research seems to be disclosing that meditation can be a path to better health (later in the chapter some of this scientific inquiry will be examined in more detail).

TYPES OF MEDITATION

Having made a rather thorough examination of the literature on meditation, I have been able to identify more than 20 meditational systems. Interestingly enough, although there are many meditation techniques, research tends to show that one technique is about as good an another for improving the way we handle stress.

I have arbitrarily selected for discussion here, four types of meditation: (1) Christian meditation, (2) meditative running, (3) strategic meditation, and (4) transcendental meditation.

Christian Meditation

If you ask the average person about meditation the response will ordinarily be that it is concerned with "sitting and thinking," or "engaging in silent prayer." And, basically this is essentially what Christian meditation means. One feels that he or she is meditating by reflecting upon certain experiences and evaluating certain activities that have taken place in his or her life.

Meditatative Running

Two prominent researchers, Diane and Robert Hales[3], have reported on a concept that has to do with a combination of meditation and running and what I would describe as meditative running. Although running and meditation seem like completely opposite states - one strenuous and the other serene - both can be considered as paths to altered states of consciousness, and together they can profoundly affect both body and mind. It is interesting that exercisers who meditate as they work out literally change the way their heart and lungs function. They burn less oxygen and use energy more efficiently. It is known that Tibetan monks, using a similar approach and concentration on a mantra, have run distances of 300 miles over mountain trails in less than 30 hours.

Strategic Meditation

Amarjit S. Sethi[4], one of my authors in my series on *Stress in Modern Society,* has developed a concept called strategic meditation. He defines it as a process of balancing "calculative thinking" and "non-calculative thinking." In order to give specificity to this concept he has labeled it strategic meditation so that it may be distinguished from other forms of meditation. The meditational process takes place in different contexts, comprising both the facts and the values of a given environment. The study of interactions between facts and values in shaping calculative and non-calculative thinking becomes a process of strategic meditation. It is strategic because meditation examines problems, identifies their nature, and establishes perspective. It is meditational because a person transforms the problem-solving orientation through a focus on both the problem and its solution, and this begins to suggest elements of how an individual processes information in a relatively "problem-free context" which has been termed non-calculative. Another term for such a level of consciousness is *playfulness*. The emphasis, in a meditational exercise, shifts from complex calculation and sophisticated decision rules to selective perception, leading to a problem-free context.

In order to practice strategic meditation one needs to develop his or her own diagnosis of the problem. Problem-solving is utilized as a process of investigating the source of stress, and is integrated as a part of the meditational process. This phase involves perception of the environment, analysis of the problem, and design of alternative solutions. The problem-solving process is integrated with a meditational process.

Transcendental Meditation

Of the various types of meditation, transcendental meditation (TM) is by far the best known. It was introduced in the United States many years ago by Mararishi Yogi. It is believed that he used the term transcendental (a literal meaning of which is "going beyond") to indicate that it projects one beyond the level of a wakeful experience to a state of profound rest along with heightened alertness.[5]

TM involves the repitition of a *mantra* (a word or specific sound) for 15 to 20 minutes daily with the meditator in a relaxed position with eyes closed. Almost without exception those who have practiced TM attest to its positive effects. While other forms of meditation may have specific procedures, it is safe to say that most derive in some way from basic TM. The discussion that follows is based on this type of meditation.

A PROCEDURE FOR MEDITATING

Presented here is a description of a procedure for meditating that I have found has met with personal success. In addition, many of my students have reported success with its use. However, it should be mentioned that it is pretty much an individual matter, and what may be successful for one person may not necessarily be successful for another.

To begin with, there are certain basic considerations that should be taken into account. The following descriptive list of these considerations is general in nature, and the reader can make his or her specific application as best fits individual needs and interests.

Locate a Quiet Place and Assume a Comfortable Position. The importance of a quiet environment should be obvious since concentration is facilitated in a tranquil surrounding. The question of the position one may assume for meditation is an individual matter. However, when it is suggested that one assume a comfortable position, this might be amended by, "but not too comfortable." The reason for this is that if one is too comfortable there is the possibility of falling asleep, and this of course would defeat the purpose of meditation. This is a reason why one should consider not taking a lying position while meditating.

A position might be taken where there is some latitude for "swaying." This can provide for a comfortable posture and, at the same time, guard against the individual "falling into dreamland." The main consideration is that the person be in a comfortable enough position to remain this way for 15 minutes or so. One such position, would be where you sit on the floor with legs crossed and the back straight and resting on the legs and buttocks. Your head should be erect and the hands resting in the lap. If you prefer to sit in a chair rather than on the floor, select a chair with a straight back. You need to be the judge of comfort, and, thus, you should select a position where you feel you are able to concentrate and remain in this position for a period of time.

Focus Your Concentration. As mentioned before, concentration is the essential key to successful meditation. If you focus on one specific thing, such as an object or a sound or a personal feeling, it is less likely that your thoughts will be distracted. You might want to consider focusing on such things as a fantasy trip, re-experiencing a trip already taken, a place that has not been visited, or a certain sound or chant.

Use a Nonsense Word or Phrase. Some techniques of meditation, such as the popular transcendental meditation, involve the chanting of a particular word (mantra) as one meditates. While the mantra has important meaning for the meditator, I refer to it as a nonsense word because it should be devoid of any connotation that would send one thinking in many directions. This, of course, would hinder concentration, so a nonsense word would perhaps be most effective. Incidentally, I have found in my own personal experience with meditation, the practice of chanting such a word is very effective.

Be Aware of Natural Breathing Rhythm. The importance of natural breathing rhythm should not be underestimated. In fact, some clinical psychologists recommend this as a means of concentrating. One can count the number of times he or she inhales, and this in itself is a relaxing mental activity.

The Time for Meditation. Since meditation is an activity to quiet the mind it is strongly recommended that the practice not be undertaken immediately at the end of the day. At this time, the mind may be in a very active state of reviewing the day's activities. My own personal experience suggests a 15 to 20 minute period in the morning and another such period in the evening preferably before dinner, or possibly two hours after dinner.

With the above basic considerations in mind, you should be ready to experiment. To begin with, assume a comfortable position in a quiet place with as passive an attitude as possible. Try to dismiss all wandering thoughts from your mind and concentrate on a relaxed body while keeping the eyes closed. When feeling fairly relaxed, the repetition of the nonsense word or phrase can begin. This can be repeated orally or silently. Personally, I have had good success repeating it silently; that is, through the mind. Repeat your chosen word or phrase in this manner over and over, keeping the mind clear of any passing thoughts. At first, this may be very difficult, but with practice it becomes easier.

After a period of about 15 or 20 minutes have passed, (or less if you wish), discontinue repetition of the word or phrase. Become aware of your relaxed body once again. Give yourself a few moments before moving as your body will need to readjust. For successful prolonged results one might consider continuing the practice two times daily for 15 to 20 minute sessions.

If you have difficulty trying to meditate on your own, it is possible to seek the services of an experienced meditator for assistance and supervision. The recent more widespread popularity of meditation has been accompanied by the establishment of meditation centers for instruction in some communities.

USING MEDITATION WITH CHILDREN

There is available evidence to support the idea that the practice of meditation can be beneficial for children. All family members can learn meditation techniques, and children as young as 10 years of age can learn, although they meditate for less than 15 minutes. Often, younger children become interested in learning to meditate after others in the family have begun practicing the technique. (Incidentally, I want to mention a television program I once observed, called: *Special Treat; He Makes Me Feel Like Dancing,* At the end of the program some of the children were asked to give their reaction to dancing. One boy, perhaps nine or ten years of age said, "It's a bit like meditation? you let your spirit run free.")

In some cases, courses in the technique of transcendental meditation have been prepared for elementary school children and implemented by some teachers. Among other things, this type of program improves creativity, and perhaps child psychologists should investigate the effect of the children's technique of TM on early development and creativity.

There has been a great deal of research on meditation for children that has appeared in the literature in recent years, and the following is a summary of some of the findings.

1.   Children can be helped to obtain greater creativity through meditation.

2. Meditation can be used successfully with gifted, retarded, and average children.
3. Attentiveness of children can be improved through meditation.
4. Eye-hand coordination can be improved by meditation.
5. Meditation can be effective in alleviating learning disorders and enhancing the learning process.

Scientific Evidence Supporting the Benefits of Meditation

Since many people are not aware of the value of meditation and since many others suspect is as a rather "spooky" procedure, it seems fitting to impress upon the reader that it is a very important area of scientific research.

The phenomenon of meditation is not an easy one to study objectively. One of the primary reasons for this is that it is extremely difficult to control all of the variables inherent in a given situation. For example, the difference in length of meditation sessions as well as the degree of meditating experience of the subjects sometimes militates against obtaining researchable experimental and control groups. These limitations should be kept in mind when reading the following summary of research findings.

1. Meditation can slow metabolism and thus promote deep rest.
2. In some cases meditation can increase resistance to disease.
3. Meditation has been shown to improve reaction time; thus it could be speculated that it can help improve coordination of mind and body.
4. There may be a correlation between meditation and immunity.
5. In some instances the practice of meditation may improve memory.

Although most studies have shown positive effects of meditation, it is repeated that certain precautions need to be taken into account in interpreting the results, and the reader is reminded again of the limitations that were mentioned at the outset of this discussion.

In closing this chapter, it is reiterated that whether or not one chooses meditation as a technique for stress reduction is an individual matter. It might be recalled that I reported previously that a relatively small number of those in my surveys used meditation as a means of coping with stress; however, all of these respondents reported great success with the technique and recommended it for others.

Suggested Activities

1. Go to the library and look up some of the works of the German philosopher, Immanuel Kant (1724-1804). Report to the class on how his philosophy relates to modern-day meditation.
2. Hold a round table discussion on the subject of meditation and sleep.
3. Experiment with the procedure for meditating presented in the chapter and compare the results with other class members.

Chapter 14

REDUCING STRESS THROUGH BIOFEEDBACK

In the discussion of biofeedback, it should be made clear that we are dealing with a complex and complicated subject. This phenomenon will be discussed in terms of what it is supposed to be and what it is supposed to do. In should be borne in mind that, at least in the early stages of bio-feedback training (BFT), an important factor is that it should take place under qualified supervision. This means that anyone wishing to pursue an interest in, and eventually participate in BFT, should seek the services of one trained in this area.

1. How can biofeedback be described?
2. How is biofeedback related to knowledge of results?
3. What is the relationship between feedback and learning?
4. How is biofeedback concerned with the systems of perception?
5. What is electromyography?
6. What is the purpose of the electroencephalograph?
7. How is galvanic skin response (GSR) used in biofeedback?

THE MEANING OF BIOFEEDBACK

The term *feedback* has been used in various frames of reference. It may have been used originally in engineering in connection with control systems that involve feedback procedures. These feedback control systems make adjustments to environmental changes, such as the case of a thermostat controlling temperature levels in the home.

Learning theorists use the term feedback interchangeably with the expression *knowledge of results* to describe the process of providing the learner with information as to how accurate his or her reactions were. Or, in other words, feedback is knowledge of various kinds that the performer received about his or her performance. With particular reference to motor skill learning, feedback in the form of knowledge of results is the strongest, most important variable controlling performance and learning, and further, studies have repeatedly shown that there is no improvement without it, progressive improvement with it, and deterioration after its withdrawal.

According to Barbara Brown,[1] one of the foremost early authorities on the subject of biofeedback the terms *feedback* and *control systems* were borrowed by physiologists when they began theorizing about how the functions of the body were performed.

There are numerous ways in which biofeedback can be described. One description could be that it is any information that we receive about the functioning of our internal organs such as the heart, sweat glands, muscles and brain. Another description could indicate that it is a process in which information about our organism's biologic activity is supplied for perception by the same organism. This could be extended by indicating that biofeedback is the monitoring of signals from the body, such as muscle tension and hand warmth, and the feeding of this information back through the use of sophisticated machines to individuals so they can get external information as to exactly what is happening in their bodies.

There are perhaps millions of individual feedback systems in the human body, and information about the external environment is sensed by way of the five senses and relayed to a control center, usually the brain, where it is integrated with other relevant information. When the sensed information is significant enough, central control generates commands for appropriate body changes.

These senses can also be thought of as the systems of *perception;* that is, how we obtain information from the environment and what we make of it. Learning theorists agree that the forms of perception most involved in learning are *auditory* perception, *visual* perception, *kinesthetic* perception, and *tactile* perception. Auditory perception is the mental interpretation of what a person hears. Visual perception is the mental interpretation of what a person sees. Kinesthetic perception is the mental interpretation of the sensation of body movement. Tactile perception is the mental interpretation of what a persons experiences through the sense of touch. In this regard, it is common practice among learning theorists to refer to auditory feedback, visual feedback, kinesthetic feedback and tactile feedback.

BIOFEEDBACK INSTRUMENTATION

We are all aware of the fact that the human body itself is a complicated and complex biofeedback instrument, which alerts us to certain internal activity, as mentioned in the previous discussion. However, many students on the subject feel that there is still a need for sensitive instruments to monitor physiological and psychological reactivity. Following is a brief discussion of the more widely known biofeedback instruments that are used both for research and therapeutic purposes.

Electromyograph (EMG)

Electromyography is the recording of electric phenomena occurring in muscles during contraction. Needle or skin electrodes are used and connected with an oscilloscope so that action potentials may be viewed and recorded (the oscilloscope is an instrument that visually displays an electrical wave on a fluorescent screen). Before the electromyograph was available, guesswork ordinarily had to be used to try to determine the participation of the muscles in movement. When a muscle is completely relaxed or inactive, it has no electric potential; however, when it is engaged in contraction, current appears.

It is believed that EMG training can produce deep muscle relaxation and relieve tension. A person gets the feedback by seeing a dial or hearing a sound from the machine, and he or she knows immediately the extent to which certain muscles may be relaxed or tensed. A muscle frequently used in EMG training for research and other purposes is the *frontalis* located in the front of the head.

Another important aspect of EMG is that which is concerned with retraining a person following an injury or disease when there is a need to observe small increments of gain in function of a muscle.

Feedback Thermometers

Th obvious purpose of feedback thermometers is to record body temperatures. Ordinarily, a thermistor is attached to the hands or fingers. This highly sensitive instrument shows very small increments of degrees of temperature change so that the person receives the information with a visual or auditory signal. This kind of feedback instrumentation has been recommended for such purposes as reduction of stress and anxiety and autonomic nervous system relaxation.

Electroencephalograph (EEC)

The purpose of this instrument is to record amplitude and frequency of brain waves, and it has been used in research for many years. It has also been used with success to diagnose certain clinical diseases. In addition, EEC feedback has found use in psychotherapy, and in reducing stress as well as pain.

An interesting relatively recent horizon for EEC feedback is how it might be involved in creativity and learning. In fact, some individuals involved in creative activity have indicated that they can emerge from the EEC *theta* state with answers to problems that they were previously unable to solve. The theta waves are ordinarily recorded when a person is in a state of drowsiness or actually falling asleep. It is perhaps for this reason that this condition has been referred to by some as "sleep learning," Since it is a state just before sleep, others refer to it as the twilight period of "twilight learning."

Galvanic Skin Response (GSR)

There are several different kinds of GSR instruments used to measure changes in electrical resistance of the skin to detect emotional arousal. The instrument reacts in proportion to the amount of perspiration one emits and the person is informed of the changes in electrical resistance by an auditory or visual signal. One aspect of GSR is concerned with the use of the polygraph or lie detector, which is supposed to record a response that is concerned with lying. GSR feedback is oftentimes recommended for use of relaxation, reducing tension, improvement of ability to sleep, or for emotional control.

In general, the purpose of the biofeedback machinery is to provide accurate and reliable data that will increase one's awareness of how the body is functioning and demonstrate one's influence of his or her action of the body. Hopefully, this information should be useful in inspiring a person to take an active self-interest in his or her own well-being. After such information is received, if it has been obtained under the supervision of a qualified person, there may be a given number of sessions arranged for consultation and training. Perhaps the ultimate objective is for the individual to be able to gain control over his or her own autonomic nervous system.

As popular and well-advertised as biofeedback machinery has become, it is not without its critics who feel that many important purposes can be accomplished without instruments by using the body as its own biofeedback instrument. In general, they identify such factors as: (1) diverse muscle relaxation, (2) change of heart rate and body temperature, (3) change of breathing patterns, (4) decrease of stress and anxiety reactions, (5) mental relaxation, (6) autonomic nervous system relaxation, (7) pain relief for tension headaches, backaches, and other aches and pains, and (8) improved learning ability, including enhancement of concentration and recall. However, the critics would probably admit that certain of the biofeedback instruments, particularly EMG has important application for retraining of patients following disease and injury.

At the present time, it is difficult to determine unequivocally what the future of biofeedback may be. Without question, it has influenced our way of thinking with reference to a person being able to possibly to control his or her physiological functions. In view of this, perhaps one of its foremost contributions is that it creates in an individual a feeling of responsibility for his or her personal well-being.

USING BIOFEEDBACK WITH CHILDREN

Biofeedback has been used with considerable success with children, and research in this area has increased appreciably in recent years. Following is a summary of representative findings of this research.

1. Biofeedback can facilitate appropriate levels of reactivity and thereby maximize functioning.
2. Children who are not aware of their own tensed state can benefit from biofeedback training.
3. Biofeedback-induced relaxation can assist children with learning disabilities in reaching their educational potentials.
4. EMG training can be useful in the treatment of hyperactivity in children.
5. EMG training has been shown to increase attention to an academic task as well as reducing problem behavior.

Most experts in the field of biofeedback believe that such treatment can provide possibilities for increased functioning and self-regulation of body and mind in children.

In concluding this chapter, it is worth repeating that at least in the early stages the practice of biofeedback training should take place under the supervision of a qualified person. Also, if a disease syndrome is present a physician's referral may be required.

SUGGESTED ACTIVITIES

1. Some colleges and universities have biofeedback laboratories on campus. This facility may be housed in such places as the health service or counseling center. If there is such a service, arrange to take a field trip to this facility.
2. Invite a speaker from the health service, counseling center, psychology department, or health education department to discuss the various features of biofeedback training.
3. Hold a panel discussion on the various types of biofeedback instrumentation.
4. Make a list of the ways in which you think biofeedback might be used. Compare your list with the other class members.

Chapter 15

REDUCING STRESS THROUGH
SELF-MODIFICATION OF BEHAVIOR

For purposes of this discussion, *behavior* will be considered as anything that the organism does as a result of some sort of stimulation. The term *modification* means a change in the organism caused by environmental factors. Thus, when the two terms are used together - behavior modification -they are interpreted to mean some sort of change in the way a person has ordinarily reacted to a given stimulus.

It is not uncommon for some individuals to display behavior that directly or indirectly causes stress arousal, either for themselves and/or for the other person(s) toward whom the behavioral action is directed. It is the function of this chapter to provide information that will assist the reader to modify his or her own behavior for the purpose of correcting or at least improving upon this condition.

1. What is meant by behavioral self-management?
2. What is the difference between self-structure and self-concept?
3. What is meant by behavioral adjustment?
4. In behavior modification why is it important to identify one's behaviors?
5. What is the *ABC Factor* in the behavior modification approach?
6. What is the place of *reinforcement* in changing behavior?
7. In self-modification of behavior how does one evaluate the *plan of intervention?*

In recent years, behavior modification has become so broad in scope that it is used in many frames of reference. It is emphasized at this point that, for purposes here it is not being considered as a variety of psychological and/or psychiatric techniques (therapist-client relations) for altering behavior. On the contrary, the recommendations for the use of modification of behavior are confined to its possibilities as a means for individuals to reduce certain stress-connected factors involved in their various environments. This is to say that if a person manifests a behavior that provokes a stressful situation, if he or she can change that behavior, it could be possible to eliminate, or at least minimize the stressful condition. For example, let us say that if a person constantly uses what others consider to be unwarranted criticism, this can create a problem in social relationships and thus a stressful atmosphere.

In general, the practice of behavior modification involves external assistance as in the case of a teacher or counselor trying to effect a behavior change in a student or a group of students. The major concern here is in the direction of self modification with the individual attempting to improve upon his or her own behavior. This assumes that, generally speaking, a person can develop the ability to increase desirable or appropriate behavior and to decrease undesirable or inappropriate behavior. Of course, this involves self-control, which can be described as manipulation of environmental events that influence one's own behavior for the purpose of changing the behavior. Self-control can eventually lead to behavioral self-management, which can be considered as the learning and practice of new habits. Satisfactory self-control and successful self-management are obviously contingent upon some sort of understanding of self, and this is the subject of the ensuing discussion.

TOWARD AN UNDERSTANDING OF SELF

In order to put an understanding of self in its proper perspective, consideration needs to be given to the basic concept of *self-structure* and *self-concept.* Self-structure is the framework of a particular individual's complex of motives, perceptions, cognitions, feelings, and values - the product of developmental processes. Self-structure is revealed in behavior. One reveals in his or her behavior the knowledge, skills, and interests acquired, the goals he or she is seeking, the beliefs, values, and attitudes adopted, the roles learned, and the self-concept formed. Thus self-concept is an aspect of self-structure.

Among the most relevant and significant perceptions that an individual acquires are those of himself or herself in various life situations; and further, basically, the self-concept is made up of a large number of *percepts,* each of which contains one or more qualities that one ascribes to himself or herself. To be more specific, *self-percept* pertains to sense impressions of a trait one ascribes to himself or herself while *self-concept* consists of the totality of one's self-percepts organized in some sort of order.

PROCESSES OF BEHAVIOR ADJUSTMENT

The term *adjustment* can be described as the process of finding and adopting-modes of behavior suitable to the environment or to changes in the environment. Daily living involves a continuous sequence of experiences characterized by the necessity for the human organism to adjust. Consequently, it may be said that "normal" behavior is the result of successful adjustment, and abnormal behavior results from unsuccessful adjustment. The degree of adjustment that one achieves depends upon how adequately he or she is able to satisfy basic needs and fulfill desires within the framework of the environment and the pattern or ways dictated by society.

As mentioned previously, we tend to think of stress as any factor acting internally or externally that renders adaptation difficult, and induces increased effort of the part of a person to maintain a state of equilibrium within himself or herself and with his or her external environment. In Chapter 2, the following points were made and are repeated here for purposes of continuity. When stress is induced as a result of the individual's not being able to meet his or her needs (basic demands) and satisfy desires (wants or wishes), *frustration* or *conflict* results. Frustration occurs when a need is not met; and conflict results when choices must be made between nearly equally attractive alternatives or when basic emotional forces oppose one another. In the emotionally healthy person, the degree of frustration is ordinarily in proportion to the intensity of the need or the desire. That is, he or she will objectively observe and evaluate the situation to ascertain if a solution is possible, and if so, what solution would best enable him or her to achieve the fulfillment of needs or desires. However, every person has a "zone of tolerance" or limits for physical, physiological, and psychological stress within which he or she normally operates. If the stress becomes considerably greater than the tolerance level, or if the individual has not learned to cope with his or her problems and objectively and intelligently solve them, some degree of maladjustment can possible result.

SOME GENERAL PROCEDURES FOR
SELF MODIFICATION OF BEHAVIOR

Over the past decade a voluminous amount of literature has been published in the general area of behavior modification. Some of this has been directed to school administrators, teachers, counselors, and others for the purpose of utilizing the procedure to produce behavior change in students. As mentioned before, the concern here is with self modification of behavior and literature in this specific area is becoming more abundant.

Although self modification of behavior is considered to be a relatively recent innovation, one report, suggests that it was used in the early history of our country by Benjamin Franklin.[1] He is said to have used it to improve upon such virtues as temperance and frugality. He kept a record of the errors he thought he made each day in each of over a dozen virtues. At the end of the day, he would consult the information to get feedback to help him identify those virtues he may have been violating. Of course, in modern times our approach to self modification of behavior is much more sophisticated than that of Franklin, and improvement in procedures is constantly being made.

Whether one is attempting to modify behavior of another (teacher with a student) or trying to modify his or her own behavior, the general procedures of application are essentially the same. There are certain sequential steps to be taken that involve the following: (1) identification and description of one's behaviors, (2) counting behaviors, (3) attempting to effect a change in behavior, and (4) evaluating the procedures used to change behaviors. The following discussion will take into account some of the important features involved in these various steps.

Identifying Behaviors

The first step in the process is concerned with identification of a behavior that one wishes to modify. This process is also referred to as *pinpointing, targeting,* or *specifying* a behavior. Essentially, this involves trying to define a particular behavior (target) that one wishes to change. This is not always an easy matter because sometimes a person may manifest a behavior that is annoying to others, but he or she may be completely unaware of it.

When a person is able to identify a behavior and admit that such a behavior may be interfering with social relationships, a strong beginning can be made in the direction of behavioral change. In other words, recognizing that one has a problem is the first prerequisite to solving it.

In many instances, the identification of a behavior emerges when one is dissatisfied with what he or she may be doing. For example, a person may find that he may be performing a behavior he does not want to perform, or that he may not be performing a behavior he wants to perform.

In the discussion that follows, a hypothetical model of self modification of behavior depicts a college senior in elementary education - Alice Brown - who is in the process of student teaching and currently taking a require course in "The Psychology of Teaching." The reader is asked to think of a personal situation in which he or she might utilize the procedure shown in the model.

Ms. Brown has been assigned as a sixth grade student teacher. She is also enrolled in the late afternoon required course "The Psychology of Teaching." In one class session on the general topic of "student attention," the discussion focused upon inappropriate teacher response to student behavior. It was brought out that one form of inappropriate behavior is the command given contingent upon the occurrence of a student behavior. That is, when there is a noise the teacher commands, "Be quiet!" Or, when students are out of their seats, the teacher commands, "Sit down!" It was also revealed that contingent "sit down" commands actually increase the frequency of standing behavior among students.

Ms. Brown not only recognized that she had been performing this behavior in her student teaching, but that also on occasion it had degenerated into a "shouting match" with students, creating a stressful situation. Inwardly she had been dissatisfied with herself for performing this behavior, but had neglected to anything about it. Upon learning that this form of behavior could make a bad situation worse, she felt desperately in need to try it correct it. She had identified an inappropriate behavior, and thus, theoretically, she was ready for the next step in self modification of behavior, that of *counting* behaviors.

Counting Behaviors

The second step in self modification of behavior is concerned with actually counting how often a target behavior occurs. This means that one obtains a frequency count of the behavior to be improved. If this step is not taken, it is difficult to learn the extent to which the behavior is being performed. Sometimes, simply counting a behavior, will tend to improve it because the person is becoming involved in self-awareness of the behavior. This is to say that counting a behavior calls one's attention to it and how often it is occurring.

In addition to determining the frequency of a behavior, another aspect of this step is what is sometimes called the *ABC Factor* in the behavior modification approach. That is, Antecedent of the behavior, the Behavior itself, and the Consequence of the behavior. *Antecedent* is concerned with any event that preceded the behavior and *consequence* is what happens as a result of the behavior. Following are some examples of ABCs of behaviors that occurred in Ms. Brown's student teaching experience.

Antecedent	Ms. Brown's Behavior	Consequence
Item 1. Student gets out of seat.	Ms. Brown shouts at student to "Sit Down!"	Class laughs at Ms. Brown.
Item 2. Student talks out to another student.	Ms. Brown shouts at student to "Be quiet!"	Student gives Ms. Brown a bored look.
Item 3. Student falls asleep.	Ms. Brown claps hands close to student's ears and awakens him.	Disruption of class by guffaws of other students.

Obviously it is most important that a person develop an awareness of antecedents and consequences of behaviors. The main reason for this is that an antecedent gets a behavior started and a given behavior can result in an unsatisfactory consequence, as in the above illustration.

Attempting to analyze an antecedent becomes important in terms of a manifested behavior. That is, why did the antecedent occur in the first place: In the case of the above example, questions such as the following might be raised.

Item 1. Why did the student leave his seat? Was he justified in doing so? Did Ms. Brown react too quickly?

Item 2. Why did a student talk out to another student? Was this a persistent behavior of this particular student?

Item 3. Why did the student fall asleep? Was he ill? Has he been doing this before, or was it the first time? The information derived from step two in self modification of behavior is usually designated as *baseline data*. If the information is valid and the behavior frequency is accurate, the person has a base from which to operate. This means that one should be in a position to see if attempts at improving a given behavior - step three, *changing behavior* is meeting with satisfactory results.

Changing Behaviors

Any effort to change a behavior that has been identified, described, counted, and recorded is referred to as a *plan of intervention*. The person intervenes with one or more procedures designed to modify the inappropriate behavior. Any plan to replace an inappropriate behavior with an appropriate one involves some sort of reinforcement procedure. Generally, speaking, *self* reinforcement is concerned with changing behavior through *self-produced* consequences, and these consequences may be overt or covert. Examples are statements to oneself or the acquisition of an item as a reward for one's efforts.

To help in the clarification of step three in self modification of behavior, let us return to the case of Ms. Brown. It will be recalled that she was dissatisfied with her constant criticism of, and shouting at, some of her sixth graders. She had gone through steps one and two by identifying a target behavior and gathering information in the way of frequency of occurrence, along with an analysis of antecedents and consequences.

In her course in "The Psychology of Teaching" one of the topics for discussion was "teacher praise versus teacher criticism" in dealing with students. Recognizing that her behavior with her sixth grade class was predominantly characterized by criticism, she took as her term project a study of these two factors - teacher praise and teacher criticism. Her investigation into the literature on the subject revealed the following information.

1. Teacher behavior in such forms as smiles, praise and words of encouragement, if made contingent upon an appropriate student behavior tend to increase the frequency of that behavior; therefore, these forms of teacher behavior operate as reinforcers for many student behaviors (this suggested to Ms. Brown that she might consider minimizing criticism of inappropriate student behavior and maximizing praise for appropriate behavior).

2. Teacher behavior that ignores inappropriate student behavior can be effective in diminishing that behavior. This, of course, depends upon how disruptive and/or dangerous the behavior might be. Obviously, some types of student behavior cannot be ignored (this suggested to Ms. Brown that the time she was using to criticize one student for inappropriate behavior might well be spent praising another for appropriate behavior).

3. Teacher behavior such as criticism should not be neglected entirely, but rather there should be a ratio between praise and criticism, with the former predominating about five times as often as the latter (it has been demonstrated that such a ratio can achieve success; moreover, it has been shown that when things are going poorly in the classroom, teachers criticize students about four or five times more than they praise them; Ms. Brown's behavior had been almost entirely one of criticism).

4. When a teacher criticizes a student, it can be done quietly. Conversely, when praise is given it can be done with emphasis. Thus, a general principle might be, *maximize the tone of praise* and *minimize the tone of criticism.* The importance of this has been borne out in studies showing that a loud tone of criticism may likely cause more inappropriate behavior of some students while soft tones may contribute to better control situations for students. (Ms. Brown remembered that in most all cases she had resorted to shouting at students).

5. It may be a good practice for a teacher to criticize an inappropriate behavior without heaping too much criticism on a student. For example, a teacher could emphasize the fact that the student is a "good person" but that the behavior was not so good. Or, from a negative point of view "You are not a bad person, but what you did was not good behavior."

With the above information to use as a general guideline, Ms. Brown was ready to set about formulating a plan of intervention. The major objective was to make an effort to reduce or eliminate the inappropriate behavior of criticism accompanied by shouting, and replace it with a more appropriate behavior.

Ms. Brown's task was to intervene with activities that would have some influence on the above situation, and, in addition, to provide for self-reinforcement when such behaviors were performed. Following are some of the items used in the intervention plan.

1. An effort was made to use less criticism, based upon the undesirability of a given student behavior.

2. An effort was made to use praise for appropriate behavior, not only of a verbal nature but also in the form of smiling, nods of approval, and the like.

3. A new voluntary seating plan was devised for the purpose of separating those students who tended to talk out to each other.

4. Cooperative assistance of some of the students was enlisted. This took the form of notifying Ms. Brown when she tended to perform an inappropriate behavior. This action on the part of Ms. Brown indicated to her students that she was "human" after all.

The next point of concern was that of self-reinforcement. It should be recalled that self-reinforcement is concerned with overt or covert consequences in the form of statements to one's self or the acquisition of an item as a reward for one's efforts. Ms. Brown decided that the major form of self-reinforcement would involve self-praise, or what is referred to as "stroking." That is, there is a human need to be applauded for a successful effort, if not by someone else, then by one's self.

In our hypothetical model, a plan was introduced by Ms. Brown whereby when any member of the class did well in something, that person literally have himself or herself a pat on the back. This also included Ms. Brown, and it became a common practice for her, as well as the class members, to applaud themselves for a job well done. As far as overt consequences were concerned, occasionally, Ms. Brown treated herself to certain luxuries that she had previously been denying herself, such as dining out or, purchasing a pair of exotic earrings (Note: The reader is cautioned to remember that the above discussion is hypothetical, and perhaps to the extent that certain aspects of it boarder on "theoretical extremity" for the purpose of clarifying some points).

Evaluating the Plan of Intervention

The final step in self modification of behavior is concerned with how well the plan of intervention is succeeding; that is, the extent to which the changes in behavior are achieving desired results. This process requires the development of valid evaluative criteria. These criteria can be broad in scope, and thus apply to any problem of self modification of behavior, or they can be more specific and be applied to a particular case. Some examples of general criteria might include the following.

1. In general, was there an increase in appropriate behavior and/or a decrease in inappropriate behavior?
2. What were the behaviors that achieved the most satisfactory results?
3. What forms of reinforcement appeared to be most successful?

The general evaluative criteria could be applied more specifically to our hypothetical case as follows.

1. Did Ms. Brown notice fewer instances of criticism and shouting on her part by actually keeping an account of this type of behavior? If so, how many?
2. Did the voluntary change in seating plan have any influence on the students who had been "talking out?" If so, in how many instances?

3. Did the system of "patting ourselves on the back" help as a reinforcer in behavior change? If so, in how many ways?

Whatever way one decides to evaluate the plan of intervention, there is still another decision to be made. This also concerns the extent to which the plan has achieved success. If it has met with complete and unequivocal success, it can then perhaps be terminated. Or, if it succeeds only when the behavior change is still being practiced, there may be a heed to maintain the procedure. Perhaps the ultimate goal should be to modify behavior to the extent that the problem would be completely eliminated. This can be accomplished if one conscientiously and systematically carries out the general procedures outlined above. Experience has shown that one can modify his or her own behavior not only to correct stress arousal but to avoid it as well.

SUGGESTED ACTIVITIES

1. Invite an outside speaker from the Psychology Department to discuss behavioral therapy.
2. Hold a round table discussion on the subject of behavioral adjustment.
3. Identify one of your own behaviors that you would like to change. Then proceed, using the hypothetical model of Ms. Brown as a guide. Present the results to the class.

REDUCING STRESS THROUGH SYSTEMATIC SELF-DESENSITIZATION

Systematic desensitization can be described as the process of systematically lessening a specific learned fear in an individual. It is purported to provide one means of controlling anxiety. If one can accomplish this, it becomes an extremely important factor in reducing stress. The reason for this is that the individual becomes more able to control his or her fears and anxieties. From the point of view of a clinical psychotherapeutic procedure, systematic desensitization consists of presenting to the imagination of the deeply relaxed person the feeblest item in a list of anxiety-evoking stimuli repeatedly, until no more anxiety is evoked. The next item of the list is presented, and so on, until eventually, even the strongest of the anxiety-evoking stimuli fails to evoke any stir of anxiety in the person. It is the purpose of this final chapter to provide information for the reader that should help him or her understand the process of this technique and at the same time give consideration to self-administration for the ultimate purpose of reducing stress.

1. What is the relationship between relaxation and systematic self desensitization?
2. What are conditioned reactions?
3. What is meant by "hierarchy of anxiety-evoking stimuli"?
4. What are the various steps to take in the use of systematic self desensitization?
5. Why is it difficult to discuss something rationally with a person who is involved emotionally in a situation?

Originally, the focus of systematic desensitization was primarily upon counselor-client, therapist-patient, or teacher-student relationships, and was used as a behavior therapy technique. In recent years, systematic desensitization has gained some favor as a self-administered technique. Although the value of it as a means of lessening stress-provoking situations has not been completely established by behavioral scientists, some of the research findings are indeed encouraging. For example, studies have shown that systematic self desensitization can be very effect in overcoming severe public speaking anxiety, test anxiety, and a host of other stress-invoking stimuli.

Systematic self desensitization efforts are not likely to be harmful, even if they fail. However, self desensitization should be approached as an experimental procedure and it should be discontinued if the course of anxiety-reduction is not relatively smooth, and it should be discontinued immediately if any increase in anxiety is experienced.

Systematic desensitization can be introduced with the idea that many anxieties that people experience are due to what are termed *conditioned reactions*. These conditioned reactions are identified as stimuli that occur together in our experience and become associated with each other so that we respond to them in the same way, or in a highly similar way, when they occur again. This is to say that if we are made anxious in the presence of certain stimuli these same stimuli will make us anxious later when they occur, even if the situation in reality no longer poses an actual threat. An example is a person who may have had a number of experiences as a child in which a person in authority, such as a school principal, policeman, or guard frightened the child and perhaps punished him or her in some way. Such a person's reactions as an adult to one in authority may produce considerably more anxiety than the situation really justifies. This is because the previous conditioning of strong anxiety to an authority figure.

Many of our emotions seem to be based on such conditioned reactions. And, these reactions are somewhat similar to reflexes, but they are learned rather than inherited (the reader is asked to refer back to the discussion of learned and unlearned tensions in Chapter 1). Their automatic "reflexive" character, however, explains why it is difficult to discuss things rationally with someone who is emotionally involved in a situation. The person is responding more with his or her conditioned reactions to the present stimuli than relating to the actual realities of the situation.

The recommendation for overcoming anxieties in the form of conditioned reactions is the use of systematic self desensitization and a highly persuasive case can be made for its effectiveness - provided in it done properly.

After a particular problem as been identified, the process consists of three sequential steps: (1) developing a hierarchy of anxiety-evoking stimuli, (2) complete relaxation, and (3) desensitization sessions. Using the previously mentioned authority figure example, let us make application of this to a college student who has difficulty with this problem where relationship with the student's department chairperson is concerned. Incidentally, my surveys show that it is not uncommon for some college students to have what they designate as a "fear of the administrator" without being aware of the reasons for it.

The first step is to take several index cards, writing a different situation or experience on each card that makes for anxiety concerning the problem. The cards are then stacked in order with the one causing the least anxiety on the top and the one causing the greatest anxiety at the bottom. This is the hierarchy of anxiety-evoking stimuli and might resemble the following.

1. Entering school parking lot and seeing department chairperson's car.
2. Greeting fellow students and discussing department chairperson.
3. Greeting fellow student who mentions his coming meeting with the department chairperson.
4. Conferring with a fellow student after his meeting with the department chairperson.
5. Walking by department chairperson's office when door is closed.
6. Walking by department chairperson's office when door is open (no verbalization or eye contact.)

7. Walking by department chairperson's office when door is open using eye contact and nodding.
8. Arranging meeting with department chairperson's secretary.
9. Talking with department chairperson's secretary about the department chairperson.
10. Pre-arranged meeting with department chairperson with secretary present.
11. Pre-arranged meeting with department chairperson with only self present.
12. Other meetings with department chairperson with only self present.

Another possible stress-inducing situation that concerns many students is that of making a report in front of the class. A hierarchy that could be used for self desensitization follows.

1. Reading an article about giving reports.
2. Reading report alone.
3. Reading report in front of mirror.
4. Reading report into tape recorder and playing back.
5. Reading report to roommate.
6. Reading report to roommate with one other present.
7. Reading report with three others present.
8. Reading report to two or three others where there is a large gathering, such as the lunch room.
9. Entering the classroom.
10. Member of audience while other reports are given.
11. Giving report to entire class.

Of course the reader must understand that the above hierarchies of anxiety-evoking stimuli are general in nature and each individual would make out his or her own list in more specific detail and pertaining more to specific anxieties,

The second step is to try to develop a condition of complete relaxation (the reader is referred back to Chapter 12 for a review of the various relaxation procedures). It is recommended that the person go through each of the muscle groups in sequential order to learn to relax them one by one.

After the person is complete relaxed, the next step is the beginning of systematic self desensitization. This is done as follows. Look at the top card on the pile - the one that is the least anxiety provoking. Close the eyes, and using the imagination, visualize as vividly as possible the situation described on it. That is, one imagines the situation occurring and that he or she is actually there. At this point, if some anxiety is experienced, the imaginary scene should cease immediately and the person should go back to relaxing. After complete relaxation is again obtained, the person is ready to proceed. This procedure is continued until the scene can be imagined without anxiety. This may take only one or two times, or it could take 15 to 20 times, but it should be repeated until no anxiety is felt. The entire procedure is continued until one has gone through all the cards.

It is recommended that one work on the scenes in this manner for approximately one half hour at a time. It can be done daily, every other day, or a couple of times a week, depending upon the amount of time one is willing or able to spend, and how quickly one wants to conquer the anxiety. It appears to be a good practice to overlap one or two items from one session to another; that is, beginning a session by repeating an item or two from the previous session that were imagined without anxiety.

One variation of the above procedure is to tape record a description of each scene in advance. One then relaxes and listens to the tape. If anxiety appears, the recorder is turned off and the person goes back to relaxing. When relaxation is again accomplished the individual proceeds as before. A value of using the tape recorder is that there is likely to be better pronunciation, enunciation, and intonation of words. In addition, it may be easier for the individual to concentrate, since he or she has provided his or her own auditory input on tape and does not have the additional task of verbalizing and trying to concentrate on the scene at the same time. If desired, the sequence of relaxation procedures can be taped as well.

After one has been desensitized, there can be a review in his or her own mind the preferred action to take in the situation that caused anxiety. Plans can then be made to do the right thing the next time the situation occurs.

Obviously, the success one experiences with this procedure will depend largely upon the extent to which one is willing to make the painstaking effort involved in the approach. Many persons who have tried it have been so delighted; by its effects that they have deliberately sought out situations that previously had caused them great anxiety, frustration, and failure. This is certainly a true test of faith in the approach.

USING DESENSITIZATION WITH CHILDREN

Systematic desensitization has been used with success in terms of lessening fears and anxieties among children. An example of such an experiment is one in which a six and one-half-year-old boy as unsuccessful in classroom verbalization.[1] Medical and psychiatric reports did not show any known reason for his unwillingness to talk in the classroom. Although the child's test results revealed that he had ability above average, his school progress failed to reach his level of potential. A six-week desensitization program of two sessions per week was developed to try to reduce or eliminate his fear of verbalization in class. The following hierarchy of anxiety-evoking stimuli was used in the experiment.

1. Reading alone to investigator.
2. Reading to roommate.
3. Reading to two classroom aides.
4. Reading to teacher and classroom aides.
5. Reading to teacher, classroom aides, and small group of class peers.
6. Reading to entire class.
7. Asking questions or making comments at weekly meetings when all children, teachers, and staff were present.

This program of desensitization met with success in alleviating the child's fear of verbalization in the classroom. Other programs of this same general nature have been used to advantage in reducing test-taking anxiety, conquering the phobia of school attendance, fear of medical settings, fear of the dark, water and insects - in fact most fears of children can be alleviated by systematic desensitization if the procedure is carried out properly.

With reference to conquering the phobia of school attendance, it has been found that many school children who are not reading and writing as well as they should may be just too frightened to do any better. As mentioned in Chapter 9, otherwise "normal" children have fears of certain school subjects, as other people irrationally fear height or the sight of blood.

Many of the fears connected with reading and writing result from conditioned reactions. After a time, the original problem may be resolved, but the barrier to learning which was removed has been replaced by another one, the fear. Since the child could not read or write well, he or she was probably a failure in school. Children may associate reading and writing with failure and most of them are afraid of failing. In time, the fear can grow and the child really needs help, and this help almost always comes by systematically desensitizing the fear.

Although systematic desensitization has proved to be a very successful procedure to use to desensitize children to fear, its use as a "self" administering device is not always applicable for fairly obvious reasons. This means that the child does not make up his or her own hierarchy of anxiety-evolting stimuli, but on the other hand, this is done by an adult, sometimes in collaboration with the child.

Although some fears are serious enough to warrant clinical intervention by a professional therapist, in many instances an "untrained" adult can be successful in the use of systematic desensitization with children. As a matter of fact, parents, without even being aware of it, sometimes actually practice systematic desensitization with their children. Take for example the first trip to the beach - a child may have a fear not only of the water but of the noise and vastness of the environment as well. A parent may desensitize the child's fear by unknowing practicing the following hierarchy of anxiety-evoking stimuli. The child, accompanied by the parent, may play near the water for a time. Next, one foot is placed in the water, followed by both feet immersed to the ankles, then to the thighs, waist and finally immersion up to the neck.

Another example where a parent may unwittingly practice systematic desensitization with a child is when there is fear of the dark. The child may be permitted to sleep with a light on in his or her room for several nights. This is followed by turning out the light in the child's room but leaving one on in a nearby room with the door left open. On successive nights the door is closed more and more until the fear is eliminated and the child is encouraged to sleep with the light off and the door closed.

Some Things to Consider When Using Systematic Desensitization with Children

If systematic desensitization is to meet with success when applied to children, there are certain considerations that need to be taken into account by adults. Most of these concerns center around the level of cognitive development of the child. In this regard, it has already mentioned the responsibility an adult should take in developing the hierarchy of anxiety-evoking stimuli.

Another cognitive factor to consider is the extent to which a child can apply his or her imagination to the stress-invoking scenes implied in the hierarchy of anxiety-evoking stimuli. In this particular regard, the late Jean Piaget, the world famous child development specialist, felt that developmentally imagery is thought to first occur in late infancy when "deferred imitation" takes place.[2] Mental imagery apparently cannot occur before this time. In "deferred imitation" the child is able to distinguish a mental image from the actual event it represents. However, Piaget felt that the image is very specific to the event it is imitating and is concrete rather than conceptual. Therefore, it is questionable whether four or five year old children can manipulate imagery in the ways required for systematic desensitization. The younger child may be able to attend to only a limited number of characteristics of the stimulus because of his or her stage of development.

It could be that using such procedures in place of imagining scenes may be best for these children. For example, in what is called "in-vivo" desensitization, the child can use toys to play out a hierarchy of fear situations; or, the child can be allowed to draw the feared scenes.

What is called "anticipatory imagery" develops around age seven or eight. The imagery allows for manipulation of the mental representation so that it can be moved about in space or changed in form. It is plausible that seven or eight year olds could use systematic desensitization effectively. However, not too many studies using traditional systematic desensitization have been done with children under ten years of age. With many children, reinforcement may also be necessary to motivate the child to attempt and then practice visualizing.

It is important to recognize that the concrete images used by children below age seven or eight have a very high degree of affect associated with them. This means that there should be caution in the use of imagery of an aversive nature, due to the possibility that the child might imagine such an aversive scene and experience further trauma rather than alleviation of the fear.

Another factor to take into account when using systematic desensitization with children is the extent to which they are able to learn relaxation techniques, as well as whether they are capable of relaxing in a short period of time. Of course, if relaxation procedures are presented to children in the same manner as they are for adults, they will have difficulty in learning how to relax.

In those cases where adults do have difficulty getting children to relax, a technique called "emotive imagery" has been used with success for many years. This technque replaces relaxation as the anxiety inhibiting response in systematic desensitization. It is meant to arouse feelings of bravery, pride, and assertiveness in the child. Like systematic de- sensitization a graduated hierarchy of the child's fears is developed. However, instead of imagining the scene concurrent with relaxing, the child is guided by the adult in imagery of the feared scene and credible events woven around a favorite hero. This could be one of the Muppets, a cartoon character or a television hero.

In summary, it should be very clear that when a given procedure can be used satisfactorily with adults, it does not follow automatically that it will be successful with children if used in the same way. Therefore, adults should exercise judgment and caution when making application of systematic desensitization with children.

SUGGESTED ACTIVITIES

1. Prepare a list of incidents that arouse fear. Select one from this list, and using the material in the chapter as a guide, construct a "hierarchy of anxiety-evoking stimuli." Practice the procedure and share the results with the class.

2. Develop a relaxation procedure using imagery as a means to assist you in systematic self desensitization. Share this with the class.

*   *   *

It has been the purpose of this book to provide college students with valid information about the phenomenon of stress - not only for the present, but in the future as they pursue their goals in a complex society.

REFERENCES

Introduction
1. Schiraldi, Glenn R. and Brown, Stephen L., Primary Preventions for Mental Health: A Stress Inoculation Training Course for Functional Adults, *American Journal of Health Education,* 32, September/October, 2001, p. 279-287.
2. Humphrey, James H., *Profiles in Stress,* New York, AMS Press, Inc., 1986, p. 107-110.

Chapter 1
1. Selye, Hans, *Stress Without Distress,* New York, New American Library, 1975, p. 18.
2. Walker, C. Eugene, *Learn to Relax: 13 Ways to Reduce Tension,* Englewood Cliffs, NJ, Prentice-Hall, Inc., 975, p. 16.
3. Viscot, David, *The Language of Feelings,* New York, Arbor House, 1976, p. 93.
4. Thomas, William C., Avoiding Burnout: Hardiness as a Buffer in College Athletes, Reston, VA *Research Quarterly for Exercise and Sports,* Supplement, 69, 1998, p. 116-117

Chapter 2
1. Selye, Hans, *Stress Without Distress,* New York, New American Library, 1975, p. 24.
2. Cannon, Walter B., *The Wisdom of the Body,* New York, W. W. Norton, 1932.
3. Posner, Israel and Leitner A., Eustress vs. Distress: Determination by Predictability and Controllability *of* the Stressor, *Stress, The Official Journal of the International Institute of Stress and Its Affiliates* Summer 1981, Vol. 2, No. 2, p. 10-12.
4. Mikhail, Anis, Stress: A Psychological Connection, *The Journal of Human Stress,* June 1981, p. 33-34.
5. Holmes, T. H., and Rahe, R. H., The Social Readjustment Scale, *Journal of Psychosomatic Research,* 11, 1967.
6. Lazarus, Richard S. Little Hassles can be Hazardous to Your Health, *Psychology Today,* June 1981, p. 16-22.
7. Friedman, Meyer and Rosenman, Ray H., *Type A Behavior and Your Health,* New York, Alfred A. Knopf, 1974, p. 77.
8. Annual Meeting of the American Psychiatric Association, Dallas, May 1985.

9. Newberry, Benjamin, et al., A Holistic Conceptulization of Stress and Disease, No. 7 in the series *Stress in Modern Society*, James H. Humphrey, Editor, New York, AMS Press, Inc., 1991.

Chapter 3

1. Whitehead, D'Ann, et al., Use of Systematic Desensitization in the Treatment of Children's Fears, No.1 in series *Stress in Modern Society*, James H. Humphrey, Editor, New York, AMS Press, Inc., 1984, p. 213-215.
2. Watson, J. B. and Raynor, R., Conditioned Emotional Reactions, *Journal of Experimental Psychology*, 3, 1920, p. 1-14.
3. Mowrer, O. H., A Stimulus-Response Analysis of Anxiety and its Role as a Reinforcement Agent, *Psychological Review*, 46, 1939, p. 553-565.

Chapter 4

1. Morse, Donald R. and Pollack, Robert L., *The Stress-Free Anti-Aging Diet*, No. 3 in the Series on *Stress in Modern Society*, James H. Humphrey, Editor, New York, AMS Press, Inc. 1989, p. 129.
2. Palm, J. Daniel, *Diet Away Your Stress, Tension & Anxiety*, New York, Doubleday & Company, Inc., 1976.
3. Morse, Donald R. and Pollack, Robert L., The *Stress-Free Anti-Aging Diet*, No. 3 in the Series on *Stress in Modern Society*, James H. Humphrey, Editor, New York, AMS Press, Inc. 1989, p. 170.
4. Rosch, Paul J., Supplement to Reduce Stress, *Health and Stress, The Newsletter of the American Institute of Stress*, No. 6, 1997, p. 5.
5. Lowry, R., Physical Activity Food Choice and Weight Management Goals and Practices Among U. S. College Students, *American Journal of Preventive Medicine*, 18, 2000, p. 18-27.
6. Diagnostic and Statistical Manual of Mental Disorders, 4th edition, Washington, DC, American Psychiatric Association, 1994, p. 544-545.
7. Diagnostic and Statistical Manual of Mental Disorders, 4th edition, Washington, DC, American Psychiatric Association, 1994, p. 549-550

Chapter 5

1. McQuade, Walter and Aikman, Ann, *Stress*, New York, E. P. Dutton and Co., Inc., 1974, p. 130.
2. Jencks, Beata, *Your Body Biofeedback at Its Best*, Chicago, Nelson-Hall, Inc., 1977, p. 51 and p. 172.
3. Walker, C; Eugene, *Learn to Relax, 13 Ways to Reduce Tension*, Englewood Cliffs, NJ, Prentice-Hall, Inc., 1975, p. 76-77.
4. Driscoll, Richard, Exertion Therapy, *Behavior Today*, VI, 1975, p. 27.

Chapter 6

1. Vedantam, Shanker, Study Links 8 Hours' Sleep to Shorter Life Span, *The Washington Post*, February 15, 2002, p. A2
2. Rosch, Paul J., Sleep, Memory and Brain Function, *Health and Stress, The Newsletter of the American Institute of Stress*, No. 8, 1996, p. 3.

Chapter 7

1. Greenberg, Jerrold S. *Stress and Sexuality,* New York, AMS Press, Inc., 1987, James H. Humphrey, Editor.
2. Kearney, Helen, Female Stress: An Overview, *Practical Stress Management, The Newsletter of the American Institute of Stress,* May/June, 1985.
3. McQuade, Walter and Aikan, Ann, *Stress,* New York, E. P. Dutton and Company, Inc., 1974.
4. Frankenhaeuser, Marianne, Women and Men Said to Differ in Their Responses to Stress, *Psychiatric News,* June 18, 1975.
5. Humphrey, Joy and Everly, George, Perceived Dimensions of Stress Responsiveness in Male and Female Students, *Health Education,* November/December, 1980.
6. Rosch, Paul J., Are Women More Stressed Out Than Men? *The Newsletter of the American Institute of Stress,* No. 7. 1997.
7. de Beauvoir, Simone, *The Second Sex,* New York, Vintage, 1974.
8. *The Columbia Encyclopedia,* New York, Columbia University Press, 2000, p. 862, Editor, Paul Lagasse'.
9. Furst, M. Lawrence, and Morse, Donald R., *The Women's World,* New Yor, AMS Press, Inc., 1988, No. 16 in series *Stress in Modern Society,* James H. Humphrey Editor.
10. Sullivan, John and Foster, Joyce Cameran, *Stress and Pregnancy,* New York, AMS Press, Inc., 1989, No. 8 in series *Stress in Modern Society,* James H. Humphrey Editor.
11. Sullivan, John, et al., Stress, Symptom Proneness and Minor Symptoms During Pregnancy, In *Human Stress; Current Selected Research,* Vol. 1, New York, AMS Press, Inc., 1986, James H. Humphrey, Editor.
12. Baldwin, Sharon, Sexual Harassment: Cracking Down, American College Network, *National College Newspaper,* February 1992.
13. Thakkar, R. R. and McCanne, T. R., The Effects of Daily Stressors on Physical Health of Women with and Without a Childhood History of Sexual Abuse, *Child Abuse & Neglect,* Vol. 24, February, 2000, p. 209-221.

Chapter 8

1. Roueche', Berton, *Alcohol; Its History, Folklore, Effects on the Human Body,* New York, Grove, 1960, p. 23-24.
2. Associated Press, April 5, 1995.
3. Humphrey, James H., Yow, Deborah A., and Bowden, William W., *Stress in College Athletics,* Binghamton, New York, The Haworth Press, Inc., 2000, p. 47.
4. Flynn, H. A., Comparison of Cross-sectional and Daily Reports in Studying the Relationship Between Depression and Use of Alcohol in Response to Stress in College Students, *Alcoholism - Clinical and Experimental Research,* Vol. 24, January 2000, p. 48-52.
5. Rosch, Paul J., Alcohol and Your Heart: What's the Bottom Line? *The Newsletter of the American Institute of Stress,* No. 12, 1994, p. 1.
6. Rosch, Paul J., Stress and Alcohol, *The Newsletter of* the American Institute of Stress, No. 11, 1996, p. 1.
7. Smoking and Women's Health, *National Women's Health Resource Center,* Washington, DC, November/December 1994.

8. Rosch, Paul J., More on Smoking and Sex, *The Newsletter of the American Institute of Stress,* No. 2, 1996, p. 7.
9. Update, American Alliance for Health, Physical Education, Recreation, and Dance, *Heart Association Issues Statement on Effects of Smoking on Children,* Washington, DC, January/February, 1995.

Chapter 9

1. Rosch, Paul J., Stress of Sexual Abuse Weakens the Immune System, *The Newsletter of the American Institute of Stress,* No. 10, 1994, p. 6.
2. Gullotta, Thomas P. and Donohue, Kevin D., Families, Relocation, and the Corporation, *New Directions for Mental Health Services,* December 1983, No., p. 15.
3. Yang, B. and Clum B. A., Childhood Stress Leads to Later Suicidality via its Effects on Cognitive Functioning, *Suicide and Life Threatening Behavior,* Vol. 30, Fall, 2000, p. 183-198.

Chapter 10

1. Luboudrov, S., Congressional Perceptions of the Elderly: The Use of Prototypes in the Legislative Process, *The Gerentologist,* 27, 1989.
2. U. S. Bureau of Censis Current Population Reports, Series P-23, No. 138, *Demographic and Socioeconomic Aspects of Aging in the United States,* Washington, DC, Government Printing Office.
3. Austad, Steven, Solving the Aging Problem, *Smithsonian,* January 1998.
4. Ross, Catherine, Religion and Psychological Distress, *Journal of the Scientific Study of Religion,* 29, June 1990.
5. Trumping Father Time - But Don't Toss Away Your Gym Shoes, *Modern Maturity,* February/March, 1991, p. 88.
6. Uson, P. P. and Larrosa, V. R., Physical Activity in Retirement Sge, *Sport in Perspective,* J. Partington, J. Orlick, and J. Samela, Editors, Canada Association of Canada, 1982, p. 149-151.
7. Bennett, J., et al., The Effect of a Program of Physical Exercise on Depression in Older Adults, *Physical Educator,* 39, 1980, p. 21-24.
8. Frekacy, G. A. and Leslie, D. K., Effects of an Exercise Program on Selected Flexibility Measurements of Senior Citizens, *The Gerentologist,* 15(2), 1987, p. 182-183.
9. Bassett, C., et al, A 10-week Exercise Program for Senior Citizens, *Geratric Nursing,* March/April, 1983, p. 103-105.
10. Chapman, E. A., et al, Joint Stiffness: Effects of Exercise on Young and Old Men, *Journal of Gerentology,* 27 (2) p. 218-221
11. Perri, H., and Templer, D. I., The Effects of an Aerobic Exercise Program on Psychological Variables in Older Adults, *The International Journal of Aging and Human Development,* 20(3), p. 167-172.

Chapter 11

1. Steps Urged to Cut Stress on the Job, *National Underwriters (Property and Casualty/Risk Benefits Management Edition)* August 1992, p. 7.

2. Heaney, Catherine, et al., Industrial Relations, Worksite Stress Reduction and Employee Well-Being: A Participatory Action Research Investigation, *Journal of Organizational Behavior,* September 1993, p. 14-17.

3. Karosek, R. and Theroell, T., Healthy Work: Stress Productivity and the Reconstruction of Working Life, New York, *Basic Books,* 1990.

4. Sims, Henry and Manz, Charles, *Business Without Bosses: How Self-Managing Teams Are Producing High-Performing Companies*, New York, John Wiley and Sons, 1993.

5. Lawyers in Distress Reflect Displeasures with Working Conditions. *A Weekly Journal of Medicine, Sciency and Society,* March 1992.

Chapter 12

1. Benson, Harbert, *The Relaxation Response,* New York, William Morrow and Company, Inc., 1975.

2. Jacobson, Edmund, *You Must Relax,* 4th ed., New York, McGraw-Hill, 1962.

Chapter 13

1. Pelletier, Kenneth, *Mind As Healer Mind As Slayer,* New York, Dell, 1977.

2. Woolfolk, Robert L., and Richardson, Frank C., *Stress, Survival & Society,* New American Library, Inc., 1978, p. 41.

3. Hales, Diane and Hales, Robert, Exercising the Psyche, *Health, Weekly Journal of Medicine, Fitness, and Psychology,* June 5, 1985.

4. Sethi, Amarajit, S, *Meditation as an Intervention in Stress Reactivity,* New York, AMS Press, Inc., No. 12 in series *Stress in Modern Society,* James H. Humphrey, Editor, 1989, p. 88-101.

5. Bloomfield, Harold H., et al., *TM Discovering Inner Energy and Overcoming Stress,* Boston, G. K. Hall, 1976, p. 7.

Chapter 14

1. Brown, Barbara B., *New Mind New Body,* New York, Bantam Books, Inc., 1975, p. 5.

Chapter 15

1. Knapp, T. J. and Shodahl, S. A., Ben Franklin as a Behavior Modifier: A Note, *Behavior Therapy,* 5, 1974.

Chapter 16

1. Kravetz, R. and Forness, S., The Special Classroom as a Desensitization Setting, *Exceptional Children* 37 (5), p. 389-391.

2. Piaget, Jean, *Les Mecanismes Perceptits,* Presses Universitares, de France, 1961.

SUGGESTIONS FOR FURTHER READING

Abela, J. R. Z. and Seligman, M. E. P., The Hopelessness Theory of Depression: A Test of the Diathesis-Stress Component in the Interpersonal and Achievement Domains, *Cognitive Therapy and Research,* 24, August 2000.

Alcohol and Stress, *Alcohol Alert,* National Institute of Alcohol Abuse and Alcoholism, 32, April 1996.

American Association of University Women, Hostile Hallways: Bullying, Teasing and Sexual Harassment, *American Journal of Health Education,* 32, September/October 2001.

Bond, Frank W., and Bunce, David, Job Control Mediates Change in a Work Organization Intervention to Stress Reduction, *Journal of Occupational Health Psychology,* 6, October 2001.

Bray, N. J. Braxton, J. M. and Sullivan, A. S., The Influence of Stress-Related Coping Strategies on College Student Departure Decisions, *Journal of College Student Development,* 40, November/December 1999.

Chang, E. C. and Rand, K. L., Perfectionism as a Predictor of Subsequent Adjustment: Evidence for a Specific Diathesis-Stress Mechanism Among College Students, Journal of Counseling *Psychology,* 47, January 2000.

Chang, E. C., Rand, K. L., and Strunk, D. R., Optimism and Risk for Job Burnout Among Working College Students: Stress as a Mediator, *Personality and Individual Differences,* 29, August, 2000.

Colder, Craig R., Life Stress, Physiological and Subjective Indexes of Negative Emotionality, and Coping Reasons for Drinking: Is There Evidence for a Self-Medication Model of Alcohol Use? *Psychology of Addictive Behavior,* 15, September 2001.

Dunkley, D. M., et al, The Relation Between Perfectionism and Distress: Hassles, Coping, and Perceived Social Support as Mediators and Moderators, *Journal of Counseling Psychology,* 47, October 2000.

Edwards, K. J., Stress, Negative Social Change, and Health Symptoms in University Students, *Journal of American College Health,* 50, September 2001.

Fischer, K. E., et al, The Relationship of Parental Alcoholism and Family Dysfunction to Stress Among College Students, *Journal of American College Health,* 48, January 2000.

Gandee, Robert N., Knierim, Helen, and McLittle-Marino, Doris, Stress and Older Adults: A Mind-Body Relationship, *Journal of Physical Education, Recreation and Dance,* 69, November/ December, 1998.

Graham, Stephanie, et al. Religion and Spirituality in Coping with Stress, *Counseling & Values,* 46, October 2001.

Ingram, K. M., Supportive Responses from Others Concerning a Stressful Life Event: Development of the Unsupportive Social Interactions Inventory, *Journal of Social and Clinical Psychology,* 20, Summer 2001.

Jackson, T., Weiss, K. E., and Lundquist, J. J., Does Procrastination Mediate the Relationship Between Optimism and Subsequent Stress? *Journal of Social Behavior and Personality,* 15, May 2001.

Johnson, E. L. and Lutgendorf, S. K., *Contributions of Imagery Ability to Stress and Relaxation,* 23, Fall 2001.

King, Keith A., Wagner, Donald I., and Hedrick, Bonnie, Parents Reported Needs in Preventing Their Children from Engaging in Alcohol, Tobacco, and Other Drug Use, *American Journal of Health Education,* 33, March/April, 2002.

Lanier, C. A., Nicholson, T., and Duncan, D., Drug Use and Mental Well Being Among a Sample of Undergraduate and Graduate College Students, *Journal of Drug Education,* 31, March 2001.

McCarthy, C. J., Moller, N. P., and Fouladi, R. T., Continued Attachment to Parents: Its Relationship to Affect Regulation and Perceived Stress Among College Students., *Measurement and Evaluation in Counseling and Development,* 33, January 2001.

Meijer, Joost, Stress in the Relation Between Trait and State Anxiety, *Psychological Reports,* 88, June 2001.

Paik, I. H., Psychological Stress May Induce Increased Humoral and Decreased Cellular Immunity, 26, *Behavioral Medicine,* 26, Fall 2000.

Penland, E. A., et al, Possible Selves, Depression and Coping Skills in University Students, *Personality and Individual* Differences, 29, November 2000.

Plante, Thomas G., Coscarelli, Laura, and Ford, Maire, Does Exercising with Another Enhance the Stress-Reducing Benefits of Exercise? *International Journal of Stress: Management,* 8, July 2001. Salmon, Peter, Effects of Physical Exercise on Anxiety, Depression, and Sensitivity to Stress, *Clinical Psychology Review,* 21, February 2001.

Sandier, M. E., Career Decision-Making Self-Efficacy, Perceived Stress and an Integrated Model of Student Persistence : A structural Model of Finances, Attitudes, Behavior, and Career Development, *Research in Higher Education,* 41, October 2000.

Segrin, C., Social Skills and Negative Life Events: Testing the Deficit Stress Generation Hypothesis, *Current Psychology,* 20, Spring 2001.

Sinha, Rajita, How Does Stress Increase Risk of Drug Abuse and Relapse? *Psychopharmacology,* 158, December 2001.

Struthers, C. W., Perry, R. P., and Menec, V. H., An Examination of the Relationship Among Academic Stress, Coping, Motivation, and Performance in College, *Research in Higher Education,* 41, October 2000.

Tennabtm Christopher, Work-Related Stress and Depressive Disorders, *Journal of Psychosomatic Research,* 51, November 2001.

Vollrath, M. and Torgersen, S., *Personality Types and Coping, Personality and Individual Differences*, 29, August 2000.

Yow, Deborah A., Humphrey, James H., and Bowden, William B., Alcohol Use Among College Student Athletes, *Athletics* Administration, 34, October 1999.

INDEX

A

ABC Factor, 167, 170
abnormal behavior, 23, 42, 168
abortion, 67
abusive working environment, 77
academic problems, 17, 104
accomplishments, x, 129
acute fatigue, 59
addiction, 91, 96
addictive drug, 91
adrenal cortex, 10
adrenal glands, 9, 14
AdrenoCorticoTropic Hormone (ACTH), 9, 10
adult health problems, 125
adultery, 74
age groups, 113
aggressive behavior, 27, 152
aging process, 112-114, 117
AIDS, 76
air pollution, 93
alarm reaction, 10
alcohol consumption, 83, 87, 89, 90, 140
alcoholic beverage, 63, 83, 85, 86, 88, 121
alcoholism treatment program, 90
Alzheimer's disease, 117
amenorrhea, 44
American Cancer Society, 91
American Institute of Stress, vii, xiii, 184-186
American Psychiatric Association, 18, 44, 183, 184
anger responses, 27
anger, 6, 17, 21, 22, 24, 25, 27, 29, 32, 99, 103, 120, 128
anorexia nervosa, 44
antisex-education forces, 81
anxiety, xii, 1, 3, 5-7, 17, 18, 25, 26, 55, 56, 66, 71, 73, 88, 100, 103, 105-108, 110, 116, 118, 127, 128, 132, 134, 136, 151, 153, 156, 163, 164, 175-180
appropriate behavior, 168, 172, 173
assertive behavior, 27
autonomic nervous system, 10, 22, 90, 108, 163, 164
aversive affective sensitivity, 72
avoidance behavior, 108, 153

B

babies, 70, 80
balanced diet, 40, 41
Basal Metabolic Rate (BMR), 70
behavior modification, 167-170
behavior patterns, 71
behavior problems, 71, 103
behavior therapy technique, 175
behavioral adjustment, 167, 174
behavioral explanations, 25
behavioral reactions (to stress), 9, 12, 19
behavioral self-management, 167, 168
behavioral therapy, ix, 174
belief systems, x, 121, 155
biofeedback instrument, 162, 164, 165
bio-feedback training (BFT), 161, 164, 165
biofeedback, 144, 150, 161-165
biofeedback-induced relaxation, 164
biological component of sexuality, 66
bladder, 22, 67, 94
blue collar workers, ix, 125, 129, 131
body builds, 50
body reactivity, 13
body segments, 51
body tension, 28, 150
body types, 47, 50
breasts, 68, 77, 84
bulimia nervosa, 44

C

calculative thinking, 157
caloric needs, 39
cancer, 16, 17, 88, 92-94
carbohydrates, 34, 35, 37, 38, 42, 89, 90
carpal tunnel syndrome, 128
causes of stress, 9, 16, 100, 102, 129, 136
changing behavior, 167, 171
characteristics of emotionality, 21, 23
child abuse, 102, 103
child bearing, 68, 69
child development, 49, 100, 110, 179
child sexual abuse, 79
childhood stress, 99, 101, 110
children, xi, xii, 15, 23, 24, 26-28, 43, 45, 47, 49,
    66, 67, 70, 73, 75, 80, 81, 85, 92, 97, 99-110,
    114, 115, 120, 133, 139, 140, 148-153, 159,
    160, 164, 178-180
cholesterol level, 41
cholesterol, 41, 42, 89
Christian meditation, 156, 157
chronic alcoholism, 90
chronic bronchitis, 94
chronic fatigue, 53, 59-61
chronic insomnia, 63
chronic obstructive bronchlopulminary diseases,
    94
chronic psychological stress, 13
chronological age, 113
cigarette smoking, 93, 94
circulatory-respiratory endurance, 48
cirrhosis of the liver, 17
classroom stress, 107
clitoris, 68
cocaine, 83, 91, 96
cognitive abilities, 121
cognitive processes, 90, 155
college students, ix-xii, 1, 2, 4, 17, 26, 27, 29, 39,
    43, 44, 53, 54, 62, 72, 75, 79, 83, 85-87, 91,
    92, 97, 110, 118, 176, 181
communication enhancements, 132
communication of a sexual nature, 78
compensation for job stress, 128
components of sexuality, 65
computer terminals, 132
concentration, 42, 84, 91, 107, 155-158, 164
concept(s) of stress, 2-4, 118
conception, 18, 67-69
concepts of emotional stability, 28
conditioned reactions, 175, 176, 179
conditioned reflex, 61
conditioned stimulus, 26

constructive stress, xii
continuing stress, 14
continuous self-evaluation, x
controllability, 13
controlling the emotions, 23
coping behavior, 13
coping with stress, ix, 86, 92, 99, 131, 160
coronary heart disease, 17, 18, 89, 94
corticoids, 10
counting behaviors, 169, 170
creative relaxation, 143, 148, 153
cultural component of sexuality, 66

D

daily stressors of children, 101
deep muscle relaxation, 143, 163
defensive behavior, 12
degree of frustration, 12, 23, 169
degree of maladjustment, 23, 169
dehumanization, 132
dementia, 117
depression, xii, 1, 5, 6, 63, 77, 78, 86, 88, 103,
    122, 127-129, 132, 133, 185-187, 189
desirable and undesirable stress, 12
diabetes, 17
digestive disturbance, 39
digestive process, 34, 35
digestive system, 39
digestive tract, 39
dirty jokes, 78
distress, 2, 4, 9, 12, 13, 19, 25, 104, 107, 118, 121
dizziness, 25
drinking behavior, 90
drug abuse, 95
drug addiction, 96
drug education, 97
drug therapy, 73
dysfunctional behavior, 12
dysmenorrhea, 69

E

eating habits, 33, 43, 46
economic conditions, 15, 73, 102
ectomorph, 51
educative process, 105
effects of aging, 111
effects of stress, 7, 9, 13, 14, 17
ejaculation (discharge of semen), 67
elderly, 112, 117, 119, 122
electroencephalograph (EEC), 161, 163
electromyograph (EMG), 162-164
electromyography, 161, 162

EMB training, 164
embryo, 68, 69
emergency medical personnel, 133
emergency reaction, 11, 151, 152
emergency stress, 14
EMG training, 163, 164
emotional arousals and reactions, 23
emotional aspect of personality, 21, 22
emotional behavior, 21, 22
emotional patterns, 21, 22, 25
emotional reactivity, 21, 22, 120
emotional response, 22, 24, 25, 27, 28, 31
emotional situations, 24
emotional stability, 21, 23, 28-32
emotional stress, 21-23, 32, 40, 92, 114
emotionality, 21, 23
emotionally charged situation, 23
emotionally healthy person(s), 21, 23, 31, 32, 169
emphysema, 94
endocrine gland, 10, 67
endocrine system, 10, 22, 34
endometrium, 68
endomorph, 50, 51
energy, 3, 6, 13, 14, 34-39, 55, 60, 70, 89, 93,
    107, 114, 156, 157
environmental experience, 29-31
erection, 91
essential nutrients, 33
estrogen, 68
ethical component of sexuality, 67
eustress, 9, 13, 19
exercise program, 54, 122
exhaustion stage, 10
expressive behavior, 12
external sexual parts of the female, 68
extramarital affairs, 76
extramarital sex, 67, 76
extroverted, 71

F

factors that influence emotionality, 21, 23
fallopian tube, 69
fat-soluble vitamins, 38
fear reduction, 26
feedback thermometers, 163
female behavior, 74, 102
female menstrual cycle, 69
female orgasm, 68
female personality, 74
female sex glands, 68
female sex hormone, 68
female sexual excitation, 68
fertilized egg, 69

fight or flight response, 11, 22, 150, 151
financial problems, ix, 17, 119
financial worries, 90, 119
Food and Drug Administration, 42
food faddists, 45
food, ix, 11, 33-41, 43-46, 48, 50, 61, 63, 70, 84,
    92, 100
foreskin, 68
form of relaxation, 143
frustration, 3, 7, 12, 17, 21, 23, 107, 108, 132,
    133, 168, 178
functional age, 113

G

gall bladder, 22
Galvanic Skin Response (GSR), 161, 163
gastrointestinal sensitivity, 72
gender differences, 65, 67, 81, 119, 123
gender equity programs, 71
General Adaptation Syndrome, 10, 19, 90
general causes of stress, 9, 102
genital herpes, 76
geriatrics, 117
gerontology, 113, 115, 117
good night's sleep, 63

H

hardiness, 7
hate, 22
health care providers, 133
health care work environments, 128
heart attack, 18, 36, 41, 62, 90, 127, 128
heart disease, 17, 18, 36, 37, 89, 91, 94
heartbeat, 22, 25, 36, 37
heavy breathing, 25
heavy smokers, 93, 95
heavy smoking, 88, 92, 93
heroin, 83, 91, 96
hierarchy of anxiety-evoking stimuli, 175, 176,
    178-180
high blood pressure, 17, 18, 37
high cholesterol levels, 41
high-cholesterol sources, 40
high-density lipoproteins (HDL), 41, 89
high-tech environment, 132
home and family stress on children, 102
hormonal conditions, 65, 70, 71
hormone, 10
hostile working environment, 77
human emotion, 22, 25
Humphrey Stress Inquiry Form, 118, 129, 135

I

imagery, 149, 188
immediate work environment, 56
importance of emotional control, 23
impotency in male smokers, 91
impotency rates, 91
impulsive, 21, 27
inappropriate behavior, 168, 170-173
incest, 79
information-processing, 156
inhibited, 21, 27
insomnia, 6, 62, 63, 153
intercourse, 68, 74, 76, 79
International Labor Office, 125
irrational fears, 25
isometric exercises, 47, 57

J

jealousy, 21, 22, 25, 27
job stress problems, 127

L

labia majora, 68
labia minora, 68
learned tensions, 5
learning disorders, 160
learning principles, 25
learning problems, 152
learning process, 160
length of life, 117
life events, 16, 100, 102-104, 106, 110
life expectancy, 111, 112, 117
Life Style Inventory, xii
liver, 17, 22, 35, 39, 87
low-density lipoproteins (LDL), 41, 89
lung cancer, 93, 94
lung disease, 17, 92

M

maintenance program, 54
major stress inducing factors, 17
male reproductive system, 67
male sex hormones, 67
management style, 126
mantra, 155, 157, 158
marijuana, 96
masturbation, 75
maximum sexuality, 69
meaning of stress, 1, 2, 5
medical problems of children, 153

medical procedures, 25
meditation for children, 159
meditation techniques, 156, 159
meditation, 121, 144, 155-160
meditational exercise, 157
meditational process, 157
meditative running, 156, 157
medulla, 9, 10
megavitamin therapy, 42, 46
memory and brain function, 59, 62
menopause, 69, 114
menstrual cycles, 44, 69
menstrual flow, 69
menstruation, 66, 68, 69, 74
mental activity, 6, 150, 156, 159
mental functioning, 115
mental health problems, 17
mental practice, 149
mental stress, 128
mesomorph, 50
metabolic process, 34, 35
metabolism, 36, 87, 90, 114, 156, 160
middle age, 112
migraine headaches, 17, 78
mineral elements, 36
moderate smoking, 92
modern society, ix, 10, 23, 31, 74, 85, 100, 109, 111
modern-day meditation, 160
multiple sclerosis, 17
multiple stressors, 102
muscular endurance, 48
muscular reactivity, 70
muscular strength, 48
muscular structure, 70
muscular tension, 5, 25, 55, 107, 144, 150

N

National Cholesterol Education Program Coordinating Committee, 41
natural breathing rhythm, 159
negative attitude, 15, 106, 122, 140
negative emotional responses, 25
nerve connections, 68
nervous indigestion, 39
nervous system, 10, 22, 55, 61, 62, 83, 84, 90, 108, 155, 156, 163, 164
nervous tension, 15
neurological climax, 67
neutral stimulus, 25, 26
nocturnal emission, 67
non-calculative thinking, 157
nonsmokers, 91-94

normal behavior, 23
nurses' stressors, 135
nutrients, 33, 34, 37, 41, 68
nutritional supplements, 42

O

objective fears, 25
occupational stress, 127
older adults, 17, 111, 118-123
older people, 37, 38, 60, 112, 113-116
older women, 113, 119
oldest old, 112
openness about sex, 81
operant conditioning, 25, 26
orgasm (neurological climax), 67, 68
ovaries, 68
overt behavior, 12, 21, 25, 153
ovulation, 68, 69

P

painful emotional reaction, 6
panel discussion, xii, 19, 46, 64, 81, 98, 110, 123, 165
parental divorce, 103
participatory action research (PAR), 126
passive relaxation, 143
passive smoking, 83, 92
penis, 67, 68, 91
personal health practices, x
Personal Life Style Survey, xii
personality conflicts, 130, 131, 138, 139
perspiration, 22, 38, 48, 151, 163
physical activity, x, 14, 28, 29, 47, 49, 53-56, 96, 117, 131, 149
physical and emotional trauma, 6, 55
physical disorders, 6
physical exercise, 22, 47, 54, 121, 131
physical fitness, 47-50, 52, 57, 59
physical health, 3, 17, 105
physical performance, 47, 51
physical stress, 9, 12, 14, 15
physical symptom, 79, 80, 153
physiologic or unlearned tensions, 5
physiological age, 113
physiological arousal, 153
physiological changes, 76, 153
physiological reactions (to stress), 9, 11, 12
physiological stressors, 10
physiological symptoms, 6
pituitary, 10
placenta, 68, 69
pleasant emotion(s), 21, 22, 28-30

pleasant emotional patterns, 21
pleasantness, 22
positive attitude(s), x, 15, 108
positive effects of meditation, 160
Post Traumatic Stress Disorder, ix, 133
post-partum period, 103
predictability, 13
pregnancy gingivitis, 77
pregnancy, 66, 68, 76, 77, 185
pregnant woman, 76
premarital sexual activities, 76
premarital sexual relations, 76
prescribed exercises, 54
principles of living, ix
problems of memory, 116
problem-solving process, 157
process of aging, 112, 114
processes of nutrition, 33
procrastination, xi
professional groups, 133
professional personnel, 133
progesterone, 68
progressive relaxation, 143-145
prolonged climax, 68
prolonged emotional stress, 40
prostate gland, 67
psychological component of sexuality, 66
psychological safety, 13
psychological stress, 5, 9, 10, 12, 13, 15, 19, 76, 169
psychological tension, 1, 5
psychological variables, 13
psychomatic disorders, 15
puberty, 66-69
public speaking anxiety, 175
pulse rate, 14, 22

Q

quiet environment, 158
Quieting Reflex (QR), 143, 150-152
quieting techniques, 152
quivering, 25

R

rapid eye movements (REM), 61, 62
rapid heartbeat, 25
recovery rate, 156
recreation, 144, 186, 188
recreational activities, 121, 131
recreational sports, 51, 54
reduce stress, xi, 42, 56, 98, 100, 121, 131, 143, 152, 155

reinforcement, 26, 54, 167, 171- 173, 180
relaxation procedures, 152, 153, 177, 178, 180
relaxation response, 143, 144
relaxation technique(s), 12, 144, 145, 180
relaxation training, 152, 153
relaxed state, 143, 150
releasing aggression, 29
religious groups, 34, 121
repetitive stress injuries, 127
resistance stage, 10
respondent conditioning, 25, 26
round table discussion, xii, 7, 19, 46, 57, 64, 81,
     98, 110, 123, 141, 160, 174

S

school sex education, 81
scientific community, 43, 116, 156
self modification of behavior, 169-171, 173
self-concept, 29, 123, 152, 167, 168
self-conscious, 50
self-control, 168
self-managing teams, 127
self-produced consequences, 171
self-reinforcement, 172, 173
self-reliance, 27
self-stimulation, 67, 75
self-structure, 167, 168
semen, 67
seminal vesicles, 67
senility, 117, 120
separation anxiety, 100, 106
serious diseases, 15, 40, 94, 125
serious health problems, 13, 17
sex discrimination, 74, 77, 78
sex education programs, 81
sex education, 80, 81, 97
sexual abuse, 79, 80
sexual activity, 65, 75, 76
sexual attitudes and values, 80
sexual behavior, 65, 66, 74, 81
sexual characteristics, 68
sexual discrimination, 65, 81
sexual excitation, 67, 68
sexual fantas(y)ies, 66
sexual harassment, 77-79, 81
sexual intercourse, 76, 79
sexual interest, 69
sexual morality, 65
sexual revolution, 76
sexual self-stimulation, 75
sexual thoughts, 66
sexuality, 65-67, 69, 80, 89
sexually experienced man, 74

sexually transmitted diseases, 76
Simon Says, 148, 149
sleep deprivation, 62
sleep disorders, 62
sleep environment, 63
smoke free, 92
smoking behavior, 94, 98
social and health problems, 17
social interactions, 15, 27
social problems, 15
social relationships, 15, 167, 169
social stress(ors), 9, 12, 15, 19, 77
societal norms, 72
speed of data acquisition, 132
sperm cells, 67
spleen, 22
stage fright, 15
stimulation, 12, 66-68, 88, 96, 143, 155, 167
stimuli, 5, 10, 21, 31, 61, 132, 175-180
strategic meditation, 156, 157
stress among lawyers, 141
stress among nurses, 141
stress and alcohol, 90
stress coping techniques, 91
stress exercises, 57
stress formula vitamins, 42
stress in children, 99, 109
stress in older adults, 119
stress in the teaching profession, 141
stress management, xii, 9, 121
stress reducing technique, 121
stress response situation, 72
stress responsiveness, 72
stress ridden, 133, 156
stress-burnout relationship, 7
stressful conditions, ix-xi, 15, 22, 56, 90, 125,
     129, 139
stressful life events, 103, 104, 106
stressful situations, xi, 12, 33, 56, 103, 106, 108,
     130, 134, 138, 152, 153, 156, 167, 170
stress-inducing factors, 105, 109, 129, 130, 132,
     134, 137-140
stress-initiated disorders, 42
stress-invoking stimuli, 175
stressology, 9
stressors of sexual activity, 65
stressors, 5, 10, 13, 65, 72, 77, 79, 90, 101-103,
     129, 132, 134-136, 141
stress-reducing technique, 155
stress-related conditions, 17, 125
stress-related disorders, 156
stress-related illnesses, 13
stress-related origins, 17

stress-related psychological and physiological disorders, 17
stress-related terms, 1, 5
student behavior(s), 137, 140, 170, 172
study of stress (stressology), 9, 10
substance abuse, 97, 98, 133
suicidal behavior, 110
suicide rate among students, 140
suicide, 94, 133, 140
surveillance, 132
sweating, 11, 25
systematic desensitization, 175, 176, 178
systematic self desensitization, 175-177, 181

T

teacher behavior, 172
teacher criticism, 171
teacher praise, 171
teacher stress factors, 137
team concept, 127
techniques for coping with stress, ix
techniques of meditation, 144, 158
technostress, 125
temper tantrums, 23, 106
temporary insomnia, 63
tensing-relaxing cycle, 153
tension, 1, 3, 5-7, 15, 17, 25, 28, 29, 55, 57, 60, 61, 88, 107, 118, 119, 143-146, 150-153, 162-164
terrorist attack on September 11, ix
test anxiety, 71, 108, 110, 175
testes, 67, 68
testicles, 67
textbooks, 17, 71
theories of aging, 111, 113
theories of stress, 10
time budgeting, xi
time constraints, 17
tolerance level, 23, 169
tranquilizers, 73, 95, 98, 121, 152
transcendental meditation (TM), 155-159, 187
two-factor theory of learning, 25
types of meditation, 156, 157

types of personality, 18
types of relaxation, 143

U

umbilical cord, 68
undesirable stress, ix, 6, 12-14, 16, 99
United States Bureau of the Census, 111
United States Department of Education, 75
unpleasant emotional patterns, 21
unpleasant emotions, 21, 28-30
unpleasant events, 14
unpleasantness, 22
unrelaxed sleep, 61
unwanted sexual solicitation, 78
urine, 38, 67, 75
use of contraceptives, 67
uterine wall, 69
uterus, 68, 69

V

vagina, 67, 68
vaginal opening, 68
vegetable foods, 35
vegetable products, 45
vegetarians, 34, 45
verbal harassment, 78
violent emotional reaction, 24
virginity, 74
vitamin pills, 38
vitamins, 34, 35, 37, 39, 42

W

water-soluble vitamins, 38
wet dream, 67

Y

younger smokers, 95

Z

zone of tolerance, 23, 169